READING ANSELM'S *PROSLOGION*

Anselm's *Proslogion* has sparked controversy from the time it was written (c. 1077) to the present day. Attempts to provide definitive accounts of its argument have led to a wide and contradictory variety of interpretations. In this book, Ian Logan goes back to basics, to the Latin text of the *Proslogion* with an original parallel English translation, before tracing the twists and turns of this controversy. Helping us to understand how the same argument came to be regarded as based on reason alone by some and on faith alone by others, as a logically sound demonstration by its supporters and as fatally flawed by its opponents, Logan considers what Anselm is setting out to do in the *Proslogion*, how his argument works, and whether it is successful.

ASHGATE NEW CRITICAL THINKING IN RELIGION, THEOLOGY AND BIBLICAL STUDIES

The *Ashgate New Critical Thinking in Religion, Theology and Biblical Studies* series brings high quality research monograph publishing back into focus for authors, international libraries, and student, academic and research readers. Headed by an international editorial advisory board of acclaimed scholars spanning the breadth of religious studies, theology and biblical studies, this open-ended monograph series presents cutting-edge research from both established and new authors in the field. With specialist focus yet clear contextual presentation of contemporary research, books in the series take research into important new directions and open the field to new critical debate within the discipline, in areas of related study, and in key areas for contemporary society.

Other Titles in the Series:

Exodus Church and Civil Society
Public Theology and Social Theory in the Work of Jürgen Moltmann
Scott R. Paeth

Eucharistic Sacramentality in an Ecumenical Context
The Anglican Epiclesis
David J. Kennedy

Reading Anselm's *Proslogion*

The History of Anselm's Argument and its Significance Today

IAN LOGAN
Blackfriars Hall, Oxford, UK

ASHGATE

Published by

Ashgate Publishing Limited
Wey Court East
Union Road
Farnham
Surrey, GU9 7PT
England

Ashgate Publishing Company
Suite 420
101 Cherry Street
Burlington
VT 05401-4405
USA

www.ashgate.com

British Library Cataloguing in Publication Data

Logan, Ian

Reading Anselm's Proslogion : the history of Anselm's argument and its significance today. – (Ashgate new critical thinking in religion, theology and biblical studies)

1. Anselm, Saint, Archbishop of Canterbury, 1033–1109. Proslogion 2. God – Proof, Ontological – History of doctrines – Middle Ages, 600–1500

I. Title

189.4

Library of Congress Cataloging-in-Publication Data

Logan, Ian.

Reading Anselm's Proslogion : the history of Anselm's argument and its significance today / Ian Logan.

p. cm. — (Ashgate new critical thinking in religion, theology, and biblical studies)

Includes bibliographical references.

ISBN 978-0-7546-6123-8 (hardcover : alk. paper) 1. Anselm, Saint, Archbishop of Canterbury, 1033–1109. Proslogion. 2. God—Proof, Ontological. I. Anselm, Saint, Archbishop of Canterbury, 1033–1109. Proslogion. English & Latin. II. Title.

B765.A83P8722 2008
212'.1—dc22

2008047920

ISBN: 978-0-7546-6123-8

Mixed Sources
Product group from well-managed forests and other controlled sources
www.fsc.org Cert no. SA-COC-1565
© 1996 Forest Stewardship Council
FSC

Printed and bound in Great Britain by
MPG Books Ltd, Bodmin, Cornwall.

Contents

Acknowledgements

This work has been in gestation over many years. In that time innumerable people have helped me (often unwittingly) to develop the theme of, and arguments contained in, this book. They are too many to mention. However, my particular thanks go to the Regent and Moderators of Blackfriars, Oxford, for providing me with an academic home. Most especially, I would like to thank my wife, Mandy Wood, without whose clear sense, attention to detail and encouragement this book would never have been completed. It is dedicated to her.

List of Abbreviations

Anselm's works are abbreviated as follows:

CDH	*Cur Deus Homo*
DC	*De Concordia*
DCD	*De Casu Diaboli*
DG	*De Grammatico*
DIV	*De Incarnatione Verbi*
DLA	*De Libertate Arbitrii*
DPSS	*De Processione Spiritus Sancti*
DV	*De Veritate*
E	*Epistolae*
M	*Monologion*
OM	*Orationes sive Meditationes*
P	*Proslogion*
R	*Responsio*

Other abbreviations:

AA	F.S. Schmitt *et al.* (eds), *Analecta Anselmiana*, vols I–V, Minerva Verlag, Frankfurt 1969–1978
AFQI	K. Barth, *Anselm, Fides Quaerens Intellectum: Anselm's Proof of the Existence of God in the Context of his Theological Scheme*, translated by I.W. Robertson, SCM Press, London 1960
B	Ms Bodley 271
CPR	*Immanuel Kant's Critique of Pure Reason*, translated by N. Kemp Smith, 2nd impression with corrections, Macmillan, London 1933
G	*Pro Insipiente*
PL	J.-P. Migne, *Patrologiae cursus completus. Series Latina*, vols 1–221, Paris 1844–1865
ScG	Thomas Aquinas, *Summa contra Gentiles*
ST	Thomas Aquinas, *Summa Theologiae*

References take the following form:

*CDH*I:3	*Cur Deus Homo*, Book I, Chapter 3
*E*10	*Epistolae* 10
*P*2	*Proslogion*, Chapter 2
*PL*64 col. 73A	Migne, *Patrologiae Latina*, vol. 64 column 73 section A

Chapter 1
Introduction

Back to the Text

Presenting an account of Anselm's *Proslogion* argument, its background and its subsequent history in later thought is more than an exercise in intellectual archaeology. Work still needs to be done to understand what Anselm was trying to achieve and how he was trying to achieve it. Anselm's argument presents an important paradigm for the history of ideas, since it has been treated directly or indirectly by so many different thinkers in subsequent centuries, and it provides a direct challenge to the way philosophy has been done over those centuries. That Anselm has been consistently misunderstood and misrepresented is a central thesis of this book. It is only by returning to and reading Anselm's text that we can hope to establish what he was trying to say and understand how he was trying to say it. Anselm's argument has fascinated and continues to fascinate philosophers and theologians, to such an extent that it is no longer possible in a single work to review exhaustively the history of its reception. Thus, the account of the reception in this book is selective, particularly in Chapter 8 where I limit myself in the main to its reception amongst modern English speaking philosophers. It is these philosophers who have been particularly concerned with the logical form, validity and soundness of Anselm's argument, and to whom it is necessary to respond, if one wishes to discover whether Anselm still has something of philosophical interest to say to us in the *Proslogion*.

There has been a natural tendency amongst modern thinkers to adhere, wittingly or unwittingly, to a Whig view of history, to see the history of ideas as the steady progress of enlightened thought over benighted ignorance. The past is a bad or at best confused place, in which people concerned themselves 'with a lot of outdated foolishness', such as questions about the existence of God, which we now correctly consider to be irrelevant.[1] It is my hope that the study of Anselm's argument and its subsequent reception will help to counter such views, not because everything in the past was good, but because some things were, and it may just be that some of those good things are what 'we' now consider outdated and irrelevant.

Anselm's argument is frequently identified with later ontological arguments. It is one of my tasks in this work to show how that has happened, and that Anselm's argument has to be addressed in its specificity, that 'that than which a greater cannot

---

[1] See R. Rorty, 'The historiography of philosophy: four genres', in R. Rorty et al. (eds), *Philosophy in History: Essays on the historiography of philosophy*, Cambridge 1984, pp. 49–75, p. 52.

be thought' is the irreplaceable middle term of Anselm's argument, which for Anselm functions as the 'natural or proper word' for God. This is not simply a question of scholarship, but also of philosophy, for in my view the latter is aided by the former.

In this book I seek to create an 'audit trail' which stretches from (i) a pre-history of the text (Chapter 2) to (ii) the manuscript tradition and a translation which seeks to remain faithful to Anselm's Latin text (Chapter 3), presenting the Latin and English texts in parallel to (iii) a commentary on the text (Chapter 4) to (iv) an exposition of the debate that immediately followed its 'publication' (Chapter 5) to (v) a review and evaluation of the historical and ongoing reception of the *Proslogion* (Chapters 6, 7 and 8). It concludes with an assessment of the significance of Anselm's argument.

Anselm of Aosta, Bec and Canterbury

Anselm was born in Aosta, Italy, in 1033 and died in Canterbury in 1109. He arrived in Bec c. 1059 to study under its prior, Lanfranc, before joining the monastery in 1060. He became prior after Lanfranc left Bec in 1063, and then abbot after the death of the monastery's founder, Herluin, in 1078. In 1093, he was made Archbishop of Canterbury. Anselm had been teaching at Bec for seventeen years before he wrote his first book, the *Monologion*, in 1076.[2] The *Proslogion* followed in 1077/78.

Anselm was first and foremost a monk of the Order of St Benedict. It is evident in his writings that Anselm's worldview is shaped by the rhythms of the monastic life, in particular by the divine office and the *lectio divina*. As part of his training as a novice, he learnt by heart the Psalms and the prayers of the church and his monastery. They were constantly repeated during the years of his formation. He imbibed them, and when he came to write, their imagery and language infused his thinking. Anselm regarded intellectual activity as a form of meditation and he called the *Monologion* 'an example of meditating on the rationality of the faith'.[3] Anselm regarded his writings as pertaining to the study of scripture.[4] Although he was concerned that what he wrote should be consistent with authority,[5] he did not appeal to authority. Rather he sought to discover what he called 'necessary reasons'[6] for the beliefs of Catholics and was willing to operate 'by reason alone'[7]

---

2 Anselm was teaching at Bec even before he entered the community in 1060. See Eadmer, *The Life of Saint Anselm, Archbishop of Canterbury*, edited with introduction, notes and translation by R.W. Southern, Oxford 1972, p. 8.

3 *P*Preface.

4 *DV*Preface.

5 See *M*Preface.

6 See *M*1. These have only an interim necessity unless they are confirmed by authority. See also *CDH*I:18.

7 *M*1. See also *CDH*I:20, II:11, II:22.

and 'without reference to Christ'.[8] This can mislead us into thinking that Anselm was simply a rationalist who believed that starting with a *tabula rasa* we can 'discover' revelation without God's aid.[9] Such a view is the opposite of the one Anselm actually held. We can see this in his use of the statement based on a reading of *Isaiah* 7:9: 'unless you believe, you shall not understand'. Anselm operated within the context of God's revelation and did not seek to depart from it, but rather considered that insofar as we can be properly rational (for we are limited and fallen), we can demonstrate with God's help the reasonableness and even necessity of whatever the church teaches about God. Anselm, as a philosopher, fails to meet the criterion established by Wittgenstein that the philosopher does not belong to a community of ideas.[10] Anselm was most definitely a member of a community of ideas, and when he could not understand what Catholic belief teaches about God he bowed his head in reverence, unlike those he called the 'heretics of dialectic'.[11] But he was also a brilliant philosopher, who discovered and successfully articulated the wonderfully original argument of the *Proslogion*.

The Text

The texts of the *Proslogion*, *Pro Insipiente* and *Responsio* that are transcribed and translated in this work are taken from a manuscript originating from the scriptorium of Christ Church Priory, Canterbury, and now residing in the Bodleian Library in Oxford: Ms Bodley 271 (SC1938). It is made up of two manuscripts: one written on parchment in the early twelfth century, the works of Anselm; the other written on paper in the fifteenth century, an exposition of the 'Song of Songs' wrongly attributed to Anselm. The genuine Anselm manuscript equates to the first ii + 166 folios of Ms Bodley 271. From now on, when I speak of this part of Ms Bodley 271, I shall refer to it as B. The script of B is written mainly in the Christ Church hand.[12] My reason for employing this text rather than that contained in Schmitt's edition[13] is based on my belief that an edition of Anselm's works was produced with the involvement of Anselm at the end of his life, and that B is to be identified

---

8 *CDH*Preface.

9 That even his contemporaries would have found his approach unusual can be seen in the response of Lanfranc to the *Monologion*, which he criticised, because it did not reference Augustine in the body of the text. See *E*77.

10 See Ludwig Wittgenstein, *Zettel*, 2nd edn, Oxford 1981, §455, p. 80.

11 *DIV*1.

12 This style of writing is found primarily in manuscripts from Christ Church Priory, Canterbury, in the late eleventh to the mid-twelfth century, but also employed in other monastic scriptoria, e.g. Rochester.

13 F.S. Schmitt, *Sancti Anselmi cantuariensis archiepiscopi Opera Omnia*, vols I–VI, Edinburgh 1946–1961.

with this edition.[14] Thus, it is from this manuscript, probably written between 1107 and 1114 at Christ Church Priory, Canterbury, that the text is taken. In fact, the outcome of the attempt in the last century, led by Dom A. Wilmart and Dom F.S. Schmitt, to distinguish the authentic works of Saint Anselm of Canterbury from later accretions,[15] following on from which Schmitt produced his critical edition of the works of Anselm, was to produce a set of works and a text which were virtually identical to that of B. B represents the closest thing we have to a definitive edition of Anselm's works.

I have chosen not to include here the text of the *Sumptum*, which follows the *Proslogion* and precedes the *Pro Insipiente*, since it simply reiterates with some minor changes in punctuation the text of *P*2–4. It is important, however, to note the presence of the *Sumptum* in B, since it confirms that the *Pro Insipiente* was viewed as a response to *P*2–4, and not to the remainder of the *Proslogion*. The *Pro Insipiente* begins, '*Quid adhaec respondeat quidam…*'. '*Haec*' here refers to the words of the *Sumptum*.

B contains all Anselm's major writings, but not his correspondence. References to his letters follow the numbering contained in Schmitt's edition.

The Transcription

The purpose of the transcription of that part of B that contains the *Proslogion*, the *Pro Insipiente* and Anselm's *Responsio* is to convey accurately the original without expecting the reader to be experienced in reading medieval scribal hands or acquainted with scribal shorthand and punctuation. Thus, the transcription expands the shorthand, placing the expanded text in square brackets, e.g. *e[st]*. The punctuation as it exists in the manuscript is retained. It should be noted that medieval punctuation is not as grammatically or syntactically significant as modern punctuation. Throughout our text a 'corrector' has scratched out the punctus employed in the *est*/*esse* abbreviations. This will not be noted in the text.

Punctuation is transcribed thus:

Punctus on the line or medial punctus followed by capital letter – **.**
Medial punctus not followed by capital letter – ,
Double punctus – **:**
Punctus elevatus – **;**
Punctus exclamativus – **!**
Punctus interrogativus – **?**

14 See I. Logan, 'Ms Bodley 271: Establishing the Anselmian Canon?' in *The Saint Anselm Journal*, 2 (2004) 67–80.

15 For the numerous articles by Schmitt, Wilmart and others, see K. Kienzler, *International Bibliography – Anselm of Canterbury*, Lewiston/Queenston/Lampeter 1999.

A characteristic feature of the text is the elision of a preposition with its object, e.g. *inipso* for *in ipso*. This has been retained in the transcription. Medieval spelling has also been retained, e.g. *nichil* for *nihil*.

I have broken up the chapters of the *Proslogion*, *Pro Insipiente* and *Responsio* with subsections in order to aid the task of commentary and citation. To assist the reader, I have also inserted the chapter headings into the body of the text of the *Proslogion*, although in B they only occur between *P*Preface and *P*1.

The Translation

It is necessary to say something about the principles behind the translation, especially as there are already several translations into English. If we are to undertake a philosophical reading in any language other than the original then ideally we would employ a translation which presents the philosophical meaning with all its nuances just as they occur in the original. But, of course, there is a problem with this ideal. For the meaning and the nuances are subject to interpretation even within the original language, so first one must decide which of the possible sets of meaning and nuances occurring in the original text most accurately captures the author's intention, and then determine how best to convey it in the receptor language. So translation presumes interpretation.[16] There is no such thing as a definitive translation of a given text, precisely because there is no such thing as a definitive interpretation of a text. All translation must be understood in the light of the original text, and where it is important that a philosophical meaning is conveyed and maintained, this is best done by presenting the original and translated texts together, which is the procedure I follow in this book. The assumption is that serious students of a text (even those who are not linguists) will develop sufficient knowledge of the original language to be able to follow the path the translator took in moving from the original text to the translation. The translation is not intended to replace the original text but to act as an aid to the reading of the original. It seeks to avoid paraphrase insofar as that is possible. But, as Ronald Knox pointed out, translation without paraphrase is virtually impossible.[17]

Anselm does not quote Scripture in the way we do with quotation marks and chapter and verse. His readership would have been expected to recognise scriptural allusions without any such prompting. In order to retain the flow of the Anselmian text whilst providing the modern reader with the relevant reference, I have chosen not to employ quotation marks, but to simply provide in the Commentary a reference to the relevant passage in the Latin Vulgate Bible.

---

16 See George Steiner, *After Babel: Aspects of Language and Translation*, 3rd edn, Oxford 1998, p. 436.

17 See R. Knox, *The Trials of a Translator*, New York 1949, p. 14.

Quotations from Anselm's other works and from other sources are my own, unless otherwise indicated by reference to the work from which the translation is taken.

Translation and Abbreviation of 'Quo maius cogitari non potest' and Variants

In the *Responsio*, in particular, Anselm uses the phrase '*quo maius cogitari non potest*' (and variants) without prefixing either *aliquid* or *id*. Where this is the case I generally assume the less specific *aliquid* in the translation.

I use the abbreviation X for both 'something than which a greater cannot be thought' and 'that than which a greater cannot be thought'. Although there is a clear distinction between the two, the former being indefinite and the latter definite, where the distinction is not of significance for the argument I simply use X. Where the distinction might be considered significant I use 'something X' or 'that X' as appropriate.

The subjunctive frequently occurs in the variants of Anselm's formula, for example, '*aliquid quo nichil maius cogitari possit*'. I generally translate this by the indicative 'can', rather than the subjunctive 'could'.

Chapter 2
The Pre-text: The dialectical origins of Anselm's argument

Anselm belongs to a tradition of learning with its roots in the early church fathers and the ancient schools of Greece and Rome. Although much important material had been lost or mislaid prior to the early medieval period (most of Aristotle and almost all of Plato), what remained enabled the development of the teaching of the liberal arts in the schools. This paucity of material meant a focus on relatively few texts and encouraged the development of a limited, standardised curriculum around the seven liberal arts (the *trivium* and *quadrivium*). Anselm stood in this tradition as a Catholic and a monk, for whom the secular learning of the *trivium* had a particular purpose as a preamble to the specialised studies of the *quadrivium* and, more importantly, to the study of sacred scripture.[1] Particular authority was given in the early medieval period to Augustine and Boethius, who not only exerted a profound influence on theological thought, but also provided much of the foundation for the study of the liberal arts. Like Boethius, Anselm was greatly influenced by Augustine. But he followed Boethius along a specific form of Augustinianism that gave great weight to a limited Aristotelianism based on Aristotle's logical works. This was not imposed on Augustine from without, but recognized the importance of dialectic in Augustine's own thought. It was this Boethian/Aristotelian outlook that coloured Anselm's Augustinianism, his view of the function of grammar, dialectic and rhetoric in the education of Christians, and his appreciation of how faith and reason interacted in the understanding of the faithful Catholic scholar. It also assisted him in developing his capacity to harmonise, without confusing, theology and dialectic.

The purpose of this chapter is to enquire into the origins of Anselm's argument and the texts and people who influenced his writing of the *Proslogion*. In order to achieve this, I will look firstly at what we can understand about Anselm's sources directly from his writings (both his correspondence and his major works) and indirectly from the works that may have been in the library at Bec, and from the curriculum that he is likely to have taught. What emerges is the importance of dialectic in Anselm's thought, particularly as it is developed in the work of Boethius. Secondly, I will look at how Boethian dialectic influences what Anselm is doing in the *Proslogion*. An investigation of the key notions of the topics, argument and argumentation, middle terms, and definition and description reveals

---

[1] See Anselm's statement that the dialogues, *DV*, *DLA* and *DCD*, pertain to the study of sacred scripture: '*Tres tractatus pertinentes ad studium sacrae scripturae*' (*DV*Preface).

a great deal about what Anselm would consider a successful argument for God to consist in. However, Anselm is not simply a dialectician, but also a man of faith, so, thirdly, bearing in mind that the original title of the *Proslogion* was '*Fides quaerens intellectum*', I will address the question of Anselm's understanding of the relation between faith and reason, particularly under the influence of Augustine.

Anselm's Reading

Anselm tells us little about his reading. Nevertheless, there are some allusions to, and citations from, other authors in his letters and writings. It is also possible to obtain some indications concerning the works he may have read from the extant catalogues of the library at Bec, and from an understanding of the curriculum he studied and taught.

Anselm's Correspondence

In Anselm's letters, we find references to the following works: Gregory's *Moralia in Job* (*E*23 and *E*25 to Lanfranc, and *E*26 to Abbott O., in which he indicates that the Bec copy has been loaned to Caen), Gregory's *Registrum Epistolarum*, XIV (*E*161 and *E*162; see also *E*65), Bede's *De temporibus* (*E*42, in which Anselm is seeking a copy he can use to correct the copy held at Bec), Lanfranc's *Commentary on Paul's Epistles* (*E*66 to Lanfranc, in which he sends the volume to Lanfranc and requests that Lanfranc make a copy for Bec), and a *Musica* (*E*146).[2] *E*425 contains a reference to a story concerning the paralysis of the misogynist Abbot Paul in Cassian's *Collationes*, VII, 26. Anselm explicitly refers to his teaching of declination[3] (and to his lack of enthusiasm for doing so) in *E*64 and suggests to the monk, Maurice, that under Arnulf at Canterbury he should study the writings of Virgil and other profane authors that Anselm did not teach him. Whilst it is possible that there was a lack of such material at Bec, the suggestion of phrases borrowed from both Virgil (*Eclogues*, IX, 25) and Horace (*Satires*, I, 4, 34) in *E*2, indicates, as we would expect in a school whose curriculum centred on the *trivium*, that such material was known and used in the teaching of grammar at Bec. On this point, it is worth noting that in *E*19, Avesgotus asks Anselm to teach his nephew grammar, confirming Anselm's involvement in the teaching of this subject. In his reply (*E*20),

---

[2] Note the volume on music contained in G. Becker, *Catalogi bibliotecharum antiqui*, Bonn 1885, p. 266, item 158, and H. Omont, *Catalogue général des mss. des bibilothèques publiques de France, départements*, vol. II, Paris 1888, p. 394, item 160.

[3] By declination is meant more than declining nouns. For a late Latin account of how the teaching of grammar proceeded, which is indicative of what Anselm means by declination, see Priscian, *Partitiones Duodecim Versuum Aeneidos Principalium*, I, 9ff. This involves a detailed analysis of each word of the portion of the text being studied, broadened out to address related issues of a literary, historical or grammatical nature.

Anselm identifies the source of a quotation in Avesgotus's letter as Persius Flaccus. Anselm sends a *Flores Psalmorum* along with seven of his own prayers to Adelaide (*E*10). He also speaks of obtaining works of Ambrose and Jerome for Lanfranc (whether getting them copied from works in Bec or from elsewhere is unclear – see *E*23). In *E*43 and *E*60 Anselm asks that Maurice should copy the work, *Aforismus* (presumably that of Hippocrates[4]) and the glosses in it, and in *E*60 mentions another work Maurice is working on, *De Pulsibus* (Galen), indicating an interest in the study of medicine. In *E*39 to Lanfranc, Anselm seeks to obtain the *Vita* and *Instituta* of Saint Dunstan (see also *E*42). In *E*115, Anselm quotes a well-known aphorism from Lucan's *Pharsalia*, I, 281: '*semper nocuit differe paratis*'.

Apart from references to Augustine and the *De Trinitate* in *E*77, *E*83 and *E*204, Anselm's letters do not provide any strong clues as to the influences on his thought. They support what we would expect, that he is well educated and widely read. I will now turn to Anselm's major writings to determine whether they can provide us with more definite evidence of the influences on him.

Anselm's Major Writings

In addition to the references in his correspondence, Anselm mentions Augustine three times in his major works. In *M*Preface, Anselm claims that his argument is consistent with Augustine and that any doubters should read the latter's *De Trinitate*. In *DIV*6, Anselm refers to the impregnable proofs for the doctrine of the Trinity to be found particularly in Augustine, and refers again to the *De Trinitate* in *DIV*16.

The only other explicit reference to another author is to Aristotle, whose name occurs eleven times in *DG* and once in *CDH*.[5] In *DG*17, Anselm writes of Aristotle's 'principal intention' in writing the *Categories*, and refers to the followers of Aristotle who wrote on dialectic. He makes it clear that both the teacher and the student are well acquainted with these works. Anselm quotes from Aristotle in this chapter, taking the quotation from Boethius's translation in his *Commentary on the Categories*, 1.[6]

The use of the terms *enuntiatio*, *oratio*, *propositio, affirmatio* and *negatio* in *DV*2 is derived from Boethius's usage throughout his commentaries on Aristotle and his work on the topics.[7] The discussion in *M*10 of *naturalia verba*, which 'are the same amongst all peoples', can be traced to Boethius's first *Commentary on*

---

[4] See L. MacKinney, *Bishop Fulbert and Education at the School of Chartres*, Notre Dame 1957, p. 32, on Richer's account of how he was urged to go to Chartres to read Hippocrates' *Aphorisms*.

[5] The reference to Plato in *DG*20 is simply the employment of a name in an example.

[6] '*Cum ergo Aristoteles ita dicat, eorum quae secundum nullam complexionem dicuntur, singulum aut substantiam significat aut quantitatem.*' See *PL*64 col. 162B.

[7] See, for example, *De Topicis Differentiis*: 'A proposition (*propositio*) is an expression (*oratio*) signifying what is true or false; for example, when someone says that the heaven is revolvable, this is called a statement (*enuntiatio*) and an assertion (*proloquium*) ....

De Interpretatione, I.[8] Anselm's designation of eternity as 'unending life existing simultaneously and perfectly complete' in *M*24 is derived from Boethius's *De Consolatione Philosophiae*, V, 6.[9] Anselm's use of the example of blindness in his discussion of 'dead faith' in *M*78 borrows the metaphor and the language from Boethius's translation of Aristotle's *Categories*, X.[10] In the following chapter (*M*79), Anselm takes his definition of 'person' as an 'individual rational nature' from Boethius.[11] In *P*Preface, Anselm talks of trying to find one argument – 'if one argument could be discovered [*inveniri*]' – reminding us of Boethius's edition of Cicero's preface to his *Topica*, where he refers to the topics as the 'discipline of discovering arguments' ['*disciplinam inveniendorum argumentorum*'].[12] A trace of Anselm's famous phrase in the *Proslogion*, '*aliquid quo nichil maius cogitare possit*' (*P*2.3), can be found in Boethius's *De Consolatione Philosophiae*, III, 10: '*cum nihil Deo melius excogitari queat*'.[13]

Apart from Augustine, Aristotle and Boethius it is difficult to find any other obvious sources in Anselm's major works. In the Preface to the *Monologion*, he does advert to the writings of the Catholic fathers, but other than that concerning Augustine and Boethius there is no direct evidence as to who is to be included in this category. Anselm was well read and would have included Ambrose, Jerome and Gregory the Great, as well as others, amongst these authorities. However, it is clear that the major influences on him were Augustine, Aristotle and Boethius (the latter as both dialectician and 'theologian').

The Library at Bec

Another place where we might hope to identify possible sources for Anselm's thinking in the *Proslogion* is in the library at the abbey of Bec, where Anselm was both a student and teacher. However, Anselm did not arrive in Bec until c. 1059 at the approximate age of 26, having spent three years wandering in Burgundy and France. We may surmise, therefore, that Anselm had already been educated in other centres of learning prior to his arrival at Bec. This would explain the fact that he acted as teacher as well as student from his earliest days there. It is possible that he had received a different or wider training in the liberal arts that that provided by Lanfranc, and that some, at least, of his knowledge of dialectic was gained outside the school at Bec. Southern's claim, that Anselm 'still had almost everything to

---

There are two species of proposition: the one, affirmation [*affirmatio*]; the other, negation [*negatio*]' (E. Stump, *Boethius's De topicis differentiis*, Ithaca/London 1978, p. 30).

8 *PL*64 col. 297C-D. See also the discussion in the following section, '*De nomine*', and in the second Commentary (*PL*64 col. 403A).

9 *PL*63 col. 858A.

10 *In Categorias Aristotelis*, IV (*PL*64 col. 270A).

11 *Contra Eutychen et Nestorium*, III (*PL*64 col. 1343C-D).

12 Boethius, *In Ciceronis Topica*, I (*PL*64 col. 1042A).

13 *PL*63 col. 765A.

learn'[14] when he arrived at Bec, underestimates the likely level of learning he achieved in the previous ten or more years.

With the caveat that this would not have constituted the sole source of Anselm's reading prior to his authorship of the *Proslogion*, it is still worthwhile looking at the contents of the library at Bec. In fact, there are two extant catalogues relating to books held at Bec in the twelfth century, which are contained in a manuscript from the Abbey of Mont Saint Michel.[15] On their own, they are only suggestive of what books might have been at Bec in Anselm's time.[16] The bulk of the material contained in the catalogues is patristic, and, unsurprisingly, the main author is Augustine, followed by Jerome and Ambrose. Nevertheless, the wide-ranging nature of the contents of the library is clear from a brief list of some of the non-patristic authors represented there, such as Cicero, Palladius, Vegetius, Macrobius and Quintillian. The library contained Lanfranc's *De Corpore et Sanguine Domini* and a collection of his letters, but there is no reference in the catalogues to any volumes which might have contained Lanfranc's glosses, even though Anselm had asked Lanfranc to have a copy made for the Bec library. Nor is there any reference to Lanfranc's lost works, *De Dialectica* and *Questiones*.[17]

If we wish to understand what texts Anselm might have used in his teaching at Bec, there are two items in the larger catalogue that might be of assistance. These are:

(i) a manuscript[18] containing Martianus Capella's *De Nuptiis Philologiae et Mercurii*, a commentary of Remigius on Martianus, both parts of Priscian's *Institutiones*, a two volume work on rhetoric, a three volume work on dialectic,[19] Boethius's commentary on Porphyry's *Isagoge*, his commentary on the *Categories*, his two commentaries on the *De Interpretatione* and his commentary on Cicero's *Topica*;

(ii) a manuscript[20] containing a volume on arithmetic, a volume on music, Macrobius's commentary on Cicero's *Somnium Scipionis*, two more volumes on arithmetic, Gilbertus's *Geometria* (presumably that of Gerbert d'Aurillac), a three volume *Propositiones* of Boethius,[21] a two volume Macrobius, a three volume Plato, and Calcidius's commentary on Plato's *Timaeus*.

---

14 R.W. Southern, *Saint Anselm: A Portrait in a Landscape*, Cambridge 1990, p. 16.

15 Bibliothèque d'Avranches Ms 159 folios 1^v-3. See Becker, pp. 199–202 and 257–66, and Omont, pp. 385–98.

16 See the discussion in G. Gasper, *Anselm of Canterbury and his Theological Inheritance*, Aldershot 2004, pp. 92–6.

17 M. Gibson, *Lanfranc of Bec*, Oxford 1978, pp. 49 and 241.

18 Becker, p. 266, item 157; Omont, p. 393, item 159.

19 S. Nelis suggests that this is Boethius's *De Syllogismo Hypothetico*. See S. Nelis, 'What Lanfranc Taught, What Anselm Learned', in *The Haskins Society Journal*, 2 (1990) 75–82, 78.

20 Becker, p. 266, item 158; Omont, p. 394. Item 160.

21 This would appear to be Boethius's three volume work *De Syllogismo Hypothetico*, which deals with propositional logic.

There in no record in the catalogue of the *De Decem Categoriis*, although Lanfranc was acquainted with it[22] and was highly likely to have used it in his teaching at Bec. The fact that Lanfranc's glosses on Augustine's *De Civitate Dei*, (XIII, 16) include a quotation from Calcidius' translation of the *Timaeus* (41A-B)[23] might suggest the manuscript containing the Calcidius was present at Bec during Lanfranc's (and therefore Anselm's) time. It seems unlikely that all the eleventh century manuscripts would have disappeared from Bec.

The Curriculum: the Liberal Arts and the Logica Vetus

Eadmer records approvingly that Pope Urban II regarded Anselm as a master who was steeped in the liberal arts.[24] By the term 'liberal arts' is meant the traditional curriculum, which was divided into the *trivium*: grammar, dialectic and rhetoric, and the *quadrivium*: arithmetic, geometry, music and astronomy. Given the role that the disciplines associated with the *trivium* played in the understanding of the scriptures and Catholic doctrine, it is unsurprising that Anselm's knowledge of the liberal arts should have been particularly focused on the *trivium*. From the limited number of books that were employed in the teaching of the *trivium*, it is possible to grasp the material Anselm would have studied and taught.

Works which expounded on the liberal arts as traditionally conceived were Augustine's *De Ordine* and *De Doctrina Christiana*, Martianus Capella's *De Nuptiis Philologiae et Mercurii* with the related books on each of the liberal arts (the fourth book, of which, *De Arte Dialectica*, contains a paraphrase of parts of Aristotle's *Categories*[25]), Cassiodorus's *De Artibus ac Disciplinis Liberalium Litterarum*, Isidore of Seville's *Etymologiae* and Rabanus Maurus's *De Institutione Clericorum*. Anselm is likely to have been acquainted with some, if not all of these works. Only the Cassiodorus and the Rabanus Maurus are not listed in the twelfth century Bec catalogue.

The central texts of the *trivium* were as follows:[26]

(i) Grammar: Priscian, *Institutiones Grammaticae*; Donatus, *Ars Grammatica*.

---

22 See R. Hunt, 'Studies on Priscian in the eleventh and twelfth centuries', in *Mediaeval and Renaissance Studies*, I (1943) 194–231, 208. One of the reasons for the influence of *De Decem Categoriis* was the fact that it had been incorrectly attributed to Augustine by Alcuin.

23 Gibson suggests that this note was written about 1050: M. Gibson, 'The Study of the "Timaeus" in the eleventh and twelfth centuries', in *Pensamiento*, 25 (1969) 183–94, 184.

24 Eadmer, *Life*, p. 105.

25 See L. Minio-Paluello, 'The Text of the Categoriae: The Latin Tradition', in L. Minio-Paluello, *Opuscula: The Latin Aristotle*, Amsterdam, 1972, pp. 28–39, pp. 30–31.

26 See S. Ebbesen, 'Ancient Scholastic Logic as the source of medieval scholastic logic', in N. Kretzmann et al. (eds), *The Cambridge History of Later Medieval Philosophy*, Cambridge 1982, pp. 101–27, esp. pp. 105–9.

(ii) Dialectic: the *logica vetus*, i.e. Aristotle's *Categories* and *De Interpretatione*, Porphyry's *Isagoge*, and Cicero's *Topics*, and Boethius's commentaries on these works; Pseudo-Augustine, *De Decem Categoriis* (which contains part paraphrase and part literal translation of Aristotle's *Categories*); Augustine, *De Dialectica*.

(iii) Rhetoric: Cicero, *De Inventione* and Marius Victorinus's commentary on *De Inventione*, and *Rhetorica ad Herennium*, which was attributed to Cicero.

Other important works were Plato's *Timaeus* in the part translation by Calcidius with the latter's commentary on lines 31c–53c, Macrobius's commentary on Cicero's *Somnium Scipionis*, *Asclepius* and *Peri hermeneias* – attributed to Apuleius, Marius Victorinus's *De Definitionibus* (attributed to Boethius), and Boethius's *De Divisione*, *De Syllogismo Categorico*, *Introductio ad Syllogismos Categoricos*, *De Syllogismo Hypothetico* and *De Topicis Differentiis*.

Although there is no guarantee that Anselm was acquainted with all the works associated with the *trivium*, he had studied some of them, in particular the works of Boethius. It is also clear that Anselm taught the *trivium* (and possibly elements of the *quadrivium*) at Bec, and must certainly be regarded as a teacher of dialectic as well as, as has already been noted, a teacher of grammar. The dialogue, *De Grammatico*, is a work of dialectic that has its origins in the school-room, where the teacher analyses and criticises the arguments of the pupil, laying particular emphasis on the need to employ syllogistic proofs. Anselm instructs the pupil to 'construct the syllogism' using the common or middle term.[27]

What we know of the works Anselm was familiar with and the likely content of the curriculum he studied and taught supports this picture of Anselm as the teacher of dialectic. This is not to say that he was constrained in his writings by the formal methods of dialectic. Anselm was not interested in displaying his skill in logic by constructing syllogisms for the sake of it. His purpose was to find logically sound arguments and to employ them in furthering his and his reader's understanding of the teachings of scripture and the church. For this task the skills of the dialectician were required, and of paramount importance in this regard was the work of Boethius.

The Anselm of Dialectic

The Influence of Boethius

A comparison of Anselm's writings and those of Boethius (see above), shows that Anselm was well acquainted with Boethius's works, in particular his commentary on Aristotle's *Categories*, the two commentaries on Aristotle's *De Interpretatione*, the two commentaries on Porphyry's *Isagoge*, the commentary on Cicero's *Topica*, *De Consolatione Philosophiae*, at least two of the theological tractates,

---

[27] *DG*4. See M. Grabmann, *Die Geschichte der scholastischen Methode*, vol. 1, Darmstadt 1969, p. 313.

De Trinitate and *Contra Eutychen et Nestorium*, and, possibly, the *Introductio ad Syllogismos Categoricos* and/or *De Syllogismo Categorico*. The presence of the three volume book of *Propositions* (and the three volume work on dialectic) in the Bec catalogue hints at the possibility that Anselm was also acquainted with Boethius's *De Syllogismo Hypothetico*. Much of what Anselm writes is also consistent with Boethius's *De Topicis Differentiis*.

Charlesworth argues that it is not Neo-platonism that is distinctive of Anselm's thought, but rather a dialectical or 'rationalist' approach that bears the influence of Aristotle and Boethius.[28] In fact, Anselm's relationship with Boethius and Neo-platonism is complex, particularly given the strength of Boethius's own Neo-platonism and the commitment of both Boethius and Anselm to the thought of Augustine. However, there exists in Boethius's Neo-platonism (following Porphyry), a clear distinction between Plato and Aristotle that permits him to regard the two as consistent with each other. Aristotle's logic addresses the world of sense experience, whilst that of Neo-platonic metaphysics addresses that of intelligible realities.[29] Of course, in Boethius's influential *De Consolatione Philosophiae*, 'Philosophy' has an ambivalent role. She is not quite Christian, and so must be treated with caution. Nevertheless, in the *De Grammatico*, Anselm's debt to Boethius's dialectical inheritance is revealed clearly, in particular in the discussions relating to Aristotle's *Categories*. L. Steiger has shown how the initial exchange between student and teacher in *De Grammatico* bears the imprint of Boethius's discussion concerning the nature of argument in Book 1 of his commentary on Cicero's *Topics*.[30] It is Boethius's theory of topics, the '*scientia inveniendorum argumentorum*' ['the science of finding arguments'],[31] that is of particular significance in understanding the argument of the *Proslogion*, which is the product of Anselm's attempt to find or discover (*invenire*) the *unum argumentum*.

The Topics

The purpose of the topics is to provide an exhaustive framework for the discovery of arguments. Although originating in Aristotle's *Topica*, the subject matter of the topics was transmitted to the early medieval period through Boethius, Aristotle's book not being extant at this time. The implications of this are significant, since Boethius developed the topics in a specific direction. They were no longer 'a general strategy for argumentation', but a specific method for the discovery of middle terms in syllogistic arguments.[32] According to Boethius, 'every argument

---

28 M.J. Charlesworth, *St.Anselm's Proslogion*, Oxford 1965, p. 24.

29 See J. Marenbon, *Boethius*, 2003, p. 12.

30 L. Steiger, 'Contexe Syllogismos: Über die Kunst und Bedeutung der Topik bei Anselm', in *AA*, I, pp. 107–43, p. 136.

31 Boethius, *In Ciceronis Topica* (*PL*64 col. 1043A).

32 See E. Stump, *Dialectic and its Place in the Development of Medieval Logic*, Ithaca/London 1989, p. 57.

is expressed by a syllogism or an enthymeme'.[33] An 'argument is nothing other than the discovery of an intermediate [term], for an intermediate will be able to conjoin the extremes, if an affirmation is being maintained, or to disjoin them, if a negation is being asserted'.[34] In other words, in the syllogism, '*a* is *b*, *b* is *c*, therefore *a* is *c*', the aim of the topics is to discover *b*, the term that conjoins *a* and *c*. An example of such a syllogism is as follows:

(1) Every man is an animal,
(2) Every animal is a substance,
(3) Therefore, every man is a substance.

Here, (1) is the minor premise, in which the minor term is the subject and the middle term is the predicate, (2) is the major premise, in which the middle term is the subject and the major term the predicate, thus enabling the conjoining of the minor and major terms in the conclusion (3).[35] Boethius holds that 'where there is something greater and lesser, there must also be something greatest or maximal', drawing the inference that there exist maximal propositions, which are the topics (i.e. the *loci*, the places) where the other propositions are located, in the same way as bodies are located in physical places. These maximal propositions are the 'universal and most known propositions from which the conclusion of syllogisms is derived'.[36] It is these maximal propositions that give force to the middle terms of syllogisms and hence to the syllogism itself. Cicero seeks to categorise these maximal propositions or topics according to their *differentiae*. The maximal propositions are divisible into *genera* which contain all other propositions. The *differentiae* or classifications of maximal propositions can be regarded as containing all 'argumentations'. In other words, they represent the 'ultimate seat' of arguments.[37] What this means in practice is that it is possible to derive all middle terms from the topics, if one has sufficient knowledge and skill. It is the purpose of dialectic to teach and apply this skill in argumentation.

Argument and Argumentation

In his *De Topicis Differentiis*, Boethius distinguishes between the terms 'argument' and 'argumentation' as follows:[38]

---

33 E. Stump, *Boethius's In Ciceronis Topica*, Ithaca/London 1988, p. 31.

34 Ibid., p. 32.

35 *PL*64 col.1051A. Unfortunately, part of the text is missing in Stump's translation of this passage (see Stump, *In Ciceronis*, p. 32)

36 Stump, *In Ciceronis*, p. 33.

37 *PL*64 col.1053B.

38 Stump, *De topicis*, p. 30.

> Argument and argumentation are not the same, however; for the sense (*vis sententiae*) and the reason enclosed in discourse (*oratio*) when something [that was] uncertain is demonstrated is called the argument; but the expression (*elocutio*) of the argument is called the argumentation. So the argument is the strength (*virtus*), mental content (*mens*), and sense of argumentation; argumentation, on the other hand, is the unfolding of the argument by means of discourse (*oratio*).

However, the distinction between the two terms is not as straightforward as this passage might suggest, for in *In Ciceronis Topica* Boethius suggests that there are four different ways of making the distinction. In fact, in one of the distinctions argument and argumentation are synonymous. Thus, when looking at Anselm's usage, we should be careful not to assume that for Anselm there is a straightforward Boethian distinction pervading all his work.[39] In the place where we might expect to have an explicit statement of such a distinction (*De Grammatico*), it is lacking. Anselm uses *argumentum* in *DG*2, *DG*11, and *DG*21, where it appears to incorporate *argumentatio*. He uses *argumentatio* in *DG*7, and *DG*8, and again there is no clear distinction between *argumentatio* and *argumentum*. Nor elsewhere in his writings is a clear distinction made explicit. This does not mean that we can ignore what Boethius says on the matter, since, when Boethius defines an argument as 'a reason [*ratio*] which brings about belief [*fidem*] concerning something in doubt'[40] and writes that 'an argument is nothing other than the discovery of an intermediate',[41] i.e. a middle term, we have perhaps the clearest indication available of the senses in which Anselm employed the term '*argumentum*'. In fact, Anselm's statement in *DG*4, that it is the meaning (*sententia*) that gives force to a syllogism rather than the words,[42] suggests that Anselm has in mind the view of argument put forward by Boethius in the above quotation from *De Topicis Differentiis*. Nevertheless, one must be careful not to suppose that this means that Anselm's employment of the terms *argumentatio* and *argumentum* always reflects such a technical Boethian usage, where the *argumentatio* represents the external form of the argument and *argumentum* the meaning of the argument.

For Boethius, arguments can be categorised as probable and necessary, probable and not necessary, not probable and necessary, and not probable and not

---

[39] As perhaps is the case with P. Boschung, *From a Topical Point of View: Dialectic in Anselm of Canterbury's* De Grammatico, Leiden/Boston 2006, p. 62, who claims that Anselm 'depends on' a Boethian distinction between argument and argumentation.

[40] In both *De Topicis Differentiis* and *In Ciceronis Topica*. *See PL*64 cols 1174D, 1180C, and 1048B.

[41] Stump, *In Ciceronis*, p. 32.

[42] The sense of this statement is easily grasped. It is in the understanding of what the words mean that the force of the syllogism lies, not in the words themselves. The same word can have different meanings and different words can have the same meaning. It is the meaning that is really operative in the syllogism.

necessary. The necessary is that which cannot be otherwise, whilst the probable involves an *ad hominem* appeal, for example to expertise or to views held by one's dialogue partner (regardless of their truth or falsity).[43] Dialectic is concerned with probable arguments, that is, arguments that the other partner in the dispute accepts, whether necessary or not, since its purpose is to win over the other party. Necessary arguments that are not probable are the concern of philosophers, rather than dialecticians, although necessary and probable arguments are the concern of both. The primary purpose, then, of argument and argumentation in dialectic is to convince, to bring about belief where there was doubt.[44]

The Middle Term

The topics involve the discovery of arguments concerning matters that are in doubt. The method of achieving a successful argument is the identification of a middle term, which will be categorised according to one of the maximal propositions. However, this can only work in disputation if one's opponent accepts the application of the middle term, both as the predicate of the minor term and the subject of the major term. From the perspective of dialectic even a logically sound demonstration will not be successful, if the opponent does not accept all of the premises. Anselm as a dialectician has to employ a strategy that firstly makes his argument acceptable to his opponent (a probable argument) and secondly establishes its demonstrative soundness (a necessary argument). It is not difficult to see that this is how Anselm proceeds in the *Proslogion*. He is setting out to establish that God exists, and begins by identifying to his wider audience (the observers of the disputation) that his middle term will be 'that than which a greater cannot be thought' (=X). He then begins the argument by identifying that God's existence is being called into question, and sets out to get his opponent, the 'fool', to accept the middle term (X), and the major premise: X exists in the understanding (*in intellectu*) and in reality (*in re*).[45] Once he has established the major premise, he argues for the minor premise: God is X. If God is not this, then something is greater than Him, which would mean the creature would be greater than the Creator, which is impossible. Here he reaches the limits of the dialectic art, because a necessary argument such as this can still be denied by the fool, just as someone foolish can deny that if you take an even number from an even number you are left with an even number, i.e.

---

43 *PL*64 col. 1180C-D.

44 Anselm's use of the term 'necessary reasons' would suggest that for him necessary arguments are more important than this general account of Boethian dialectic might suggest. But in Anselm's account, necessary reasons do not always possess the necessity of thoroughgoing logical demonstrations.

45 See Stump, *De topicis*, p. 161: 'Part of the questioner's art is to conceal from the answerer which are the necessary premises crucial for producing the conclusion, because in this way the answerer is more likely to answer as he thinks and less likely to balk perversely or ingeniously at the important questions.'

the fool can deny maximal propositions. At this point the fool has no further part to play in Anselm's argument since he is moving from the art of dialectic (probable arguments) to that of demonstration (necessary arguments). Having established both his premises, he is able to draw the conclusion that God exists.

Definition and Description

Boethius can also assist us in understanding whether X is, as frequently stated by commentators, a definition of God.[46] In *De Divisione*, Boethius writes:[47]

> Of things some are higher, others lower, others intermediate. The higher ones no definition embraces since for them no higher genera can be discovered; at the same time, the lower things, i.e. individuals, lack specific differentiae, so that they too are excluded from definition. The intermediate ones, then, which both have genera and are predicated of other things, be they genera, species, or individuals, *are* able to come under a definition.

In *De Topicis Differentiis*, Book II, Boethius states that the difference between definition and description lies in the fact that 'a definition contains genus and differentiae', whilst a description involves an 'understanding of the subject' through accidents or differentiae 'apart from the appropriate genus'.[48] In saying that a definition 'contains' a genus, Boethius means, for example, that the definition of man ('rational, mortal animal') contains the genus, animal. Thus, when Porphyry says that genus is that to which species is subordinated,[49] it is clear that God cannot fall under a genus, otherwise He would be a species, an intermediate thing, falling under a higher classification. The highest genera are the ten categories, and none of these can be employed to define God. Furthermore, since definition requires the application of differentiae to genera, even the categories themselves cannot be defined in the strict sense. Finally, a genus is predicable of more than one thing, which could not be the case of any 'genus' under which God falls, since God must be one. Thus, in the strict sense, X cannot be a definition of God in the Boethian tradition in which Anselm is operating.

---

[46] For example, W. Kneale and M. Kneale, *The Development of Logic*, Oxford 1962, p. 201.

[47] *Anicii Manlii Severini Boethii De divisione liber*, critical edition, translation, prolegomena and commentary by John Magee, Leiden 1998, pp. 33f. Reprinted with permission of Koninklijke Brill N.V.

[48] Stump, *De topicis*, pp. 49f.

[49] '*Aliter autem rursus dicitur genus, cui supponitur species*.' (Boethius's second commentary on Porphyry's *Isagoge*, PL64 col. 90C.)

The Anselm of Faith and Reason

Anselm is not simply a dialectician; he is also a man of faith. In order to understand what this means, we need to look at how that faith informed his thinking, always being aware that there could be no conflict between faith and reason for him, other than that arising from human ignorance and sinfulness. And yet, it did appear to some that such a conflict could exist, and it is easy to see how from the writings of Boethius. In *De Topicis Differentiis*, III, discussing the topic 'from antecedents to consequents', Boethius writes:[50]

> From an antecedent an argument is taken [in this way]. If she has borne a child, then she has lain with a man. I take the antecedent: but she has borne a child; I conclude the consequent: therefore she has lain with a man. From consequents in this way. I take the consequent: but she has not lain with a man; I conclude the antecedent: therefore, she has not borne a child.

The example provided by Boethius clearly has implications for the doctrine of the virgin birth and would appear to constitute a rejection of this doctrine, even though in *De Fide Catholica* Boethius explicitly subscribes to it. Unsurprisingly, given the apparent conflicts that could arise between dialectic and Catholic doctrine, dialectic was viewed with suspicion by some. Nevertheless, dialecticians such as Boethius and Anselm were men of faith, and it is the balance between reason and faith that Anselm is at pains to maintain in a way that is faithful to the authority of scripture and the church.

Scriptural Authority and Dialectic

The influence of the scriptures is felt throughout Anselm's writings. He was a monk whose daily life was governed by the rhythms of monastic prayer in the divine office and the *lectio divina*. He was also a student of the church fathers, whose 'rhetorical' style included frequent references to scripture, and much of whose subject matter was dictated by the scriptures. Even where Anselm claims to be addressing questions *sola ratione*[51] or *remoto Christo*,[52] he continues to employ the language of scripture. Nevertheless, Anselm did not produce glosses on scripture in the way that Lanfranc, his teacher, did. The dialogues he wrote, 'pertaining to the study of sacred scripture',[53] do not involve a line by line reading

---

50 Stump, *De topicis*, p. 68. See Stump, *In Ciceronis*, p. 129. See also Cicero, *De Inventione*, I, 29.

51 *M*1. Nothing is to be argued on the authority of scripture, see *M*Preface. In Boethius's theory of topics, the argument from authority is regarded as inferior to all the other topics. See *De Topicis Differentiis*, III, and *In Ciceronis Topica*, II.

52 *CDH*Preface.

53 *DV*Preface.

of and commentary on a particular text. They are responses to questions that are touched on but not fully answered in scripture, or represent attempts to clarify the true meaning of the text where it is concealed by the 'impropriety of words'.[54]

The monastic, prayerful Anselm, the author of the *Orationes sive Meditationes*, who reads scripture for spiritual nourishment, is not to be too strongly distinguished from the Anselm who applies the skills of the grammarian and dialectician to scripture. These are not for him incompatible approaches, but represent two sides of a single approach, characterised in Augustine's *De Doctrina Christiana*, Cassiodorus' *Institutiones*, in the writings of Isidore of Seville, and even present, if more sceptical of secular learning, in the work of Gregory the Great.[55] But what is characteristic of Anselm's approach in comparison to those who went before him is the lack of restraint he feels concerning the use of the liberal arts. He is aware of the dangers of dialectic, but does not see these as inherent in dialectic. The right person can use dialectic correctly. He applies the term 'heretics of dialectic'[56] not to dialecticians as opposed to anti-dialecticians, but to those who use dialectic incorrectly in matters of faith as opposed to those who use it correctly. To employ dialectic correctly it is essential to have (i) a thorough training in the liberal arts and (ii) climbed the 'ladder of faith'.[57] The acceptance of the authority of scripture, the church and the fathers is a prerequisite for the proper use of dialectic, but there is a proper use. Nowhere in Anselm's writings do we find an apology for this approach, because he took it for granted. Thus, it appears to be even less of an issue for him than it was for so many of his precursors. In his response to the *Monologion*, Lanfranc appears to have felt a need to point out to Anselm the possible 'conflict' between reason and authority.[58] The real problem of dialectic for Anselm does not concern any such conflict. Rather, it is why, given its success as the means to the discovery of his *unum argumentum*, dialectic has not brought him closer to God. In spite of its success the dialectical method in practice achieves relatively little, and consequently there is no risk for Anselm of overestimating its place in the scheme of faith.[59]

---

[54] *DCD*1.

[55] Gregory's authorship of the work, *In Librum Primum Regum*, in which he appears to be most supportive of the application of secular studies to scripture has been called into question by A. de Vogüé, 'L'auteur du Commentaire des Rois attribué à saint Grégoire: un moine de Cava?', in *Revue Bénédictine*, 106 (1996) 319–31.

[56] *DIV*1.

[57] Ibid.

[58] See Steiger, p. 125. Nevertheless, in his *Commentary on Paul's Letter to the Colossians*, Lanfranc accepts that it is not dialectic, but its perverse use that is the problem: '*non artem disputandi vituperat, sed perversum disputantium usum*' (*PL*150 col. 323B).

[59] See T. Holopainen, 'Logic and Theology in the Eleventh Century: Anselm and Lanfranc's Heritage', in G. Gasper and H. Kohlenberger (eds), *Anselm and Abelard: Investigations and Juxtapositions*, Toronto 2006, pp. 1–16, p. 15.

Augustine and Authority

Apart from scripture and the doctrine set out by the church in its creeds, *the* authority and source of ideas for Anselm (as for Boethius) was Augustine. Anselm states explicitly in *M*Preface that he cannot find anything in the *Monologion* that conflicts with the writings of the church fathers, especially Augustine, and requests that anyone who thinks he is being too novel or original should read Augustine's *De Trinitate*. This reveals precisely Anselm's attitude to authority and to that of Augustine in particular. Gibson goes so far as to state that neither Anselm (or Boethius) say anything that is not said in more detail in Augustine's *De Trinitate*.[60] This view of Anselm's relation to Augustine is supported by the fact that, in the letter to Lanfranc, in which he is responding to Lanfranc's criticism of his lack of references to authorities,[61] Anselm states that the *Monologion* proved the same points as Augustine's *De Trinitate*, although by a briefer process of argumentation, and that he sought to say nothing that could not be defended from scripture or Augustine. Nevertheless, the only reference to Augustine in the *Monologion* is in the Preface, and may well have been added in the light of Lanfranc's criticism.[62]

Anselm's relation to Augustine is not straightforward, as Lanfranc's response to the *Monologion* suggests. Southern expresses the problem precisely:[63] 'Anselm's greatest and most characteristic phrases can always be traced back in the direction of Augustine, but the trail disappears before it reaches him.' Anselm presents arguments that are not found in Augustine. His concern is to be consistent with Augustine, not to repeat what he said. If one were to distil Augustine's work, one would not come up with the *Monologion*. Moreover, given Anselm's determination not to appeal to scriptural authority in the *Monologion*, we should be cautious of what it means for Anselm to regard Augustine as an authority. In fact, Boethius (and Cicero) had identified the argument from authority as one of the topics which, unlike the others, falls outside the art of dialectic:[64] 'There remains the Topic ... from without. This depends on judgement and authority and is only readily believable [*probabilis*], containing nothing necessary.' For Anselm, authority is not the source of argument and argumentation, it is extrinsic to dialectic, providing the rule against which results of the dialectical examination of the relation of subjects and predicates should be measured. In two identical passages, in what seems to be a standard Anselmian formula,[65] Anselm states clearly the provisional nature of whatever he appears to prove by reason (*ratione probare*) in matters of

60 M. Gibson, 'The *Opuscula Sacra* in the Middle Ages', in M. Gibson (ed.), *Boethius: His Life, Thought and Influence*, Oxford 1981, pp. 214–34, p. 214.

61 *E*77.

62 Apart from the *Monologion* and *E*77, Anselm only mentions Augustine by name in *DIV*6 and 16, and in two other letters, *E*83 and *E*204.

63 R.W. Southern, *Saint Anselm and his Biographer*, Cambridge 1966, p. 32.

64 Stump, *De topicis*, p. 70. See ibid., p. 200.

65 *CDH*I:2 and 18.

faith: confirmation is required from a greater authority before the outcome of his rational proof is to be accepted. In *M*1, Anselm speaks of a quasi or interim necessity which again remains provisional until support is provided by a greater authority. However, this does not mean that the matter remains in doubt, for as he says in *CDH*I:25, if something is deduced by means of necessary reason, it ought not to be doubted, even if the reason for it is not properly understood.

Whilst dialectic is not given free reign, but must be consistent with authority, authority cannot be employed in that area of dialectic whose results are intended to be 'necessary', since these must be derived from the 'first principles' of dialectic, the maximal propositions. Anselm's 'necessary reasons' are intended to be independent of, but consistent with, authority. Anselm's 'rationalism' is then constrained by his faith, not because his faith rejects dialectic, but because it constrains it by the rule of consistency. It is consistency and not repetition that is the rule.

'Faith Seeking Understanding' and Dialectic

The key methodological principle that Anselm derives from Augustine is that of '*fides quaerens intellectum*', a notion that permeates the thought of Augustine. This principle does not involve a rejection of reason.[66] As Augustine says in *De Ordine*, authority and reason constitute the two ways of learning. Whilst authority has priority insofar as it precedes reason in the learning process, reason has priority in terms of learning itself.[67] Although later, in his *Retractiones*, Augustine was to take the view that he had over-stressed the importance of the liberal arts in *De Ordine*,[68] he did not reject the notion expressed in *De Doctrina Christiana*, that dialectic was not a mere human invention, but reflected the 'divinely instituted system of things'.[69]

Augustine defends his use of dialectic in *Contra Cresconium*, where he identifies the Greek word *dialectica* with the Latin work *disputatio*, and states that the Apostle Paul is a *disputator* and a *dialecticus*.[70] In *De Doctrina Christiana*, he says explicitly that dialectic (*disputationis disciplina*) is extremely valuable as a means of resolving problems or questions that arise from scripture.[71] It allows for

---

66 See Augustine, *Epistola* CXX, 1, 3: 'Let no one think that God hates in us that in respect of which he made us superior to all other living beings. Let no one think, I say, that we should believe in such a way as not to accept or seek reason, since we could not even believe if we did not have rational souls.' (N. Kretzmann, 'Faith Seeks, Understanding Finds: Augustine's Charter for Christian Philosophy', in T. Flint (ed.), *Christian Philosophy*, Notre Dame, Indiana, 1990, pp. 1–36, p. 24.)

67 *De Ordine*, II, 9, 26.

68 *See Retractiones*, I, 3.

69 *De Doctrina Christiana*, II, 32, 50 (Saint Augustine, *On Christian Teaching*, translated with an Introduction and Notes by R.P.H. Green, Oxford 1997, p. 59).

70 *Contra Cresconium*, I, 17.

71 *De Doctrina Christiana*, II, 31, 48 (*On Christian Teaching*, p. 58).

the application of valid logical forms to propositions. It does *not* supply the truth of those propositions. According to Augustine, it is in scripture that the truth of propositions is to be found.[72] The point is to use dialectic correctly, as Augustine attempts to do in Book V of *De Trinitate* in his deployment of Aristotle's *Categories* against the Arians.[73]

It is in the context of his view of the validity and limitations of dialectic that we need to approach Augustine's notion of '*fides quaerens intellectum*'. He derives this principle from *Isaiah* 7:9 in the Old Latin translation: '*Nisi credideritis, non intelligetis*' ['If you do not believe, you will not understand']. He was aware of the different translation of Jerome in the Vulgate, '*Nisi credideritis, non permanebitis*' ['If you do not believe, you will not remain'], and in *De Doctrina Christiana* sought to harmonise the two. However, it was to the Old Latin version of this text that Augustine returned again and again.[74] Norman Kretzmann has analysed many of these references, and come to the conclusion that there are distinctions to be made between propositional faith and propositional understanding, and between faith as a way of life (the way of faith) and as supernatural understanding. He determines that we need to understand Augustine's view of the relation of faith to understanding as that of the way of faith to propositional understanding.[75] According to Augustine, 'The hidden things and secrets of the Kingdom of God first seek out believing men, that they may make them understand. For faith is understanding's ladder, and understanding is faith's reward.'[76] Just as it is not possible to go from a state of unlearning to a state of learning without first accepting the authority of one's teachers, without taking what they say on trust, so it is impossible to attain understanding without faith's acceptance of the authority of scripture and the church. When Anselm speaks of the 'ladder of faith' in *DIV*1, he is recalling the view of Augustine, a view in which faith does not supplant reason, but provides the context, foundation and limits of reason. What Kretzmann says of Augustine can also be said legitimately of Anselm: 'The aim of Christian

---

72 *De Doctrina Christiana*, II, 31, 49 (*On Christian Teaching*, p. 59).

73 See S. Hessbrüggen-Walter, 'Augustine's Critique of Dialectic: Between Ambrose and the Arians', in K. Pollmann and M. Vessey (eds), *Augustine and the Disciplines: From Cassiacum to* Confessions, Oxford 2005, pp. 184–205, pp. 202ff. Augustine's well-known criticism of Aristotle's *Categories* in *Confessiones*, IV, 16, may appear to be inconsistent with its use in *De Trinitate*, but in the *Confessiones*, Augustine's criticism actually addresses his own misuse of Aristotle's work after he had first read it as a young man. He says of the liberal arts that he did not understand the source of the truths they contained.

74 A list of the large number of such references is contained in Roger Gryson (ed.), *Esaias* (*Vetus Latina*, vol. 12/1), Freiburg im Breisgau 1987, pp. 229–31. Augustine's use of the Old Latin here was very influential. See, for example, Eriugena, *Homilia in Prologum S. Evangelii secundum Ioannem* (*PL*122 col. 284D): faith as a preparation for understanding.

75 Kretzmann, 'Faith seeks', pp. 16f.

76 *Sermo* CXXVI, 1, 1. Cited by Kretzmann, 'Faith seeks', p. 12.

philosophy as Augustine sees it is to combine propositional understanding with the way of faith.'[77]

The need to scale the ladder of faith does not mean that dialectical argument can only take place between believing Christians. Augustine writes in *De Trinitate*, XV, 1, that his purpose is to demonstrate, not just to those who believe, but also to those who possess some kind of rational understanding. Augustine's argument is addressed, then, to both believers and unbelievers. The believer should accept Augustine's argument on the authority of scripture, the unbeliever on the basis of reason, but neither will get very far in understanding unless he enlists both faith and reason in his search. In his *Responsio*, Anselm too is aware that there are two audiences, one of whom should accept the argument on the basis of his Catholic faith, and it is to him he addresses his arguments in that work, having addressed the unbeliever in the *Proslogion*.[78]

Augustine's willingness to exploit Aristotle's *Categories* was to have a wide influence, particularly once it was taken up by Boethius in his *Opuscula Sacra*.[79] Boethius had already noted the problem that arose when an attempt was made to reject the use of reason in investigating the world: 'Therefore it was necessarily the case that those who rejected the science of disputation would fail in their investigation of the nature of things.'[80] Dialectic could not be rejected, precisely because, as Augustine had been aware, it was built into the scheme of things. Even in matters of faith it cannot be removed or supplanted. When properly understood the Augustinian principle of '*fides quaerens intellectum*' requires both faith and reason. With this in mind, let us know turn to the text of the *Proslogion*, which Anselm originally entitled '*Fides quaerens intellectum*'.

---

77 Kretzmann, 'Faith seeks', p. 18.

78 In *DIV*6, Anselm states that in the *Monologion* and *Proslogion* he had tried to answer those who do not want to believe what they do not understand.

79 See his first theological tractate, *De Trinitate*, IV. His second theological tractate, *Utrum Pater*, discusses the sense in which Father, Son and Spirit are predicated of God.

80 Boethius's second *Commentaria in Prophyrium* [*PL*64 col. 73A]: '*Quare necesse erat eos falli, qui abjecta scientia disputandi de rerum natura perquirerent*.'

Chapter 3
The Text

1. PROSLOGION

0.1 INCIPIT PROEMIUM INPROSLOGION.

0.2 POST QUAM OPUSCULUM quodda[m] velut exemplu[m] meditandi deratione fidei cogentib[us] me precibus q[uo]ru[n]da[m] fr[atru]m, inp[er]sona alicuius tacite secum ratiocinando qu[a]e nesciat investigantis edidi; considerans illud e[ss]e multoru[m] concatenatione contextu[m] argumentorum, c[o]epi mecu[m] qu[a]erere si forte posset inveniri unum argum[en]tu[m] quod nullo alio adse p[ro]bandum qua[m] se solo indigeret, & solum ad astruendum quia deus vere est et quia est su[m]mu[m] bonum nullo alio indigens, & quo om[n]ia indigent ut sint & ut bene sint, & qu[a]ecunq[ue] de divina credimus substantia, sufficeret.

0.3 Adquod cu[m] sepe studioseq[ue] cogitationem convertere[m], atq[ue] aliquando m[ihi] videretur iam posse capi q[uo]d qu[a]erebam, aliquando mentis aciem om[n]ino fugeret; tandem desp[er]ans volui cessare velut abinquisitione rei qua[m] inveniri e[ss]et impossibile. Sed cu[m] illam cogitatione[m] ne mente[m] mea[m] frustra occupando abaliis in q[ui]bus p[ro]ficere possem impediret, penitus ame vellem excludere; tunc magis

0.1 THE BEGINNING OF THE PREFACE TO THE *PROSLOGION*.

0.2 In response to the appeals of some of the brothers, I produced a certain work – an example of meditating on the rationality of the faith – in the guise of someone who investigates things he does not know by a means of a process of silent reasoning within himself. After I had completed this work, I reflected on the fact that it was constructed by a chain of many arguments, and began to ask myself if one argument could be discovered that would need no other to prove itself than itself alone, and would suffice on its own to establish that [i] God truly exists, [ii] that He is the supreme good, needing nothing else, and whom all things need that they might exist and that they might exist rightly, and [iii] whatever else we believe about the divine substance.

0.3 I would often turn my thoughts eagerly to this [question]. Sometimes it seemed to me that what I was seeking could already be grasped, but at other times my mind completely lost its grip [of the matter]. Finally, in despair, I wanted to put a stop to [my] investigation into something that could not possibly be discovered. But just when I wanted to give up this idea, in case it was distracting me from other things in which I could make progress ac magis nolenti & defendenti se c[o]epit cu[m] importunitate quada[m] ingerere.

and occupying my mind in vain, it began to impose itself upon me with increasing force, in spite of my unwillingness and resistance.

0.4 Cum [i]g[itur] quada[m] die vehementer eius importunitati resistendo fatigarer: inipso cogitationum conflictu si[c] se obtulit q[uo]d desperaveram, ut studiose cogitatione[m] amplecterer qua[m] sollicitus repellebam.

0.4 Then one day, as I tired of struggling so violently against this fixation, what I had despaired of presented itself in the very conflict of my thought, so that I enthusiastically embraced the idea that I had sought to drive out.

0.5 Estimans [i]g[itur] quod me gaudebam invenisse, si scriptum e[ss]et alicui legenti placiturum; dehoc ipso & de quib[us]dam aliis, sub p[er]sona conantis erigere mente[m] suam adconte[m]plandum d[eu]m & qu[a]erentis intelligere q[uo]d credit, subditum scripsi opusculum.

0.5 Considering that what I rejoiced at having discovered would, if it were written down, be pleasing to someone or other reading [it], I wrote the following work on this question and certain others, in the guise of someone trying to lift up his mind to contemplate God and seeking to understand what he believes.

0.6 Et q[uonia]m nec istud nec illud cuius supra memini dignu[m] libri nomine aut cui auctoris pr[a]eponeretur nomen iudicabam, nec tamen eadem sine aliquo titulo, quo alique[m] in cui[us] man[us] venirent quodamm[odo] adse legendu[m] invitarent dimittenda putabam; unicuiq[ue] suu[m] dedi titulum, ut pri[us] exemplu[m] meditandi de ratione fidei, & sequens, fides qu[a]erens intellectum diceretur.

0.6 I judged neither this work, nor the one I mentioned above, worth calling a book or having the name of the author prefixed to it. Nevertheless, I thought they should not be released without a title, which would act as an invitation to read them to anyone into whose hands they happened to fall. So, I gave each its title: the first being called, An Example of Meditating on the Rationality of the Faith, and the next, Faith Seeking Understanding.

0.7 Sed cu[m] iam aplurib[us] cu[m] his titulis utrunq[ue] transcriptum e[ss]et; coegerunt me plures & maxime reverendus archiep[iscopu]s lugdunensis hugo nomine fungens ingallia legatione apostolica, qui m[ihi] hoc exapostolica pr[a]ecepit auctoritate, ut nomen meu[m] illis pr[a]escriberem.

0.7 But when they had already been transcribed with these titles by various people, several people brought pressure to bear on me to write my name at the beginning of them – in particular the reverend archbishop of Lyons, Hugh, apostolic legate in Gaul, who commanded me to do this by apostolic authority.

0.8 Q[uo]d ut aptius fieret; illud quidem monologion id est soliloquium, istud v[ero] p[ro]slogion, id est alloquium, nominavi.

0.8 So that this would be done more fittingly, I named the former work, Monologion, that is, a soliloquy, and the latter, Proslogion, that is, an address.

INCIPIUNT CAP[ITU]LA.	BEGINNING OF THE CHAPTER HEADINGS.
I Excitat[i]o m[en]tis adc[on]te[m] plandu[m] d[eu]m.	I A raising of the mind to the contemplation of God.
II Quod vere sit deus.	II That God truly exists.
III Q[uo]d non possit cogitari non e[ss]e.	III That He cannot be thought not to exist.
IIII Quom[odo] insipiens dixit in corde, quod cogitari non potest.	IIII How the fool has said in his heart, what cannot be thought.
V Quod d[eu]s sit quicquid melius est esse qua[m] non e[ss]e, & solus existens p[er]se om[n]ia alia faciat de nichilo.	V That God is whatever it is better to be than not to be, and alone existing through Himself makes all other things from nothing.
VI Quom[odo] sit sensibilis cu[m] n[on] sit corpus.	VI How He is sensible, although He is not a body.
VII Quom[odo] sit om[ni]p[oten]s cu[m] multa n[on] possit.	VII How He is omnipotent, although there are many things He cannot [do].
VIII Quom[odo] sit misericors & impassibil[is].	VIII How He is merciful and impassible.
IX Quom[odo] totus iustus et su[m]me iustus parcat malis, & q[uo]d iuste misereatur malis.	IX How the totally just and supremely just spares the wicked, and that He justly shows mercy to the wicked.
X Quom[odo] iuste puniat, & iuste parcat malis.	X How He justly punishes and justly spares the wicked.
XI Quom[odo] univers[a]e vi[a]e d[omi]ni mis[eri]c[or]dia & veritas, & tamen iustus d[omi]n[u]s in omnibus viis suis.	XI How all the ways of the Lord are mercy and truth, and yet the Lord is just in all His ways.
XII Q[uo]d deus sit ipsa vita qua vivit, & sic de similibus.	XII That God is the very life by which He lives, and the same [can be said] concerning similar [attributes].
XIII Quom[odo] solus sit incircumscriptus & [a]et[er]nus, cum alii spirit[us] sint incircumscripti et [a]eterni.	XIII How He alone is unlimited and eternal, although other spirits are unlimited and eternal.
XIIII Quom[odo] & cur videtur & non videtur deus aqu[a]erentibus eum.	XIIII How and why God is seen and not seen by those seeking Him.
XV Quod maior sit qua[m] cogitari possit.	XV That He is greater than can be thought.
XVI Q[uo]d h[a]ec sit lux inaccessibilis quam inhabitat.	XVI That this is the inaccessible light, in which He dwells.

XVII Q[uo]d indeo sit armonia, odor, sapor, l[a]enitas, pulchritudo, suo ineffabili m[odo].	XVII That there is harmony, fragrance, flavour, gentleness and beauty in God, in His own ineffable way.
XVIII Q[uo]d indeo nec in[a]eternitate ei[us] qu[a]e ipse est null[a]e sint partes.	XVIII That there are no parts in God nor in His eternity, which He Himself is.
XIX Q[uo]d non sit inloco aut tempore, sed omnia sint inillo.	XIX That He does not exist in space or time, but all things exist in Him.
XX Quod sit ante & ult[ra] om[n]ia etia[m] [a]eterna.	XX That He is before and beyond even all eternal things.
XXI An hoc sit s[ae]c[u]l[u]m s[ae]c[u]li sive s[ae]c[u]la s[ae]c[u]lor[um].	XXI Whether this is the age of the age or the ages of ages.
XXII Q[uo]d solus sit q[uo]d est & qui est.	XXII That He alone is what He is and who He is.
XXIII Quod hoc bonum sit pariter pater & filius & spirit[us] s[an]c[tu]s, & hoc sit unum necessarium, q[uo]d est omne & totum & solum bonum.	XXIII That this good is equally the Father and the Son and the Holy Spirit; and this is the one [thing] necessary, which is the all and whole and only good.
XXIIII Coniectatio quale & q[ua]ntu[m] sit hoc bonu[m].	XXIIII A conjecture: what this good is like and how great it is.
XXV Qu[a]e & q[ua]nta bona sint fruentib[us] eo.	XXV What good things there are for those delighting in Him and how great they are.
XXVI An hoc sit gaudium plenu[m] quod promittit dominus.	XXVI Whether this is the full joy that the Lord promises.
EXPLICIUNT CAPITULA;	END OF THE CHAPTER HEADINGS.
1.1 INCIPIT PRO[S]LOGION LIBER ANSELMI CANTUARIENSIS ARCHI EP[ISCOP]I.	1.1 THE BEGINNING OF THE PROSLOGION, THE BOOK OF ANSELM, ARCHBISHOP OF CANTERBURY.
[1.2 Excitat[i]o [m[en]tis adc[on]te[m] plandu[m] d[eu]m.]	[1.2 A raising of the mind to the contemplation of God.]
•I•	•I•
1.3 EIA NUNC HOmuncio fuge paululum occupationes tuas, absconde te modicu[m] atumultuosis cogitationib[us] tuis. Abice nunc onerosas curas, & post pone laboriosas distentiones tuas.	1.3 COME NOW, little man, flee your preoccupations for a short while. Hide yourself briefly from your tumultuous thoughts. It is time to throw off your burdensome cares, and lay aside your wearisome distractions.

1.4 Vaca aliquantulum d[e]o, & requiesce aliquantulu[m] ineo. Intra incubiculum mentis tu[a]e, exclude om[n]ia pr[a]eter d[eu]m & qu[a]e te iuvent ad qu[a]erendum eum, et clauso hostio qu[a]ere eum.

1.4 Make a little time for God, and rest a while in Him. Enter the inner room of your mind. Exclude everything except God and those things that help you in seeking Him, and, with the door shut, seek Him.

1.5 Dic nunc totum cor meum, di[c] nunc deo, Qu[a]ero vultu[m] tuum, vultu[m] tuum d[omi]ne requiro.

1.5 Say now, my heart, say now to God: 'I seek Your face; for Your face, O Lord, I am searching.'

1.6 Eia nunc [er]g[o] tu d[omi]ne d[eu]s meus, doce cor meu[m] ubi & quom[odo] te qu[a]erat, ubi & q[uo]m[odo] te inveniat.

1.6 So come now, Lord my God, teach my heart where and how it should seek You, where and how it should find You.

1.7 Domine, si hic non es, ubi te qu[a]eram absentem? Si aute[m] ubiq[ue] es, cur non video pr[a]esentem?

1.7 Lord, if You are not here, where shall I seek You who are absent? If however You are everywhere, why do I not see You who are present?

1.8 Sed certe habitas lucem inaccessibilem. Et ubi est lux inaccessibil[is]? Aut quom[odo] accedam adlucem inaccessibilem? Aut quis me ducet & inducet inillam, ut videa[m] te inilla?

1.8 But surely You dwell in inaccessible light. And where is the inaccessible light? Indeed, how shall I approach the inaccessible light? Or rather, who will lead me and bring me to it, so that I may see You in it?

1.9 De inde quib[us] signis, qua facie te qu[a]eram? Numqua[m] te vidi d[omi]ne d[eu]s m[eu]s, non novi faciem tua[m].

1.9 Even then, by what signs, under what guise, shall I seek You? I have never seen You, Lord my God, I have not known Your face.

1.10 Quid faciet altissime d[omi]ne, quid faciet iste tuus longinquus exul? Quid faciet servus tuus anxius amore tui, & longe p[ro]iectus afacie tua?

1.10 What shall this distant exile of Yours do, most high Lord, what shall he do? What shall Your servant do, afflicted by love of You, and cast far away from Your face?

1.11 Anhelat videre te, & nimis ab est illi facies tua. Accedere ad te desiderat, & inaccessibilis est habitatio tua. Invenire te cupit, & nescit locum tuum. Qu[a]erere te affectat, & ignorat vultum tuu[m].

1.11 He aspires to see You, and Your face is completely absent from him. He desires to come near to You, and Your dwelling place is inaccessible. He yearns to find You, and he does not know where You are. He strives to seek You, and he does not know what You look like.

1.12 D[omi]ne, d[eu]s m[eu]s es, & d[omi]n[u]s m[eu]s es, & nunquam te vidi. Tu me fecisti & refecisti, & om[n]ia mea bona tu m[ihi] contulisti, & nondum novi te. Deniq[ue] adte

1.12 Lord, You are my God and You are my Lord, and I have never seen You. You made me and remade me. You conferred all my goods upon me, and still I have not known You. In short, I was made to videndum factus sum, & nondum feci p[ro]pter q[uo]d factus sum.

1.13 O misera sors hominis, cum hoc p[er] didit adquod factus est. O durus & dirus casus ille! Heu quid p[er]didit & quid invenit, q[ui]d abscessit & q[ui]d remansit! P[er]didit beatitudinem ad qua[m] factus est, & invenit miseria[m] p[ro]pter qua[m] factus non est.

1.14 Abscessit sine quo nichil felix est, & remansit q[uo]d p[er]se non n[isi] miserum est. Manducabat tunc homo pane[m] angelor[um] que[m] nunc esurit, manducat nunc panem dolor[um] que[m] tunc nesciebat! Heu publicus luctus hominu[m], universalis planctus filior[um] ad[a]e.

1.15 Ille ructabat saturitate, nos suspiram[us] esurie. Ille abundabat, nos mendicamus. Ille feliciter tenebat & misere deseruit, nos infeliciter egemus & miserabiliter desideramus, & heu vacui remanemus.

1.16 Cur non nobis custodivit cum facile posset, quo tam graviter careremus? Quare sic nobis obseravit lucem, & obdux[it] nos tenebris? Ut quid nobis abstulit vitam, & inflixit mortem?

1.17 Erumnosi, unde sumus expulsi, quo sumus impulsi. Unde pr[a]ecipitati, quo obruti. Apatria inexilium, avisione d[e]i inc[a]ecitate[m] n[ost]ram. Aiocunditate immortalitatis, inamaritudinem & horrore[m] mortis.

1.18 Misera mutatio. Dequanto bono inquantum malum. Grave damnu[m], gravis dolor, grave totum.

1.19 Sed heu me miserum, unu[m] de aliis miseris filiis ev[a]e elongatis adeo, quid inc[o]epi, quid effeci?

see You, and I have not yet done that for which I was made.

1.13 O miserable fate of man, since he has lost that for which he was made. O what a harsh and cruel fall! Alas, what he has lost and what he has found, what has departed and what has remained! He has lost the happiness for which he was made, and has found the wretchedness for which he was not made.

1.14 That without which nothing is happy has gone, and that which in itself is wretched has remained. Then, man ate the bread of angels, for which he now hungers; now, he eats the bread of sorrows, of which he knew nothing then! Alas, the manifest sorrow of men, the universal grief of the children of Adam.

1.15 He belched in repletion, we sigh in hunger. He was rich, we are beggars. He happily possessed and wretchedly forsook. We are unhappily destitute and wretchedly desire, and, alas, are left empty.

1.16 Why did he not preserve for us, when he easily could have, that which we would so grievously lack? Why did he block the light from us in this way, and cover us in darkness? For what purpose did he take life away from us, and inflict death?

1.17 From where we were expelled, full of woe, to where we were impelled! From where cast down, to where cast under! From a homeland into exile, from the vision of God into our blindness. From the delight of immortality into the bitterness and horror of death.

1.18 Wretched transformation! From so much good to so much evil! Grievous injury, grievous sorrow, it is all grievous.

1.19 But alas, wretched me, one of the wretched children of Eve, far removed from God. What have I begun? What

Quo tendebam, quo deveni? Adquid aspirabam, inquib[us] suspiro?

have I accomplished? Where was I aiming, where did I reach? To what was I aspiring, for what am I sighing?

1.20 Qu[a]esivi bona, & ecce turbatio. Tendebam ind[eu]m, & offendi inme ipsum.

1.20 I begged for good things, and behold, confusion. I aimed at God and I stumbled into myself.

1.21 Requiem qu[a]erebam insecreto meo, & tribulatione[m] & dolorem inveni inintimis meis. Volebam ridere agaudio mentis me[a]e, & cogor rugire agemitu cordis mei. Sp[er]abatur l[a]eticia, & ecce unde densentur suspiria.

1.21 I sought peace in my hidden place, and found confusion and sorrow in my depths. I wanted to laugh with a joyful mind and am forced to roar with a groaning heart. Happiness was my hope, and, behold, sighs abound.

1.22 Et o tu d[omi]ne usquequo? Usquequo d[omi]ne oblivisceris nos, usqueq[uo] avertis faciem tua[m] anob[is]? Quando respicies & exaudies nos? Quando illuminabis oculos n[ost]ros, & ostendes nobis faciem tua[m]? Quando restitues te nobis?

1.22 And You, O Lord, how long? How long, O Lord, will You forget us? How long will You turn Your face away from us? When will You look upon us and listen? When will You enlighten our eyes, and show us Your face? When will You give Yourself back to us?

1.23 Respice d[omi]ne, exaudi, illumina nos, ostende nobis te ipsum.

1.23 Look upon, listen to, enlighten us, Lord; show Yourself to us.

1.24 Restitue te nobis, ut bene sit nobis, sine quo tam male est nobis. Miserare labores & conatus n[ost]ros adte, qui nichil valemus sine te.

1.24 Give Yourself back to us, so that things may go well for us, for without You everything goes so badly for us. Have pity on our efforts and endeavours towards You. We are worth nothing without You.

1.25 Invitas nos, adiuva nos.

1.25 You summon us; help us.

1.26 Obsecro d[omi]ne, ne desp[er]em suspirando, sed respirem sperando. Obsecro d[omi]ne, amaricatu[m] est cor meu[m] sua desolatione, indulca illud tua consolatione. Obsecro, d[omi]ne, esuriens inc[o]epi qu[a]erere te, ne desina[m] ieiunus de te.

1.26 I pray, Lord, that I may not despair in sighing, but rejoice in hoping. I pray, Lord, that You will sweeten by Your consolation my heart, which has grown bitter in its desolation. I pray, Lord, that having begun to seek You whilst hungry, I may not give up while still deprived of You.

1.27 Famelicus accessi, ne receda[m] impastus. Paup[er] veni addivite[m], miser admis[eri]c[or]dem, ne redeam vacuus & contemptus. Et si antequa[m] comedam suspiro; da v[e]l post suspiria q[uo]d comedam.

1.27 I have approached as one famished, may I not go away unfed. Poor, I have come to the one who is rich, wretched to the one who is merciful; may I not return empty-handed and despised. And if I sigh before I eat, grant, if You will, that after [my] sighs I shall eat.

1.28 D[omi]ne, incurvatus n[on] possum n[isi] deorsum aspicere, erige me ut possi[m] sursum intendere. Iniquitates me[a]e sup[er] gress[a]e caput meu[m] obvolvunt me, & sicut onus grave gravant me. Evolve me, exonera me, ne urgeat puteus earu[m] os suu[m] sup[er] me. Liceat m[ihi] suspicere lucem tua[m], v[e]l delonge, v[e]l dep[ro]fundo.

1.28 Lord, I [am] bent over [and] can only look downwards; lift me up, so that I can direct my eyes upwards. My iniquities have gone over my head. They cover me, and like a heavy burden weigh me down. Unbind me, release me, lest the pit should force its mouth over me. Permit me to look up at Your light, be it from afar or from the depths.

1.29 Doce me qu[a]erere te & ostende te qu[a]erenti, quia nec qu[a]erere te possum n[isi] tu doceas, nec invenire n[isi] te ostendas.

1.29 Teach me to seek You, and show Yourself to the one who seeks; because I can neither seek You, unless You teach me, nor find You, unless You show Yourself.

1.30 Qu[a]eram te desiderando, desiderem qu[a]erendo. Invenia[m] amando, ame[m] inveniendo.

1.30 May I seek You in desiring You, may I desire You in seeking You. May I find You in loving You, may I love You in finding You.

1.31 Fateor d[omi]ne & gra[tia]s ago, quia creasti inme hanc imagine[m] tuam, ut tui memor te cogite[m], te ame[m].

1.31 Lord, I confess and give thanks that You have created Your image in me, so that in remembering You, I might think of You and love You.

1.32 Sed sic est abolita attritione vitior[um], sic est offuscata fumo peccator[um]; ut non possit facere ad quod facta est, n[isi] tu renoves & reformes eam.

1.32 But it is so worn away by the abrasion of vice, so obscured by the smoke of sin, that it cannot do that for which it was made, unless You renew and reform it.

1.33 Non tempto d[omi]ne penetrare altitudine[m] tua[m], quia nullatenus comparo illi intellectum meum; sed desidero aliquatenus intelligere veritate[m] tua[m] qua[m] credit & amat cor meum.

1.33 Lord, I do not attempt to penetrate Your height, for in no way do I compare my understanding to it; but I desire to understand to some extent Your truth, which my heart believes and loves.

1.34 Neq[ue] eni[m] qu[a]ero intelligere ut credam; sed credo ut intelliga[m]. Nam & hoc credo; quia n[isi] credidero n[on] intelligam.

1.34 And indeed I do not seek to understand, so that I may believe, but I believe, so that I may understand. For I also believe this: that unless I believe, I shall not understand.

[2.1 Quod vere sit deus.]
II

[2.1 That God truly exists.]
II

2.2 Ergo d[omi]ne qui das fidei intellectum, da m[ihi] ut quantu[m]

2.2 Therefore, Lord, You who grant understanding to faith, grant that I may understand (to the extent You consider it scis expedire intelligam, quia es sicut credimus, & hoc es q[uo]d credimus.

profitable) that You exist as we believe, and are that which we believe.

2.3 Et quidem credimus te e[ss]e aliquid quo nichil maius cogitari possit.

2.3 And indeed we believe You to be something than which nothing greater can be thought.

2.4 An [er]g[o] non est aliq[ua] talis natura, quia dixit insipiens in corde suo non est d[eu]s?

2.4 Or is there not anything of such a nature, since the fool has said in his heart, 'There is no God'?

2.5 Sed certe ipse idem insipiens cum audit hoc ipsum q[uo]d dico, aliquid quo maius nichil cogitari potest; intelligit quod audit, & q[uo]d intelliget inintellectu eius est, etiam si non intelligat illud e[ss]e.

2.5 But surely this same fool, when he hears this very thing that I say, 'something than which nothing greater can be thought', understands what he hears, and what he understands is in his understanding, even if he should not understand that it exists.

2.6 Aliud eni[m] e[st] rem e[ss]e i[n]i[n]tellectu, aliud intelligere rem e[ss]e.

2.6 For it is one thing for a thing to exist in the understanding, and another to understand a thing to exist.

2.7 Nam cu[m] pictor pr[a]ecogitat qu[a]e facturus est; habet q[ui]de[m] inintellectu, sed non dum intelligit e[ss]e q[uo]d non du[m] fecit. Cum v[ero] iam pinx[it]; & habet inintellectu et intelligit e[ss]e q[uo]d iam fecit.

2.7 For when a painter thinks in advance of the things which he is about to make, he has that which he has not yet made in his understanding at least, even though he does not yet understand that it exists. Once he has painted it, he both has what he has now made in the understanding and understands that it exists.

2.8 Convincitur [er]g[o] etia[m] insipiens, e[ss]e vel inintellectu aliquid q[uo] nichil maius cogitari potest; quia hoc cu[m] audit intelligit, & quicquid intelligitur inintellectu est.

2.8 Thus, even the fool is convinced that there is in the understanding at least something than which nothing greater can be thought, because he understands this when he hears it, and whatever is understood is in the understanding.

2.9 & certe id quo maius cogitari nequit; n[on] potest e[ss]e insolo intellectu.

2.9 And certainly that than which a greater cannot be thought cannot be in the understanding alone.

2.10 Si enim vel insolo intellectu est; potest cogitari e[ss]e & inre quod maius est.

2.10 For if it is in the understanding alone, it can also be thought to exist in reality, which is greater.

2.11 Si e[rg]o id quo maius cogitari non potest e[st] insolo intellectu; id ipsum quo maius cogitari n[on] potest, e[st] q[uo] maius cogitari potest. Sed certe hoc e[ss]e non potest.

2.11 If therefore that than which a greater cannot be thought is in the understanding alone, that same thing than which a greater cannot be thought is [something] than which a greater can be thought. But this cannot be the case.

2.12 Existit [er]g[o] p[ro]cul dubio aliquid quo maius cogitari non valet, & inintellectu & inre.

[3.1 Q[uo]d non possit cogitari non e[ss]e.]

•III

3.2 Quod utiq[ue] sic vere est; ut nec cogitari possit non e[ss]e.

3.3 Nam potest cogitari e[ss]e aliquid q[uo]d non possit cogitari non e[ss]e, quod maius est qua[m] q[uo]d n[on] e[ss]e cogitari potest. Quare si id quo maius nequit cogitari, potest cogitari n[on] e[ss]e: id ipsum q[uo] maius cogitari nequit, n[on] e[st] id quo maius cogitari nequit, quod convenire non potest.

3.4 Sic [er]g[o] vere e[st] aliquid quo maius cogitari n[on] potest; ut nec cogitari possit n[on] e[ss]e.

3.5 & hoc es tu d[omi]ne d[eu]s n[oste]r. Sic [er]g[o] vere es d[omi]ne d[eu]s m[eu]s; ut nec cogitari possis n[on] e[ss]e.

3.6 Et merito. Si enim aliqua mens posset cogitare aliquid melius te; ascenderet creatura sup[er] creatorem, & iudicaret decreatore, quod valde est absurdum.

3.7 & quidem quicquid e[st] aliud pr[a]eter te solu[m]; potest cogitari non e[ss]e. Solus [i]g[itur] verissime omniu[m], & ideo maxime omniu[m] habes e[ss]e; quia q[ui]cquid aliud est n[on] sic vere, & iccirco minus habet e[ss]e.

3.8 Cur itaq[ue] dixit insipiens incorde suo, n[on] e[st] d[eu]s, cu[m] tam inpromptu sit rationali m[en]ti te

2.12 Therefore without doubt something than which a greater cannot be thought exists, both in the understanding and in reality.

[3.1 That He cannot be thought not to exist.]

•III

3.2 Surely this truly exists in such a way, that it cannot be thought not to exist.

3.3 For there can be thought to exist something that cannot be thought not to exist, [and] this is greater than what can be thought not to exist. Therefore if that than which a greater cannot be thought can be thought not to exist, this same thing than which a greater cannot be thought is not that than which a greater cannot be thought, which cannot be logically consistent.

3.4 Therefore something than which a greater cannot be thought truly exists in such a way that it cannot be thought not to exist.

3.5 And You are this thing, O Lord our God. Therefore, O Lord my God, You truly exist in such a way that You cannot be thought not to exist.

3.6 And rightly so. For if some mind could think something better than You, the creature would ascend above the Creator, and would pass judgement on the Creator, which is quite absurd.

3.7 And indeed whatever is other than You alone can be thought not to exist. Therefore, You alone have being most truly of all, and thus most greatly of all, because whatever is other [than You] truly does not exist in this way, and for this reason has less being.

3.8 Why then has the fool said in his heart, 'There is no God', when it is so obvious to a rational mind that You maxime omniu[m] e[ss]e? Cur, n[isi] quia stultus et insipiens?

exist most greatly of all? Why, except that he is stupid and foolish?

[4.1 Quom[odo] insipiens dixit in corde, quod cogitari non potest.]
IIII

[4.1 How the fool has said in his heart, what cannot be thought.]
IIII

4.2 Verum q[uo]m[odo] dixit incorde quod cogitare n[on] potuit, aut quom[odo] cogitare n[on] potuit q[uo]d dixit incorde, cum idem sit dicere incorde & cogitare? Q[uo]d si vere immo quia vere & cogitavit quia dixit in corde, & n[on] dixit incorde quia cogitare n[on] potuit; non uno tantu[m]m[odo] dicitur aliquid incorde vel cogitatur.

4.2 But how has he said in his heart what he could not think, or how could he not think what he has said in his heart, when it is the same thing to say in one's heart and to think? If he has truly – or rather because he has truly – both thought it, since he has said it in his heart, and not said it in his heart, since he could not think it, something is not said in the heart or thought in only one way.

4.3 Aliter eni[m] cogitatur res cum vox eam significans cogitatur, aliter cu[m] id ipsum quod res est intelligitur. Illo itaq[ue] m[odo] potest cogitari d[eu]s n[on] e[ss]e, isto v[ero] minime.

4.3 For a thing is thought in one way when the word signifying it is thought, and in another when the thing itself is understood. Accordingly, God can be thought not to exist in the first way, but not at all in the second.

4.4 Nullus quippe intelligens id q[uo]d d[eu]s est potest cogitare quia d[eu]s non e[st], licet h[a]ec verba dicat incorde, aut sine ulla aut cu[m] aliqua ext[ra]nea significatione.

4.4 Indeed, no one who understands what God is can think that God does not exist, although he may say these words in [his] heart; be it without any, or with some extraneous, meaning.

4.5 D[eu]s enim e[st] id q[uo] maius cogitari non potest. Q[uo]d qui bene intelligit; utiq[ue] intelligit id ipsum sic e[ss]e, ut nec cogitatione queat n[on] e[ss]e. Qui [er]g[o] intelligit sic e[ss]e d[eu]m; nequit eum non e[ss]e cogitare.

4.5 For God is that than which a greater cannot be thought. Whoever understands this [that than which a greater cannot be thought] properly, understands at least that this same thing exists in such a way that not even in thought can it not exist. Therefore, whoever understands that God exists in the same way [as that than which a greater cannot be thought], cannot think that He does not exist.

4.6 Gra[tia]s t[ibi] bone d[omi]ne, gra[tia]s t[ibi], quia q[uo]d prius credidi te donante, iam sic intelligo te illuminante; ut si te e[ss]e nolim credere, n[on] possim n[on] intelligere.

4.6 I give thanks to You, good Lord, I give thanks to You, because what I first believed by Your gift, I now understand by Your illumination in such a way that even if I should not want to believe it, I would not be able not to understand that You exist.

[5.1 Quod d[eu]s sit quicquid melius est esse qua[m] non e[ss]e, & solus existens p[er]se om[n]ia alia faciat de nichilo.]

[5.1 That God is whatever it is better to be than not to be, and alone existing through Himself makes all other things from nothing.]

•V•

5.2 Quid i[gitur] es, d[omi]ne d[eu]s, quo nil mai[us] valet cogitari?

5.3 Sed quid es n[isi] id q[uo]d su[m]mu[m] omniu[m] solum existens p[er]se ipsum, om[n]ia alia fecit denichilo?
5.4 Quicquid eni[m] hoc non est; minus [est] qua[m] cogitari possit.
5.5 Sed hoc de te cogitari n[on] potest.

5.6 Q[uo]d [er]g[o] bonum de est summo bono, p[er]q[uo]d e[st] om[n]e bonu[m]?
5.7 Tu es itaq[ue] iustus, verax, beatus, & q[ui]c quid melius est e[ss]e qua[m] n[on] e[ss]e. Melius nanq[ue] est esse iustu[m] qua[m] n[on] iustum, beatum qua[m] n[on] beatum.

•V•

5.2 What therefore are You, Lord God, than whom nothing greater can be thought?

5.3 What are You if not that which, the highest of all things, alone existing through itself, made all other things from nothing?
5.4 For whatever is not this, is less than can be thought.
5.5 But this cannot be thought concerning You.

5.6 What good, then, is absent from the supreme good, through which every good exists?
5.7 You are accordingly just, truthful, blessed and whatever it is better to be than not to be. For it is better indeed to be just than not just, blessed than not blessed.

[6.1 Quom[odo] sit sensibilis cu[m] n[on] sit corpus.]
VI
6.2 Verum cum melius sit esse sensibilem, om[n]ipotentem, mis[eri]c[or]diem, impassibilem, qua[m] n[on] e[ss]e, quom[odo] es sensibilis si n[on] es corpus, aut om[ni]p[oten]s si om[n]ia n[on] potes, aut misericors simul & impassibilis?
6.3 Nam si sola corporea sunt sensibilia, q[uonia]m sensus circa corpus & incorpore sunt; quom[odo] es sensibilis cu[m] n[on] sis corpus sed su[m]mus spirit[us], qui corpore melior e[st];

6.4 Sed si sentire n[on] n[isi] cognoscere aut n[on] n[isi] adcognoscendum est, qui enim sentit cognoscit s[e]c[un]d[u]m sensuum p[ro]prietatem, ut p[er]visum

[6.1 How He is sensible, although He is not a body.]
VI
6.2 And yet, since it is better to be sensible, omnipotent, merciful, impassible, than not to be, how are You sensible if You are not a body – or omnipotent, if You cannot do everything – or merciful and impassible at the same time?
6.3 For, if bodily things alone are sensible, since the senses relate to the body and are in the body, how are You sensible, since You are not a body, but the supreme spirit, which is better than a body?

6.4 But if to sense is just to know, or is just for knowing – for he who senses knows according to the particular characteristic of the senses, as colours colores, p[er] gustum sapores; non inconvenienter dicitur aliquom[odo] sentire, quicquid aliquom[odo] cognoscit. Ergo d[omi]ne quanvis non sis corpus; vere tamen eomodo su[m]me sensibilis es, quo summe om[n]ia cognoscis, non quo animal corporeo sensu cognoscit.

through sight, flavours through taste – whatever in some way knows is said not inconsistently in some way to sense. Therefore, Lord, although You are not a body, yet truly You are supremely sensible in the way in which You know all things supremely, [but] not [in the way] in which an animal knows by bodily sense.

[7.1 Quom[odo] sit om[ni]p[oten]s cu[m] multa n[on] possit.]
VII

[7.1 How He is omnipotent, although there are many things He cannot [do].]
VII

7.2 Sed & om[ni]p[oten]s q[uo]m[odo] es, si om[n]ia non potes? Aut si n[on] potes corrumpi nec mentiri, nec facere verum e[ss]e falsum ut q[uo]d factum e[st] n[on] e[ss]e factum, & plura similiter; quom[odo] potes om[n]ia?

7.2 But how are You omnipotent, if You cannot do everything? And how can You do everything, if You cannot be destroyed or lie or cause a true thing to be false – for example, making what has happened not to have happened, and so on,?

7.3 An h[a]ec posse n[on] e[st] potentia sed impotentia? Nam qui h[a]ec potest; q[uo]d sibi non expedit & quod n[on] debet potest. Qu[a]e quanto magis potest; tanto magis adversitas & p[er]versitas possunt inillum, & ipse minus cont[ra] illas. Qui [er]g[o] sic potest; n[on] potentia potest, sed impotentia.

7.3 Or is it not a power but a lack of power to be able to do these things? For he who can do this, can do what is not advantageous to himself and what he ought not. The more he can do these things, the more adversity and perversity can do to him and the less he can do against them. Therefore, he who can act in such a way can do so not by a power but by a lack of power.

7.4 Non enim ideo dicitur posse, quia ipse possit; sed quia sua impotentia facit aliud inse posse, sive aliquo alio genere loquendi, sicut multa imp[ro]prie dicunt[ur]. Ut cu[m] ponimus esse p[ro]n[on] e[ss]e, & facere p[ro]eo quod e[st] non facere, aut p[ro]nichil facere.

7.4 For on this account he is not said 'to be able' because he himself is able to act, but because his lack of power makes another thing able to act on him – whether expressed in this or in some other manner of speaking – just as many things are said improperly: for example, when we replace 'not to be' by 'to be', and 'not to do' or 'to do nothing' by 'to do'.

7.5 Nam sepe dicimus ei qui rem aliquam e[ss]e negat, sic e[st] quemadmodu[m] dicis e[ss]e; cum magis p[ro]prie videatur dici, sic non e[st] que[m]admodu[m] dicis n[on] e[ss]e. Item dicimus, iste sedet sicut ille facit, aut iste quiescit sicut ille facit,

7.5 For often we say to him who denies that something is, 'It is thus, just as you say it is', when it would seem to be said more properly, 'It is not thus, just as you say it is not'. Likewise, we say, 'This person sits, just as that person does' or 'This person rests, just as that person cum sedere sit quiddam non facere, & quiescere sit nichil facere.

does', when 'to sit' is a kind of not doing and 'to rest' is to do nothing.

7.6 Sic itaq[ue] cum quis dicitur habere potentiam faciendi aut patiendi quod sibi non expedit, aut quod non debet; impotentia intelligitur p[er]potentiam, quia quo plus habet hanc potentiam; eo adversitas & p[er]versitas inillu[m] sunt potentiores, & ille contra eas impotentior.

7.6 Accordingly, when someone is said to have a power of doing or of allowing what is not advantageous to him or which he ought not to do, a lack of power is to be understood by the term, power, because the more he has this power, the more power adversity and perversity have over him, and the more lacking in power he is against them.

7.7 Ergo d[omi]ne deus inde verius es om[ni]p[oten]s quia nichil potes p[er] impotentia[m], & nichil potest contra te.

7.7 Therefore, Lord God, You are then more truly omnipotent, because You can do nothing through a lack of power, and nothing can act against You.

[8.1 Quom[odo] sit misericors & impassibil[is].]

VIII

[8.1 How He is merciful and impassible.]

VIII

8.2 Sed & misericors simul et impassibilis quom[odo] es? Nam si es impassibilis n[on] compateris, si n[on] compateris n[on] e[st] t[ibi] miserum cor excompassione miseri, quod est e[ss]e misericordem. At si non es misericors, unde miseris est tanta consolatio?

8.2 But how are You both merciful and impassible at the same time? For if You are impassible, You do not feel compassion. And if You do not feel compassion, You do not have a sorrowful heart out of compassion for the wretched, which is what it means to be merciful. But if You are not merciful, from where comes such great consolation to the wretched?

8.3 Quom[odo] [er]g[o] es & n[on] es misericors d[omi]ne, n[isi] quia es misericors s[e]c[un]d[u]m nos, & non es s[e]c[un]d[u]m te? Es q[ui]ppe s[e]c[un]d[u]m n[ost]r[u]m sensum, & non es s[e]c[un]d[u]m tuum. Et enim cu[m] tu respicis nos miseros; nos sentimus miseri_cordis effectum, tu non sentis affectum.

8.3 How, then, are You and are You not merciful, Lord, unless it is because You are merciful in relation to us, but not in relation to Yourself? You are indeed merciful in relation to our experience, but not in relation to Yours. For when You look upon us wretches, we feel the effect of mercy, but You do not feel any emotion.

8.4 Et misericors es [i]g[itur] quia miseros salvas & peccatorib[us] tuis parcis; & misericors non es, quia nulla miseri[a]e compassione afficeris.

8.4 On the one hand, therefore, You are merciful, because You save the wretched and spare those who sin against You; on the other hand, You are not merciful, because You are not affected by any compassion for misery.

[9.1 Quom[odo] totus iustus et su[m]me iustus parcat malis, & q[uo]d iuste misereatur malis.]

IX

9.2 Veru[m] malis quom[odo] parcis, si es totus iustus & su[m]me iustus? Quom[odo] eni[m] totus & su[m]me iustus facit aliquid n[on] iustum? Aut qu[a]e iustitia est merenti mortem [a]eterna[m], dare vitam sempiternam? Unde [er]g[o] bone d[eu]s, bone bonis & malis, unde t[ibi] salvare malos, si hoc n[on] [est] iustum, & tu non facis aliquid n[on] iustum?

9.3 Anquia bonitas tua est incomprehensibilis, latet hoc in luce inaccessibili qua[m] inhabitas? Vere inaltissimo & secretissimo bonitatis tu[a]e, latet fons unde manat fluvius mis[eri]c[or]di[a]e tu[a]e. Nam cu[m]totus & su[m]me iustus sis; tamen iccirco etia[m] malis benignus es, quia totus su[m]me bonus es.

9.4 Minus nanq[ue] bonus esses; si nulli malo esses benignus. Melior est enim qui & bonis et malis bon[us] e[st]; qua[m] qui bonis tantum e[st] bonus. & melior est qui malis & puniendo & parcendo est bonus; qua[m] qui puniendo tantum. Ideo [er]g[o] misericors es; quia totus & su[m]me bonus es.

9.5 Et cum forsitan videatur cur bonis bona, et malis mala retribuas; illud certe penitus est mirandum, cur tu totus iustus & nullo egens, malis & reis tuis bona tribuas. O altitudo bonitatis tu[a]e d[eu]s, et videtur unde sis misericors, & non p[er]videtur.

[9.1 How the totally just and supremely just spares the wicked, and that He justly shows mercy to the wicked.]

IX

9.2 But how do You spare the wicked, if You are totally just and supremely just? For how does the totally and supremely just do something which is not just? Or what justice is it to give everlasting life to someone meriting eternal death? Why then, good God, do You do good to the good and to the wicked, and why do You save the wicked, if this is not just and You do not do anything that is not just?

9.3 Or does the reason lie hidden in the inaccessible light in which You dwell, because Your goodness is incomprehensible? Truly the spring from where the river of Your mercy flows lies hidden in the highest and most secret [place] of Your goodness. For although You are the totally and supremely just, yet You are indeed kind to the wicked, because You are totally [and] supremely good.

9.4 For indeed You would be less good, if You were not kind to anyone wicked. For he who is good to both the good and the wicked is better than he who is only good to the good. And he who is good in both punishing and sparing the wicked, is better than he who is good in punishing alone. Therefore, on this account You are merciful, because You are totally and supremely good.

9.5 And although, perhaps, it is clear why You return good things to the good and wicked things to the wicked, it is certainly utterly amazing, why You, totally just and lacking nothing, give good things to Your wicked and guilty people. O the heights of Your goodness, my God. One both sees and does not perceive why You are merciful.

9.6 Cernitur unde flumen manat, & n[on] p[er]spicitur fons unde nascatur. Nam & de plenitudine bonitatis est quia peccatorib[us] tuis pius es, & in altitudine bonitatis latet qua ratione hoc es.

9.6 One sees clearly from where the stream flows, but cannot observe the spring from where it rises. For it is from the fullness of Your goodness that You are loving to Your sinful people. But the reason why You are like this lies hidden in the heights of Your goodness.

9.7 Et enim licet bonis bona & malis mala ex bonitate retribuas; ratio tamen iustici[a]e hoc postulare videtur. Cum v[ero] malis bona tribuis; & scitur quia su[m]me bonus hoc facere voluit, & mirum e[st] cur summe iustus hoc velle potuit.

9.7 For although it is out of goodness that You return good things to the good and wicked things to the wicked, the logic of justice seems to require it. But when You give good things to the wicked, one both knows that the supremely good wished to do this and is amazed why the supremely just could have wished it.

9.8 O mis[eri]c[or]dia, de qua[m] opulenta dulcedine & dulci opulentia nobis p[ro]fluis. O immensitas bonitatis dei,quoaffectuamandaespeccatorib[us]. Iustos enim salvas iusticia comitante, istos v[ero] liberas iusticia damnante. Illos meritis adiuvantib[us], istos meritis repugnantibus. Illos bona qu[a]e dedisti cognoscendo, istos mala qu[a]e odisti ignoscendo.

9.8 O mercy, from what opulent sweetness and sweet opulence You flow forth for us. O immensity of the goodness of God, with what devotion You should be loved by sinners. For You save the just when justice attends them, but free the unjust when justice condemns them. The former aided by their merits, the latter contrary to their demerits. The former knowing the good things You gave, the latter ignorant of the bad things You hated.

9.9 O immensa bonitas qu[a]e sic omne[m] intellectum excedis, veniat sup[er] me mis[eri]c[or]dia illa qu[a]e de tanta opulentia tui p[ro]cedit. Influat inme, qu[a]e profluit de te. Parce p[er] clementiam, ne ulciscaris p[er] iusticiam.

9.9 O immense goodness, You who so surpass all understanding, may that mercy come upon me, which proceeds from Your great riches. May that flow into me, which flows forth from You. Spare by Your clemency, do not take vengeance by Your justice.

9.10 Nam & si difficile sit intelligere, quom[odo] mis[eri]c[or]dia tua n[on] absit a tua iusticia; necessarium tamen est credere, quia nequaqua[m] adversatur iustici[a]e quod exundat exbonitate qu[a]e nulla est sine iustitia, immo vere concordat iustici[a]e. Nempe si misericors es quia es su[m]me bonus, & su[m]me bonus non es n[isi] quia

9.10 For, even if it is difficult to understand how Your mercy is not absent from Your justice, yet it is necessary to believe that it is in no way opposed to justice, because it flows from goodness, which is not at all without justice, but rather is truly in accord with justice. Indeed, if You are merciful, because You are supremely es su[m]me iustus, vere iccirco es misericors quia su[m]me iustus es.

good, and You are not supremely good unless You are supremely just, then truly You are merciful because You are supremely just.

9.11 Adiuva me iuste & misericors d[eu]s cuius lucem qu[a]ero, adiuva me ut intelligam q[uo]d dico.

9.11 Help me, just and merciful God, whose light I seek, help me, so that I may understand what I am saying.

9.12 Vere [er]g[o] ideo misericors es, quia iust[us]. Ergone mis[eri]c[or]dia tua nascitur exiustitia tua? Ergone parcis malis ex iustitia? Si sic est d[omi]ne, si sic est, doce me quom[odo] est.

9.12 Truly then You are merciful, because You [are] just. Does Your mercy therefore arise out of Your justice? Do You therefore spare the wicked out of justice? If it is so, Lord, if it is so, teach me how it is.

9.13 An quia iustum est te sic e[ss]e bonum, ut nequeas intelligi melior, & sic potenter op[er]ari ut n[on] possis cogitari potentius? Quid eni[m] hoc iustius?

9.13 Is it because You are just that You are so good, that You cannot be understood to be better, and act so powerfully, that You cannot be thought to be more powerful? For what is more just than this?

9.14 Hoc utiq[ue] non fieret si esses bonus tantum retribuendo & non parcendo, & si faceres de non bonis tantum bonos, & non etia[m] de malis. Hoc itaq[ue] m[odo] iustum est ut parcas malis, & ut facias bonos de mal[is].

9.14 This would surely not be the case, if You were good only in so far as You paid retribution and did not spare, and if You only made the good from the not-good and not also from the wicked. Thus in this way it is just that You spare the wicked and make the good from the wicked.

9.15 Deniq[ue] quod n[on] iuste fit non debet fieri, & quod non debet fieri iniuste fit. Si [er]g[o] non iuste malis misereris; n[on] debes misereri, & si n[on] debes misereri; iniuste misereris. Quod si nefas est dicere; fas e[st] credere te iuste misereri malis.

9.15 In short, what is not done justly ought not to be done, and what ought not to be done is done unjustly. If therefore You do not justly show mercy to the wicked, You ought not to show mercy, and if You ought not to show mercy, You show mercy unjustly. If it is sinful to say this, it is right to believe that You justly show mercy to the wicked.

[10.1 Quom[odo] iuste puniat, & iuste parcat malis.]

•X•

10.2 Sed et iustum est ut malos punias. Quid nanq[ue] iustius qua[m] ut boni bona, & mali mala recipiant? Quom[odo] [er]g[o] & iustum est ut malos punias, et iustum e[st] ut malis parcas?

[10.1 How He justly punishes and justly spares the wicked.]

•X•

10.2 But it is also just that You punish the wicked. For what is more just than that the good should receive good things and the wicked wicked things? How then is it both just that You punish the wicked and just that You spare the wicked?

10.3 An alio m[odo] iuste punis malos, et alio m[odo] iuste parcis malis? Cu[m] eni[m] punis malos iustum est; quia illor[um] meritis convenit, cum v[ero] parcis malis iustum est; nonquia illor[um] meritis, sed quia bonitati tu[a]e condecens est.

10.3 Or do You punish the wicked justly in one way and spare the wicked justly in another way? For when You punish the wicked, it is just, because it accords with their deeds. But when You spare the wicked, it is just, not because it befits their deeds, but because it befits Your goodness.

10.4 Nam parcendo malis ita iustus es s[e]c[un]d[u]m te & non s[e]c[un]d[u]m nos; sicut misericors es s[e]c[un]d[u]m nos & non s[e]c[un]d[u]m te. Q[uonia]m salvando nos quos iuste p[er]deres, sicut misericors es non quia tu sentias affectum, sed quia nos sentimus effectum; ita iustus es non quia nobis reddas debitum, sed quia facis q[uo]d decet te su[m]me bonum. Sic itaq[ue] sine repugnantia iuste punis, & iuste parcis.

10.4 For in sparing the wicked in this way, You are just according to Yourself and not according to us, just as You are merciful according to us and not according to Yourself. Whereas in saving us, whom You might justly destroy, You are merciful, not because You feel emotion, but because we feel the effect, so You are just, not because You give back to us our due, but because You do what befits You, the supremely good. So this is how You justly punish and justly spare without contradiction.

[11.1 Quom[odo] univers[a]e vi[a]e d[omi]ni mis[eri]c[or]dia & veritas, & tamen iustus d[omi]n[u]s in omnibus viis suis.]

XI

11.2 Sed nunquid etia[m] n[on] e[st] iustu[m] s[e]c[un]d[u]m te, d[omi]ne, ut malos punias? Iustum quippe est, te sic e[ss]e iustum, ut iustior nequeas cogitari. Quod nequaqua[m] esses; si tantu[m] bonis bona, & non malis mala redderes. Iustior enim e[st] qui & bonis & malis; qua[m] qui bonis tantum merita retribuit. Iustu[m] [i]g[itur] est s[e]c[un]d[u]m te iuste & benigne d[eu]s; & cum punis & cu[m] parcis.

[11.1 How all the ways of the Lord are mercy and truth, and yet the Lord is just in all His ways.]

XI

11.2 But can it really be said that it is not just according to Yourself, Lord, that You punish the wicked? Of course, it is just that You are so just, that You cannot be thought to be more just. You would by no means be this just, if You only gave good things back to the good, and not bad things to the wicked. For he who gives back what they merit to both the good and the wicked is more just than he who does so only to the good. Therefore, it is just according to Yourself, O just and benevolent God, both when You punish and when You spare.

11.3 Vere [i]g[itur] univers[a]e vi[a]e d[omi]ni mis[eri]c[or]dia & veritas, & tamen iustus d[omi]n[u]s inomnib[us] viis suis.

11.3 Truly, therefore, all the ways of the Lord are mercy and truth, and yet the Lord is just in all His ways.

11.4 Et utique sine repugnantia; quia q[uo]s vis punire n[on] e[st] iustum salvari, & q[ui]b[us] vis parcere n[on] e[st] iustu[m] damnari. Nam id solum iustu[m] est quod vis, & non iustum q[uo]d non vis. Sic [er]g[o] nascitur de iusticia tua mis[eri]c[or]dia tua; quia iustum e[st] te sic e[ss]e bonum, ut & parcendo sis bonus.

11.4 Certainly this can be said without contradiction, because it is not just that those whom You wish to punish be saved, and it is not just that those whom You wish to spare be condemned. For that alone which You wish is just, and what You do not wish is not just. Therefore, in this way Your mercy arises out of Your justice, because it is just that You are so good that You are also good in sparing.

11.5 & hoc e[st] forsitan, cur su[m]me iustus potest velle bona malis. Sed si ut cu[m]q[ue] capi potest cur malos potes velle salvare; illud certe nulla ratione comprehendi potest, cur de similib[us] malis hos magis salves qua[m] illos p[er]su[m]ma[m] bonitatem, & illos magis damnes quam istos p[er]su[m]mam iusticiam.

11.5 And this is perhaps why the supremely just can wish good things for the wicked. But if it can, to some extent, be grasped, why You can wish to save the wicked, it certainly cannot be comprehended by any reason, why from equally wicked people You save some rather than others by Your supreme goodness, and condemn the latter rather than the former by Your supreme justice.

11.6 Sic [er]g[o] vere es sensibilis, om[ni]p[oten]s, misericors & impassibilis; que[m] admodum vivens, sapiens, bonus, beatus, [a]eternus, & q[ui]cq[ui]d melius est e[ss]e quam non esse.

11.6 Therefore You are truly sensible, omnipotent, merciful and impassible, even as You are living, wise, good, blessed, eternal and whatever it is better to be than not to be.

[12.1 Q[uo]d deus sit ipsa vita qua vivit, & sic de similibus.]

XII

12.2 Sed certe quicquid es, non p[er]aliud es qua[m] p[er]te ipsum. Tues [i]g[itur] ipsa vita qua vivis, & sapientia qua sapis, & bonitas ipsa qua bonis et malis bonus es, & ita de similibus.

[12.1 That God is the very life by which He lives, and the same [can be said] concerning similar [attributes].]

XII

12.2 Truly, whatever You are, You are through none other than Yourself. You are therefore the very life itself by which You live, and the wisdom by which You are wise, and the very goodness by which You are good to the good and the wicked, and likewise concerning similar [attributes].

[13.1 Quom[odo] solus sit incircumscriptus & [a]et[er]nus, cum alii spirit[us] sint incircumscripti et [a]eterni.]

[13.1 How He alone is unlimited and eternal, although other spirits are unlimited and eternal.]

XIII

13.2 Sed omne q[uo]d clauditur aliquatenus loco aut te[m]pore; minus e[st] qua[m] quod nulla lex loci aut temporis coercet. Q[uonia]m [er]g[o] maius te nichil est; nullus locus aut tempus te cohibet, sed ubiq[ue] & semp[er] es. Q[uo]d quia de te solo dici potest; tu solus incircumscriptus es et [a]eternus.

XIII

13.2 But everything which is to some extent enclosed by place or by time is less than that which no law of place or time confines. Therefore, since nothing is greater than You, no place or time restricts You, but You are everywhere and always. Since this can be said of You alone, You alone are unlimited and eternal.

13.3 Quom[odo] [i]g[itur] dicuntur & alii sp[iritu]s incircumscripti & [a]eterni?

13.3 How then are other spirits also called unlimited and eternal?

13.4 & quidem solus es [a]eternus; quia solus omniu[m] sicut n[on] desinis, sic n[on] incipis esse.

13.4 Indeed, You alone are eternal, since alone of all things, just as You do not cease to exist, so You do not begin to exist.

13.5 Sed solus quom[odo] es incircumscriptus? An creatus sp[iritu]s adte collatus e[st] circumscriptus, ad corpus v[ero] incircumscriptus? Nempe om[n]ino circumscriptu[m] e[st] quod cum alicubi totum est, n[on] potest simul e[ss]e alibi, q[uo]d desolis corporeis cernitur. Incircu[m]scriptum v[ero]; q[uo]d simul est ubiq[ue] totum, q[uo]d de te solo intelligitur.

13.5 But how are You alone unlimited? Or is the created spirit limited relative to You, yet unlimited relative to the body? Surely, it is altogether limited, because, when it is completely somewhere, it cannot at the same time be elsewhere. This is recognised as being the case concerning bodily things alone. That is truly unlimited, which is completely everywhere at the same time. This is understood to be the case concerning You alone.

13.6 Circumscriptum autem simul & incircumscriptu[m] est; quod cum alicubi sit totu[m], potest simul e[ss]e totum alibi n[on] tamen ubiq[ue], q[uo]d de creatis spiritib[us] cognoscitur. Si eni[m] non e[ss]et anima tota insingulis membris sui corporis; n[on] sentiret tota insingulis.

13.6 But that is at the same time limited and unlimited, which, when it is completely somewhere, can at the same time be completely elsewhere, yet not everywhere. This is acknowledged to be the case concerning created spirits. For if the soul were not completely in every one of the members of its body, it would not experience sensation completely in every one of them.

13.7 Tu [er]g[o] d[omi]ne singulariter es incircumscriptus & [a]eternus, & tamen & alii sp[iritu]s sunt incircumscripti & [a]eterni.

13.7 You therefore, Lord, are uniquely unlimited and eternal, and yet other spirits are also unlimited and eternal.

[14.1 Quom[odo] & cur videtur & non videtur deus aqu[a]erentibus eum.]
XIIII•

[14.1 How and why God is seen and not seen by those seeking Him.]
XIIII•

14.2 An invenisti anima mea q[uo]d qu[a]erebas? Qu[a]erebas d[eu]m, & invenisti eum e[ss]e quiddam su[m]mu[m] omniu[m], quo nichil melius cogitari potest, & hoc e[ss]e ipsam vitam, luce[m], sapientiam, bonitatem, [a]eternam beatitudinem, & beatam [a]eternitatem, & hoc e[ss]e ubiq[ue] & semp[er].

14.2 My soul, have you found what you sought? You sought God, and you have found that He is that, the highest of all things, than which nothing better can be thought; and that this is life itself, light, wisdom, goodness, eternal blessedness and blessed eternity; and that it exists everywhere and always.

14.3 Nam si n[on] invenisti d[eu]m tuu[m], quom[odo] est ille hoc q[uo]d invenisti, & quod illum tam certa veritate & vera certitudine intellexisti? Si v[ero] invenisti, quid est q[uo]d n[on] sentis quod invenisti? Cur non te sentit d[omi]ne d[eu]s anima mea si invenit te?

14.3 For if you have not found Your God, how is He this which you have found and which you have understood Him to be with such certain truth and true certitude? If you have truly found Him, how is it that you do not experience what you have found? Why does my soul not experience You, Lord God, if it has found You?

14.4 An non invenit, que[m] invenit e[ss]e lucem et veritate[m]? Quo m[odo] nanq[ue] intellexit hoc n[isi] videndo lucem & veritatem? Aut potuit om[n]ino aliquid intelligere de te, nisi p[er]lucem tua[m] & veritatem tua[m]? Si [er]g[o] vidit lucem et veritate[m]; vidit te. Si non vidit te; non vidit luce[m] nec veritatem.

14.4 Or has it not found Him, whom it found to be the light and the truth? For indeed how did it understand this, if it did not see the light and the truth? Could it have understood anything about You at all, except through Your light and Your truth? If therefore it has seen the light and the truth, it has seen You. If it has not seen You, it has not seen the light or the truth.

14.5 An & veritas & lux est q[uo]d vidit, & tamen n[on] dum te vidit, quia vidit te aliquatenus, sed n[on] vidit te sicuti es?

14.5 Or is it that it has seen both the truth and the light, but at the same time has not yet seen You, since it has seen You to some extent, but has not seen You as You are?

14.6 D[omi]ne d[eu]s m[eu]s, formator & reformator m[eu]s, dic desideranti anim[a]e me[a]e quid aliud es qua[m]

14.6 Lord my God, my fashioner and refashioner, tell my desiring soul in what respect You are different from what it quod vidit, ut pure videat q[uo]d desiderat. Intendit se ut plus videat, & nichil vid[et] ultra hoc quod vidit nisi tenebras, immo non videt tenebras qu[a]e null[a]e sunt inte; sed videt se non plus posse videre p[ro]pter tenebras suas.

has seen, so that it may see clearly what it desires. It directs itself so that it may see more, but sees nothing beyond that which it has seen except darkness. Or more precisely, it does not see darkness, which is not in You at all, but sees that it can see no more on account of its own darkness.

14.7 Cur hoc d[omi]ne cur hoc? Tenebratur oc[u]l[u]s eius infirmitate sua, aut reverberatur fulgore tuo? Sed certe & tenebratur inse, & reverberatur a te. Utiq[ue] & obscuratur sua brevitate, & obruitur tua immensitate. Vere & contrahitur angustia sua, & vincitur amplitudine tua.

14.7 Why is this, Lord, why is this? Is its eye darkened by its infirmity or driven back by Your brightness? Truly, it is both darkened in itself and driven back by You. Without doubt it is both obscured by its smallness and overshadowed by Your immensity. Truly, it is both restricted by its narrowness, and overcome by Your breadth.

14.8 Quanta nanq[ue] est lux illa, de qua micat om[n]e veru[m] quod rationali m[en]ti lucet. Qua[m] ampla e[st] illa veritas, inqua est om[n]e q[uo]d verum e[st], & extra qua[m] non n[isi] nichil & falsum est. Qua[m] immensa e[st] qu[a]e uno intuitu videt qu[a]ecunq[ue] facta sunt, & aquo & p[er]que[m] & quom[odo] denichilo facta sunt. Quid puritatis, quid simplicitatis, q[ui]d certitudinis & splendoris ibi est. Certe plusqua[m] a creatura valeat intelligi.

14.8 For how great is that light, from which springs forth every true thing that gives light to the rational mind. How broad is that truth, in which everything which is true exists, and outside which there is only nothing and falsehood. How immense is that, which sees in one glance whatever things have been made, and by whom and through whom and how they were made from nothing! What purity, what simplicity, what certainty and splendour is there! Certainly, more than can be understood by a creature.

[15.1 Quod maior sit qua[m] cogitari possit.]

XV

15.2 Ergo d[omi]ne non solum es quo maius cogitari nequit; sed es quiddam maius qua[m] cogitari possit. Q[uonia]m nanq[ue] valet cogitari e[ss]e aliquid huiusmodi; si tu non es hoc ipsum potest cogitari aliquid maius te, q[uo]d fieri nequit.

[15.1 That He is greater than can be thought.]

XV

15.2 Therefore, Lord, not only are You [something] than which a greater cannot be thought, but You are also something greater than can be thought. For, since it can be thought that there is something of this kind, if You are not this very thing, it is possible to think of something greater than You – and this cannot be done.

[16.1 Q[uo]d h[a]ec sit lux inaccessibilis quam inhabitat.]

XVI

16.2 Vere d[omi]ne h[a]ec est lux inaccessibilis, in qua habitas. Vere eni[m] n[on] e[st] aliud quod hanc penetret, ut ibi te p[er]videat.

16.3 Vere ideo hanc non video, quia nimia m[ihi] est, & tamen quicquid video p[er]illam video, sicut infirmus oc[u]l[u]s q[uo]d videt p[er] lucem solis videt, qua[m] inipso sole nequit aspicere.

16.4 Non potest intellectus m[eu]s adillam. Nimis fulget, non capit illam, nec suffert oculus anim[a]e me[a]e diu intendere inillam. Reverberatur fulgore, vincitur amplitudine, obruitur immensitate, confunditur capacitate.

16.5 O su[m]ma & inaccessibilis lux, o tota et beata veritas, qua[m] longe es a me, qui tam p[ro]pe t[ibi] sum. Qua[m] remota es aconspectu meo, qui sic pr[a]esens su[m] conspectui tuo. Ubiq[ue] es tota pr[a]esens, & non te video. Inte moveor & inte sum, & ad te n[on] possum accedere. Intra me & circa me es, & non te sentio.

[17.1 Q[uo]d indeo sit armonia, odor, sapor, l[a]enitas, pulchritudo, suo ineffabili m[odo].]

XVII

17.2 Adhuc lates d[omi]ne anima[m] mea[m] inluce & beatitudine tua, & iccirco versatur illa adhuc intenebris et miseria sua. Circu[m]spicit eni[m], & non videt pulchritudinem tua[m]. Auscultat, & non audit armonia[m] tua[m]. Olfacit, & n[on] p[er]cipit odore[m] tuum. Gustat, & non cognoscit

[16.1 That this is the inaccessible light, in which He dwells.]

XVI

16.2 Truly, Lord, this is the inaccessible light, in which You dwell. For truly there is no other thing which penetrates it to look upon You there.

16.3 Truly, I do not see [the inaccessible light] for this reason, that it is too much for me. And yet, whatever I see I see through it, just as the weak eye sees what it sees by the sun's light, although it cannot look directly at the sun.

16.4 My understanding cannot attain it. It shines too brightly. [My understanding] does not grasp it, nor can the eye of my soul bear to focus its attention on it for long. It is driven back by [its] brightness, overcome by [its] breadth, shrouded by [its] immensity, bewildered by [its] capacity.

16.5 O supreme and inaccessible light, O complete and blessed truth, how far You are from me, who am so near to You. How distant You are from my sight, whilst I am so present to Your sight. You are wholly present everywhere, yet I do not see You. In You I move, in You I exist, yet I cannot draw near to You. You are within me and around me, yet I do not experience You.

[17.1 That there is harmony, fragrance, flavour, gentleness and beauty in God, in His own ineffable way.]

XVII

17.2 You still lie concealed from my soul, Lord, in Your light and beatitude, and for this reason it dwells still in its darkness and misery. For it looks all around, and does not see Your beauty. It listens, and does not hear Your harmony. It smells, and does not perceive Your fragrance. It tastes, and does not discern saporem tuu[m]. Palpat, & n[on] sentit lenitate[m] tua[m].

17.3 Habes eni[m] h[a]ec d[omi]ne d[eu]s inte tuo ineffabili m[odo], qui ea dedisti rebus ate creatis suo sensibili m[odo], sed obriguerunt, sed obstupuerunt, sed obstructi sunt sensus anim[a]e me[a]e, vetusto languore peccati.

Your flavour. It caresses, and does not feel Your gentleness.

17.3 For You possess in Yourself, Lord God, in Your own ineffable way, these [attributes], which You have given to created things in their own sensible way. But the senses of my soul have become stiff, they have become paralysed, they are obstructed by the ancient weakness of sin.

[18.1 Q[uo]d indeo nec in[a]eternitate ei[us] qu[a]e ipse est null[a]e sint partes.]
XVIII

[18.1 That there are no parts in God nor in the eternity, which He Himself is.]
XVIII

18.2 Et it[er]um ecce turbatio, ecce it[er]u[m] obviat meror & luctus, qu[a]erenti gaudium et l[a]eticiam. Sp[er]abat ia[m] anima mea satietate[m], & ecce it[er]um obruit[ur] egestate. Affectabam ia[m] comedere, & ecce magis esurire.

18.3 Conabar assurgere adluce[m] dei, & recidi intenebras meas. Immo non m[odo] cecidi ineas, sed sentio me involutum ineis! Ante cecidi, qua[m] concip[er]et me mater mea. Certe inillis conceptus sum, & cu[m] earu[m] obvolutione natus sum. Olim certe in illo om[ne]s cecidim[us], inquo om[ne]s peccavimus.

18.4 Inillo om[ne]s p[er]didimus qui facile tenebat & male sibi & nob[is] p[er]didit, q[uo]d cu[m] volumus qu[a]erere nescimus, cu[m] qu[a]erimus n[on] invenimus, cu[m] invenimus n[on] e[st] quod qu[a]erimus.

18.5 Adiuva me tu p[ro]pter bonitate[m] tua[m] d[omi]ne. Qu[a]esivi vultu[m] tuu[m], vultum tuu[m] d[omi]ne requira[m], neavertas faciem tua[m] ame. Releva me de me ad te. Munda, sana, acue, illumina oculu[m] mentis me[a]e, ut intueatur te.

18.2 And again behold turmoil, behold again grief and mourning stand in the way of the one who seeks joy and gladness. My soul had hoped for abundance by now, and behold once more it is overwhelmed by destitution. I endeavoured to eat at last, and behold more hunger.

18.3 I tried to ascend to the light of God, and I fell back into my darkness. Or rather, not only did I fall into it, but I also feel myself enveloped in it! I fell before my mother conceived me. Indeed, I was conceived in [darkness], and was born with its shroud. Truly, we all fell a long time ago in him, in whom we have all sinned.

18.4 We have lost everything in him who easily possessed and wickedly lost for himself and for us what we do not know how to seek when we wish to, do not find when we seek it, and is not what we are seeking when we find it.

18.5 Help me on account of Your goodness, Lord. I have sought Your countenance; Your countenance, Lord, I will seek. Do not turn Your face from me. Lift me up from myself to You. Cleanse, heal, sharpen, illuminate the eye of my mind, so that it may gaze on You.

18.6 Recolligat vires suas anima mea, & toto intellectu it[er]um intendat inte d[omi]ne.

18.6 May my soul regain its strength and with all its understanding strive again towards You, Lord.

18.7 Quid es d[omi]ne, q[ui]d es, q[ui]d te intelliget cor meu[m]? Certe vita es, sapientia es, veritas es, bonitas es, beatitudo es, [a]eternitas es, & om[n]e veru[m] bonu[m] es. Multa sunt h[a]ec, n[on] potest angustus intellect[us] m[eu]s tot uno simul intuitu videre, ut omnib[us] simul delectetur. Quom[odo] [er]g[o] d[omi]ne, es om[n]ia h[a]ec?

18.7 What are You, Lord? What are You? How should my heart understand You? Indeed, You are life, You are wisdom, You are truth, You are goodness, You are blessedness, You are eternity, and You are every true good. These are many things. But my narrow understanding cannot see in a single glance so many things at the same time, that it may simultaneously take pleasure in them all. How then, Lord, are You all these things?

18.8 An sunt partes tui, aut potius unu[m] q[uo]dq[ue] horu[m] e[st] totum q[uo]d es? Nam quicq[ui]d partib[us] e[st] iunctum n[on] e[st] om[n]ino unum; sed q[uo]da[m] m[odo] plura & diversum ase ipso, & vel actu v[e]l intellectu dissolvi potest, qu[a]e aliena sunt ate quo nichil meli[us] cogitari potest.

18.8 Are they parts of You, or rather is each one of them all that You are? For whatever is joined together by parts is not entirely one but in some way several things and distinct from itself, and can be broken up either by act or by understanding. Such things are foreign to You than whom nothing better can be thought.

18.9 Null[a]e [i]g[itur] partes sunt inte d[omi]ne, nec es plura, sed sic es unu[m] quidda[m] & idem t[ibi] ipsi; ut innullo t[ibi] ipsi sis dissimilis, immo tues ipsa unitas, nullo intellectu divisibilis. Ergo vita & sapientia & reliqua non sunt partes tui, sed om[n]ia sunt unum, & unu[m] quodq[ue] horu[m] e[st] totu[m] q[uo]d es, & q[uo]d sunt reliqua om[n]ia.

18.9 Therefore, there are no parts in You, Lord, nor are You several things, but You are one thing and the same as Yourself in such a manner that in no way are You dissimilar to Yourself. More precisely, You are unity itself, divisible by no understanding. Therefore life and wisdom and the rest are not parts of You, but they are all one, and each one of them is all that You are and what all the rest are.

18.10 Q[uonia]m [er]g[o] nec tu habes partes, nec tua [a]et[er]nitas qu[a]e tues: nusqua[m] & nunqua[m] e[st] pars tua aut [a]et[er]nitatis tu[a]e, sed ubiq[ue] totus es, & [a]et[er]nitas tua tota est semp[er].

18.10 Since therefore neither You nor the eternity, which You are, have parts, in no place and at no time is there a part of You or of Your eternity. But You are wholly everywhere and Your eternity is always whole.

[19.1 Q[uo]d non sit inloco aut tempore, sed omnia sint inillo.]

XIX

[19.1 That He does not exist in space or time, but all things exist in Him.]

XIX

19.2 Sed si p[er][a]eternitate[m] tua[m] fuisti, & es, & eris, et fuisse n[on]

19.2 But if through Your eternity You were, are and will be, and to have been e[st] futuru[m] e[ss]e, et e[ss]e, n[on] e[st] fuisse v[e]l fut[ur]um e[ss]e, q[uo]m[odo] [a]eternitas tua tota est semp[er]?

19.3 An de [a]eternitate tua nichil pr[a]eterit ut iam n[on] sit, nec aliquid fut[ur]um est quasi n[on] dum sit? Non [er]g[o] fuisti heri aut eris cras; sed heri & hodie & cras es. Immo nec heri nec hodie nec cras es; sed simpliciter es extra om[n]e tempus.

19.4 Nam nichil aliud est heri & hodie & cras; qua[m] intempore, tu aute[m] licet nichil sit sine te n[on] es tamen inloco aut tempore, sed om[n]ia sunt inte. Nich[il] eni[m] te continet, sed tu contines om[n]ia.

[20.1 Quod sit ante & ult[ra] om[n]ia etia[m] [a]eterna.]

XX•

20.2 Tu [er]g[o] imples & complecteris om[n]ia, tues ante & ultra om[n]ia. Et quide[m] ante om[n]ia es; quia ante qua[m] fierent tues.

20.3 Ultra om[n]ia v[ero] quom[odo] es? Qualiter eni[m] es ultra ea qu[a]e fine[m] non habebunt? An quia illa sine te nullatenus e[ss]e possunt, tu autem nullom[odo] minus es, etia[m] si illa redeunt innichilum? Sic eni[m] quoda[m] m[odo] es ultra illa!

20.4 An etia[m] quia illa cogitari possunt habere finem, tu v[ero] nequaquam? Nam sic illa quide[m] habent fine[m] quoda[m]m[odo], tu v[ero] nullo m[odo]. & certe q[uo]d nullo m[odo]

is not to be in the future, and to be is not to have been nor to be in the future, how is Your eternity always a whole?

19.3 Or, from the perspective of Your eternity, is it not the case that nothing passes away so that it no longer exists, nor will something exist in the future as though it does not yet exist? Therefore You did not exist yesterday nor will You exist tomorrow, but You exist yesterday and today and tomorrow. Or rather, You exist neither yesterday nor today nor tomorrow, but You exist simply outside all time.

19.4 For to exist yesterday and today and tomorrow is nothing other than to exist in time; yet, although nothing exists without You, You do not exist in space or time, and all things exist in You. For nothing contains You, but You contain all things.

[20.1 That He is before and beyond even all eternal things.]

XX•

20.2 Therefore, You fill and encompass all things. You are before and beyond all things. Indeed You are before all things, because, before they were made, You exist.

20.3 How in truth are You beyond all things? In what way, in fact, are You beyond those things that will not have an end? Is it because without You they cannot exist at all, whereas You are in no way lessened, even if they return to nothingness? So, then, in a certain way You are beyond them!

20.4 Furthermore, is it because they can be thought to have an end, whereas You in no wise can? For in a certain sense they indeed have an end, whereas You in no way do. And surely that which in habet finem; ultra illud est q[uo]d aliq[uo] m[odo] finitur.

no way has an end is beyond that which is in some way limited.

20.5 An hoc quoq[ue] modo transis om[n]ia etia[m] [a]et[er]na, quia tua & illor[um] [a]eternitas tota tibi pr[a]esens est, cum illa non du[m] habeant de sua [a]et[er]nitate q[uo]d vent[ur]um est, sicut iam n[on] habent q[uo]d pr[a]et[er]itum e[st]?

20.5 Do You surpass all eternal things in this way too, because Your eternity and theirs is wholly present to You, although they do not yet possess what is to come of their eternity, just as they no longer possess what is past?

20.6 Sic quippe semp[er] es ultra illa, cum semp[er] ibi sis pr[a]esens, seu cu[m] illud se[m]p[er] sit tibi pr[a]esens, ad q[uo]d illa n[on] dum p[er]venerunt.

20.6 For thus You are always beyond them, since You are always present in that place at which they have not yet arrived, or rather since it is always present to You.

[21.1Anhocsits[ae]c[u]l[u]m s[ae]c[u]li sive s[ae]c[u]la s[ae]c[u]lor[um].]
XXI

21.2 An [er]g[o] hoc est s[ae]c[u]l[u]m s[ae]c[u]li, sive s[ae]c[u]la s[ae]c[u]lor[um]? Sicut eni[m] s[ae]c[u]l[u]m tempor[um] continet om[n]ia temporalia; sic tua [a]eternitas continet etia[m] ipsa s[ae]c[u]la tempor[um]. Qu[a]e sæculum quidem e[st] p[ro]pt[er] indivisibilem unitate[m], s[ae]c[u]la v[ero] p[ro]pter int[er]minabilem immensitate[m]!

21.3 & q[ua]nvis ita sis magnus d[omi]ne, ut om[ni]a sint te plena & sint inte; sic tamen es sine om[n]i spacio, ut nec mediu[m] nec dimidiu[m] nec ulla pars sit inte.

[21.1 Whether this is the age of the age or the ages of ages.]
XXI

21.2 Is this then the age of the age or the ages of ages? For just as the age of the times contains all temporal things, so Your eternity contains even the very ages of the times. It is indeed an age, because of its indivisible unity, and on the other hand the ages, because of its unending immensity!

21.3 And even though You are so great, Lord, that all things are full of You and are in You, yet You are completely without any spatial extension, so that in You there is neither centre nor half nor any part.

[22.1 Q[uo]d solus sit q[uo]d est & qui est.]
XXII

22.2 Tu solus [er]g[o], d[omi]ne es q[uo]d es, & tues q[ui] es. Nam q[uo]d aliud est intoto & aliud inpartib[us], & inquo aliquid est mutabile; n[on] om[n]ino e[st] q[uo]d est.

[22.1 That He alone is what He is and who He is.]
XXII

22.2 You alone then, Lord, are what You are, and You are who You are. For that which is one thing in its totality, and another in its parts, and in which something is subject to change, is not entirely what it is.

22.3 & quod inc[o]epit a n[on] e[ss]e & potest cogitari n[on] e[ss]e, & n[isi] p[er] aliud subsistat redit in n[on] e[ss]e, & quod habet fuisse q[uo]d iam n[on] e[st] & futuru[m] e[ss]e q[uo]d nondum e[st]; id n[on] [est] p[ro]p[ri]e & absolute.

22.3 And that does not exist properly and absolutely, which began from non-being and can be thought not to be, and returns to non-being if it does not subsist through another, and which has a past existence which now no longer exists, and a future existence that does not yet exist.

22.4 Tu v[ero] es q[uo]d es, quia quicquid aliquando aut aliquom[odo] es; hoc totus & semp[er] es. & tu es q[ui] p[ro]p[ri]e & simpliciter es; quia nec habes fuisse aut futuru[m] esse, sed tantum pr[a]esens e[ss]e, nec potes cogitari aliquando non e[ss]e.

22.4 You truly are what You are, because whatever You are at some time or in some way, this You are wholly and always. And You are who You are properly and simply, because You do not have past existence nor future existence, but only present existence, and cannot be thought not to exist at some particular time.

22.5 Et vita es, & lux, & sapientia, & beatitudo, & [a]eternitas, et multa huiusmodi bona, & tamen n[on] es n[isi] unum & su[m]mu[m] bonu[m], tu t[ibi] omnino sufficiens, nullo indigens, quo om[n]ia indigent ut sint, & ut bene sint.

22.5 And You are life, and light, and wisdom, and beatitude, and eternity, and the many good things of this kind, and yet You are nothing but the one and supreme good, You who are entirely sufficient to Yourself, needing nothing, and whom all things need that they might exist and that they might exist rightly.

[23.1 Quod hoc bonum sit pariter pater & filius & spirit[us] s[an]c[tu]s, & hoc sit unum necessarium, q[uo]d est omne & totum & solum bonum.]

XXIII

[23.1 That this good is equally the Father and the Son and the Holy Spirit; and this is the one [thing] necessary, which is the all and whole and only good.]

XXIII

23.2 Hoc bonum es tu d[eu]s pater, hoc est verbum tuu[m], id e[st] filius tuus. Et eni[m] non potest aliud qua[m] q[uo]d es aut aliquid maius vel minus te e[ss]e inverbo quo te ipsum dicis; q[uonia]m verbu[m] tuu[m] sic est veru[m] q[uo]m[odo] tu verax, & iccirco est ipsa veritas sicut tu non alia quam tu, & sic es tu simplex, ut de te n[on] possit nasci aliud qua[m] quod tu es.

23.2 You, God the Father, are this good; it is Your Word, that is Your Son. And indeed there cannot be anything other than what You are, or something greater or lesser than You are, in the Word by which You speak Yourself, since Your Word is true even as You are truthful, and therefore it is truth itself, just as You are, and is none other than You. And You are so simple that from You there cannot be begotten anything other than what You are.

23.3 Hoc ipsu[m] e[st] amor unus & co[m]munis t[ibi] & filio tuo, id est s[an]c[tu]s sp[iritu]s abutroq[ue] p[ro]cedens.

23.3 This [good] itself is the one Love shared by You and by Your Son, that is, the Holy Spirit proceeding from both of You.

23.4 Nam idem amor non e[st], impar t[ibi] aut filio tuo; quia tantu[m] amas te & illu[m], & ille te & se ipsum, quantus es tu & ille, nec est aliud ate & abillo q[uo]d dispar n[on] e[st] t[ibi] & illi, nec desu[m]ma simplicitate potest p[ro]cedere aliud qua[m] quod est de quo p[ro]cedit. Quod aute[m] e[st] singulus quisq[ue], hoc e[st] tota trinitas simul pater & filius & sp[iritu]s s[an]c[tu]s, q[uonia]m singulus quisq[ue] non e[st] aliud qua[m] su[m]me simplex unitas & su[m]me una simplicitas, qu[a]e nec multiplicari nec aliud & aliud e[ss]e potest.

23.4 For the same Love is not inferior to You or to Your Son. For You love Yourself and Him and He loves You and Himself to such a degree, that You are also Him. And what is not unequal to You and to Him is not different from You and from Him. And anything that is different from that from which it proceeds cannot proceed from the supreme simplicity. But what each one by itself is, the whole Trinity is at the same time, Father and Son and Holy Spirit, since each by itself is not anything other than the supremely simple unity and the supremely one simplicity, which can neither be multiplied nor be different things.

23.5 Porro unu[m] e[st] necessarium. Porro hoc est illud unu[m] necessariu[m], inquo e[st] om[n]e bonu[m], immo q[uo]d est om[n]e & unu[m] & totum & solum bonu[m].

23.5 Moreover, one [thing] is necessary. Moreover, this is that one necessary [thing], in which is every good, or rather which is every and the one and the whole and the only good.

[24.1 Coniectatio quale & q[ua]ntu[m] sit hoc bonu[m].]

XXIIII

[24.1 A conjecture: what this good is like and how great it is.]

XXIIII

24.2 Excita nunc anima mea & erige totu[m] intellectu[m] tuu[m], & cogita quantu[m] potes quale et quantu[m] sit illud bonu[m].

24.2 Awake now my soul, and rouse all of your understanding, and think, as far as you can, what this good is like and how great it is.

24.3 Si eni[m] singula bona delectabilia sunt; cogita intente qua[m] delectabile sit illud bonum, q[uo]d continet iucunditate[m] om[n]iu[m] bonor[um], & et non quale[m] inrebus creatis sumus exp[er]ti, sed tanto differentem quanto differt creator acreatura.

24.3 For if individual good things are delightful, consider intently how delightful is that good, which contains what is pleasing in all good things, and is as different from what we have had experience of in created things as is the Creator from the creature.

24.4 Si eni[m] bona e[st] vita creata, qua[m] bona e[st] vita creatrix? Si iucunda e[st] salus facta, qua[m] iucunda e[st] salus qu[a]e fac[it] omne[m]

24.4 For if created life is good, how good is creative life? If salvation secured is delightful, how delightful is the salvation that secures all salvation? If wisdom in salute[m]? Si amabilis e[st] sapientia incognitione rerum conditaru[m], qua[m] amabilis e[st] sapientia qu[a]e om[n]ia condidit exnichilo? Deniq[ue] si mult[a]e & magn[a]e delectationes sunt in reb[us] delectabilib[us], qualis et quanta delectatio [est] inillo qui fecit ipsa delectabilia?

the knowledge of constructed things is worthy of love, how worthy of love is the wisdom which has constructed all things out of nothing? Finally, if there are many great delights in delightful things, how excellent and how great a delight is there in that which makes delightful things themselves?

[25.1 Qu[a]e & q[ua]nta bona sint fruentib[us] eo.]

[25.1 What good things there are for those delighting in Him and how great they are.]

XXV

25.2 O qui hoc bono fruetur, quid illi erit, & quid illi non erit. Certe quicq[ui]d volet erit, & quod nolet non erit. Ibi quippe erunt bona corporis & anim[a]e, qualia nec oculus vidit, nec auris audivit, nec cor hominis cogitavit.

XXV

25.2 O he who delights in this good, what will he possess and what will he not possess. Certainly, whatever he shall will shall be, and whatever he shall not will shall not be. For in that place will be the good things of the body and of the soul, such as neither the eye has seen, nor the ear has heard, nor the heart of man has thought of.

25.3 Cur [er]g[o] p[er]multa vagaris homuncio, qu[a]erendo bona anim[a]e tu[a]e & corporis tui? Ama unu[m] bonu[m] in quo sunt om[n]ia bona, & sufficit. Desidera simplex bonu[m] quod e[st] omne bonu[m], & satis est.

25.3 Why then do you wander by so many ways, little man, seeking the good of your soul and your body? Love the one good, in which are all goods. That is sufficient. Desire the simple good, which is every good. That is enough.

25.4 Quid eni[m] amas caro mea, quid desideras anima mea? Ibi e[st] ibi est quicq[ui]d amatis, quicq[ui]d desideratis.

25.4 For what do you love, my flesh, and what do you desire, my soul? There, in that place, is whatever you love, whatever you desire.

25.5 Si delectat pulchritudo; fulgebunt iusti [sicut] sol.

25.5 If beauty delights you: the just will shine like the sun.

25.6 Si velocitas aut fortitudo, aut libertas corporis cui nichil obsistere possit; erunt similes angeli[s] dei, quia seminatur corp[us] animale, & surget corpus sp[irit]uale, potestate utiq[ue] non natura.

25.6 If it is speed or strength, or freedom of the body, which nothing can resist: they will be like the angels of God, because an animal body is sown and a spiritual body springs up by a spiritual power and certainly not by nature.

25.7 Si longa & salubris vita; ibi est sana [a]et[er]nitas, & [a]eterna sanitas, quia iusti inp[er]petuu[m] vivent, & salus iustor[um] a d[omi]no.

25.7 If it is a long and healthy life: there is healthy eternity and eternal health, because the just live for ever, and the salvation of the just is from the Lord.

25.8 Si satietas; satiabuntur cu[m] apparuerit gl[ori]a dei.

25.8 If it is fullness: they will be filled when the glory of God appears.

25.9 Si ebrietas; inebriabuntur abubertate domus dei.

25.9 If it is intoxication: they will be made drunk by the abundance of the house of God.

25.10 Si melodia; ibi angelor[um] chori concinunt sine fine deo.

25.10 If it is melody: there the choirs of angels sing in harmony without end to God.

25.11 Si qu[a]elibet n[on] immunda sed munda voluptas; torrente voluptatis su[a]e potabit eos d[eu]s.

25.11 If it is pure and not impure pleasure: God will give them to drink from the torrent of His pleasure.

25.12 Si sapientia; ipsa dei sapientia ostendet eis se ipsam.

25.12 If it is wisdom: the very wisdom of God will show itself to them.

25.13 Si amicitia; diligent d[eu]m plusqua[m] se ipsos, & invicem tanqua[m] se ipsos, & d[eu]s illos plusqua[m] illi se ipsos; quia illi illu[m] & se & invice[m] p[er]illu[m], & ille se & illos p[er]se ipsum.

25.13 If it is friendship: they will love God more than themselves, and each other as much as themselves, and God will love them more than they love themselves, because they love Him and themselves and each other through Him, and He loves Himself and them through Himself.

25.14 Si concordia: omnibus illis erit una voluntas, quia nulla illis erit nisi sola dei voluntas.

25.14 If it is concord: they will all possess one will, because they will possess none except the will of God alone.

25.15 Si potestas; om[n]ipotentes erunt su[a]e voluntatis ut d[eu]s su[a]e. Nam sicut poterit d[eu]s q[uo]d volet p[er]se ipsum; ita poterunt illi q[uo]d volent p[er]illu[m], quia sicut illi non aliud volent qua[m] quod ille; ita ille volet quicquid illi volent, & q[uo]d ille volet non poterit n[on] e[ss]e.

25.15 If it is power: they will be omnipotent in their will as God is in His. For just as God will be able to do what He shall will through Himself, so they will be able to do what they shall will through Him, because just as they shall not will anything other than what He wills, so He shall will whatever they shall will, and what He shall will shall not be able not to be.

25.16 Si honor & diviti[a]e; d[eu]s suos servos bonos & fideles supra multa constituet, immo filii dei & dii vocabuntur & er[un]t, & ubi erit filius eius ibi erunt & illi, heredes quidem dei, coheredes aute[m] xpi [=Christi].

25.16 If it is honour and riches: God will establish His good and faithful servants above many things. Or rather, they shall be called, and shall be, sons of God and gods, and where His Son shall be, there will they be also, heirs indeed of God and co-heirs of Christ.

25.17 Si vera securitas; certe ita certi erunt numqua[m] & nullatenus ista vel

25.17 If it is true security: then certainly they will be certain that those goods potius istud bonu[m] sibi defuturu[m]; sicut certi erunt se non sua sponte illud amissuros, nec dilectore[m] d[eu]m illud dilectorib[us] suis invitis ablaturum, nec aliquid d[e]o potentius invitos d[eu]m & illos separat[ur]um.

or rather that good will never, ever, be lacking to them, just as they will be certain that they will not lose it of their own accord, that the loving God will not take it away against the will of those who love Him, and that something more powerful than God will not separate God and them against their will.

25.18 Gaudiu[m] v[ero] quale aut quantu[m] est, ubi tale ac tantu[m] bonu[m] est? Cor humanu[m], cor indigens, cor exp[er]tum eru[m]nas immo obrutu[m] erumnis, quantum gauderes, si his omnib[us] abundares? Int[er]roga intima tua, si cap[er]e possint gaudiu[m] suu[m] detanta beatitudine sua.

25.18 Truly, what kind of joy, how great a joy, is there, where such a good, so great a good, exists? Human heart, needy heart, heart experienced in afflictions or rather crushed by afflictions, how greatly would you rejoice if you abounded in all these things? Ask your inmost being, if it could contain its joy at such great blessedness.

25.19 Sed certe si quis alius que[m] om[n]ino sicut te ipsu[m] diligeres, eandem beatitudine[m] haberet; duplicaretur gaudiu[m] tuu[m] quia non minus gauderes p[ro]eo qua[m] p[ro]te ipso. Si v[ero] duo v[e]l tres v[e]l multo plures idipsum haberent; tantunde[m] p[ro]sing[u]lis quantu[m] p[ro]te ipso gauderes, si sing[u]los sicut teipsum amares. Ergo inilla p[er]fecta caritate innumerabiliu[m] beator[um] ang[e]lor[um] & hominu[m], ubi nullus minus diliget aliu[m] qua[m] se ipsum; non aliter gaudebit quisq[ue] p[ro]singulis aliis qua[m] p[ro]se ipso.

25.19 But certainly if someone else, whom you loved in every respect just as you love yourself, should have the same blessedness, your joy would be doubled, because you would rejoice no less for him than for yourself. If truly two or three or many more should have the very same blessedness, you would rejoice just as much for each one of them as for yourself, if you loved each one of them as yourself. Therefore in that perfect love of innumerable blessed angels and men, where no one loves another less than himself, each will rejoice for every other no differently than he rejoices for himself.

25.20 Si [er]g[o] cor hominis de tanto suo bono vix capiet gaudium suu[m], quom[odo] capax erit tot & tantor[um] gaudior[um]? & utiq[ue] q[uonia]m quantum quisq[ue] diligit alique[m], tantum de bono eius gaudet; sicut inilla p[er]fecta felicitate unus quisq[ue] plus amabit sine comparatione d[eu]m qua[m] se & om[ne]s alios secum; ita plus gaudebit absq[ue] existimatione

25.20 If then the heart of man scarcely contains its joy at such great good, how will it be capable of containing so many and such great joys? Since to the extent someone loves another, he rejoices at their good, and in that perfect happiness each one will love God incomparably more than himself and every one else, so he will rejoice inestimably more at the happiness of God than at his own de felicitate d[e]i qua[m] de sua & omniu[m] alior[um] secum.

happiness and that of all others who are with him.

25.21 Sed si d[eu]m sic diligent toto corde, tota mente, tota anima, ut tamen totu[m] cor, tota mens, tota anima n[on] sufficiat dignitati dilectionis; p[ro]fecto sic gaudebunt toto corde, tota mente, tota anima; ut totu[m] cor, tota mens, tota anima non sufficiat plenitudini gaudii.

25.21 But if they love God in such a way with all their heart, with all their mind, with all their soul, that nevertheless all their heart, all their mind, all their soul would not be equal to the dignity of this love, they will surely rejoice with all their heart, with all their mind, with all their soul in such a way that all their heart, all their mind, all their soul would not be equal to the fullness of this joy.

[26.1 An hoc sit gaudium plenu[m] quod promittit dominus.]

XXVI

[26.1 Whether this is the full joy that the Lord promises.]

XXVI

26.2 D[eu]s m[eu]s & d[omi]n[u]s m[eu]s, spes mea & gaudiu[m] cordis mei, dic anim[a]e me[a]e si hoc est gaudium de quo nob[is] dicis p[er]filiu[m] tuu[m]: petite & accipietis, ut gaudiu[m] v[est]r[u]m sit plenum. Inveni nanq[ue] gaudiu[m] q[uo]dda[m] plenu[m], & plusqua[m] plenum.

26.2 My God and my Lord, my hope and the joy of my heart, tell my soul if this is the joy about which You speak to us through Your Son, 'Ask and you shall receive, that your joy may be full'. For I have found a kind of joy, which is full, and more than full.

26.3 Pleno quippe corde, plena mente, plena anima, pleno toto homine gaudio illo; adhuc supra modu[m] sup[er]erit gaudiu[m]. Non [er]g[o] totu[m] illud gaudium intrabit ingaudentes; sed toti gaudentes intrabunt ingaudium.

26.3 Indeed, with the heart full, the mind full, the soul full, the whole man full of that joy, there will still remain joy beyond measure. Therefore, not all that joy will enter into the joyful, but all the joyful will enter into joy.

26.4 Dic d[omi]ne, dic servo tuo intus incorde suo, si hoc e[st] gaudiu[m] inquod intrabunt servi tui, qui intrabunt ingaudium d[omi]ni sui.

26.4 Tell, Lord, tell Your servant in the depths of his heart, if this is the joy, into which Your servants will enter – those who will enter into the joy of their Lord.

26.5 Sed gaudiu[m] illud certe quo gaudebunt electi tui; nec oc[u]l[u]s vidit, nec auris audivit, nec in cor hominis ascendit. Nondum [er]g[o] dixi aut cogitavi d[omi]ne, quantu[m] gaudebunt illi beati tui.

26.5 Truly, neither the eye has seen, nor the ear has heard, nor has there arisen in the heart of man that joy in which Your elect will rejoice. Therefore, Lord, I have not yet spoken of or thought, how much they, Your blessed, will rejoice.

26.6 Utiq[ue] tantum gaudebunt quantu[m] amabunt, tantum amabunt quantu[m] cognoscent. Quantu[m] te

26.6 But, in so far as they will rejoice they will love, and in so far as they will love, they will know. How much cognoscent d[omi]ne tunc, & quantu[m] te amabunt? Certe nec oc[u]l[u]s vidit, nec auris audivit, nec incor hominis ascendit inhac vita, quantu[m] te cognoscent & amabunt inilla vita.

will they love You then, Lord, and how much will they know You? Certainly, neither the eye has seen, nor the ear has heard, nor has there arisen in the heart of man in this life, how much they will know and love You in that life.

26.7 Oro d[eu]s, cognoscam te, ame[m] te, ut gaudeam dete. & si non possu[m] inhac vita adplenum; v[e]l p[ro]ficia[m] indies usq[ue] dum veniat illud adplenu[m].

26.7 I pray, God, that I may know You, and that I may love You, so that I may rejoice in You. And if I cannot do so to the full in this life, may I advance daily right until that joy comes to fullness.

26.8 P[ro]ficiat hic inme noticia tui & ibi fiat plena, crescat amor tuus & ibi sit plenus; ut hic gaudiu[m] meu[m] sit inspe magnum, & ibi sit inre plenu[m].

26.8 Here may knowledge of You advance in me, and there be made full; may my love of You increase, and there be full, so that here my joy may be great in hope, and there be full in reality.

26.9 D[omi]ne, p[er] filiu[m] tuu[m] iubes immo consulis petere & p[ro]mittis accip[er]e, ut gaudiu[m] n[ost]r[u]m plenu[m] sit. Peto d[omi]ne q[uo]d consulis p[er]admirabilem consiliariu[m] n[ost]r[u]m, accipia[m] q[uo]d p[ro]mittis p[er]veritate[m] tua[m], ut gaudium meu[m] plenu[m] sit. D[eu]s verax, peto accipiam, ut gaudiu[m] meu[m] plenu[m] sit.

26.9 Lord, through Your Son You command or rather counsel us to ask and You promise we shall receive, that our joy may be full. I ask, Lord, what You counsel through our admirable Counsellor. May I receive what You promise through Your Truth, that my joy may be full. Truthful God, I ask that I may receive, so that my joy may be full.

26.10 Meditetur interim inde mens mea, loquatur inde lingua mea. Amet illud cor meu[m], sermocinetur os meu[m]. Esuriat illud anima mea, sitiat caro mea, desid[er]et tota substantia mea; donec intre[m] ingaudiu[m] d[omi]ni mei, qui est trin[us] & un[us] d[eu]s benedict[us] ins[ae]c[u]la. AMEN

26.10 In the meantime may my mind meditate on it, my tongue speak of it. May my heart love it, my mouth preach it. May my soul hunger for it, my flesh thirst for it, my whole substance desire it, until I may enter into the joy of my Lord, who is God, threefold and one, blessed for ever. AMEN.

26.11 EXPLICIT PROSLOGION LIBER ANSELMI CANTUARIENSIS ARCHI EPISCOPI.

26.11 THE END OF THE PROSLOGION, THE BOOK OF ANSELM, ARCHBISHOP OF CANTERBURY.

2. PRO INSIPIENTE

QUID ADH[A]EC RESPONDEAT QUIDAM PRO INSIPIENTE.

[1.1] Dubitanti utrum sit vel neganti quod sit aliqua talis natura qua nichil mai[us] cogitari possit, cum e[ss]e illa[m] hinc dicitur p[ri]mo p[ro]bari, quod ipse negans vel ambigens de illa iam habeat ea[m] inintellectu, cu[m] audiens illam dici id quod dicitur intelligit, de inde quia quod intelligit, necesse est ut non insolo intellectu sed etiam inre sit, & hoc ita p[ro]batur q[ui]a maius est e[ss]e & inre qua[m] insolo intellectu, & si illud insolo est intellectu, maius illo erit quicq[ui]d etia[m] inre fuerit, ac sic maius om[n]ib[us] minus erit aliquo et non erit mai[us] omnib[us] q[uo]d utiq[ue] repugnat, & ideo necesse est ut maius om[n]ib[us], q[uo]d e[ss]e ia[m] p[ro]batu[m] est inintellectu, non in solo intellectu sed & inre sit, q[uonia]m aliter maius om[n]ib[us] e[ss]e non poterit; respondere forsan potest.

HOW SOMEONE MIGHT REPLY TO THESE [WORDS OF PROSLOGION 2-4] ON BEHALF OF THE FOOL.

[1.1] It is said to someone who doubts whether there is, or denies that there is, such a nature [as that] than which nothing greater can be thought, that it is proved to exist on the following basis. Firstly, because the person who denies or doubts this [nature] already has it in the understanding, when, on hearing it said, he understands what is said. And, then, because it is necessary that what he understands does not exist in the understanding alone but also in reality, and this is proved, because it is greater to exist in reality as well [as in the understanding] rather than in the understanding alone. If it is in the understanding alone, whatever exists in reality will be greater, and in this way the greater than everything will be less than something and will not be greater than everything, which is certainly contradictory. Therefore, it is necessary that the greater than everything which has already been proved to exist in the understanding, exists not in the understanding alone, but also in reality, since otherwise it could not be greater than everything. Perhaps he can reply as follows.

[2.1] Q[uo]d hoc iam e[ss]e dicitur inintellectu meo, non ob aliud n[isi] quia id q[uo]d dicitur intelligo; nonne & qu[a]ecunq[ue] falsa ac nullo p[ro]rsus modo in se ipsis existentia inintellectu hab[er]e similiter dici possem, cu[m] ea dicente aliquo, qu[a]ecu[n]q[ue] ille diceret, ego intelligerem?

[2.1] But this is said to exist already in my understanding for no other reason than that I understand what is said. In a similar way, could I not be said to have false and absolutely non-existent things in the understanding, if I were to understand whatever someone said, when he spoke of these things?

[2.2] Nisi forte tale illud constat e[ss]e ut n[on] eo m[odo] quo etia[m] falsa qu[a]eq[ue] vel dubia haberi possit incogitatione, et ideo non dicor illud auditu[m] cogitare v[e]l incogitatione habere; sed intelligere & inintellectu habere, quia scilicet non possim hoc aliter cogitare; n[isi] intelligendo id est scientia comprehendendo, re ipsa illud existere.

[2.3] Sed si hoc est, primo quidem non hic erit iam aliud idemq[ue] tempore pr[a]ecedens habere rem inintellectu, & aliud idq[ue] tempore sequens intelligere rem e[ss]e, ut fit de pictura qu[a]e prius est in animo pictoris, de inde inop[er]e.

[2.4] De inde vix unqua[m] poterit e[ss]e credibile, cu[m] dictum & auditum fuerit istud n[on] eomodo posse cogitari non e[ss]e; quo etiam potest n[on] e[ss]e d[eu]s.

[2.5] Nam si n[on] potest, cur contra negantem aut dubitante[m] quod sit aliqua talis natura: tota ista disputatio e[st] assumpta?

[2.6] Postremo quod tale sit illud ut non possit n[isi] mox cogitatu[m] indubitabilis existenti[a]e su[a]e certo p[er]cipi intellectu, indubio aliquo p[ro]bandum m[ihi] est argumento, n[on] aute[m] isto q[uo]d iam sit hoc inintellectu meo cu[m] auditu[m] intelligo, inquo similiter e[ss]e posse qu[a]ecunq[ue] alia incerta vel etia[m] falsa abaliquo cuius verba intelligerem dicta adhuc puto, & insup[er] magis si illa deceptus ut sepe fit crederem, qui istud n[on] dum credo.

[2.2] Unless perhaps it is established that a being of this kind can be thought differently to false or uncertain things, and [that] therefore I am not said to think or to have in thought what is heard, but to understand it and to have it in the understanding, because plainly I cannot think it other than by understanding [it], that is by comprehending with knowledge that it exists in reality.

[2.3] But if this is the case, firstly, there will no longer be a difference between having something in the understanding on a prior occasion and understanding that it exists on a subsequent occasion, as happens in the case of a painting, which exists first in the soul of the painter and then in his completed work.

[2.4] Secondly, it could hardly be credible that, when this thing has been spoken and heard of, it could not be thought not to exist, given that there is a way in which even God can be thought not to exist.

[2.5] For if this [i.e. God's non-existence] cannot be thought, why is this whole disputation taken up against someone denying or doubting that there is such a nature?

[2.6] Finally, that there is something, the indubitable existence of which the understanding cannot but perceive with certainty as soon as it is thought of, is to be proved to me by some indubitable argument, but not by this one: that it exists already in my understanding, when I understand what I have heard. I still maintain that all kinds of uncertain or false things could exist in a similar way, if these were spoken of by someone whose words I understood. This would be even more so, if, as often happens, I, who do not yet believe this argument, were deceived and believed these things.

[3.1] Unde nec illud exemplu[m] de pictore pictura[m] qua[m] facturus est iam in intellectu habente; satis potest huic argumento congruere.

[3.1] Hence, the example of the painter having a painting which is about to be created in his understanding cannot be satisfactorily adapted to this argument.

[3.2] Illa eni[m] pictura ante qua[m] fiat inipsa pictoris arte habetur, & tale quippiam inarte artificis alicuius nichil e[st] aliud qua[m] pars qu[a]eda[m] intelligenti[a]e ipsius, quia & sicut s[an]c[tu]s AUGUSTINUS ait, cu[m] faber arcam facturus inop[er]e, prius habet illa[m] inarte; arca qu[a]e fit inop[er]e n[on] e[st] vita, arca qu[a]e est inarte vita e[st]; quia vivit anima artificis, inqua sunt ista om[n]ia antequa[m] p[ro]ferantur.

[3.2] For before he creates it, the painting is possessed in the very art of the painter, and such a thing in the art of some artisan is nothing other than a part of his intelligence, because, as Saint Augustine also says: ‘When, in doing [his] work, a craftsman is about to make a box, he first possesses it in [his] art. The box which is created in his work is not alive. The box which is in his [art] is alive, because the soul of the artisan is alive. In this [soul] all these things exist before they are produced.’

[3.3] Ut quid eni[m] invivente artificis anima vita sunt ista, n[isi] quia nil sunt aliud qua[m] scientia, vel intelligentia anim[a]e ipsius?

[3.3] How are these things alive in the living soul of the artisan, unless they are nothing other than the knowledge or intelligence of his soul?

[3.4] At v[ero] q[ui]cquid extra illa qu[a]e adipsam mentis noscuntur p[er]tinere natura[m], aut auditum aut excogitatu[m] intellectu p[er]cipit[ur] veru[m]; aliud sine dubio e[st] verum illud, aliud intellectus ipse quo capitur.

[3.4] But no matter what is perceived as true by the understanding, when it understands or thinks it, it is without doubt [the case that] what is true is one thing and the understanding itself which grasps it is another, if one excludes those things that are known to pertain to the very nature of the mind.

[3.5] Quo circa etia[m] si verum sit e[ss]e aliquid quo maius quicq[ua]m nequeat cogitari; non tamen hoc auditu[m] & intellectu[m] tale est qualis n[on] dum facta pictura in intellectu pictoris.

[3.5] Thus, even if it were true that there existed something than which something greater cannot be thought, still this thing, when heard and understood, is not the same kind of thing as the yet to be created painting in the understanding of the painter.

[4.1] Huc accedit illud quod pr[a]etaxatum e[st] sup[er]ius, quia scilicet illud om[n]ib[us] qu[a]e cogitari possint maius, quod nichil aliud posse e[ss]e dicitur qua[m] ipse d[eu]s, ta[m] ego s[e]c[un]d[u]m re[m], vel exspecie m[ihi] v[e]l exgenere notam, cogitare auditu[m], vel inintellectu habere non

[4.1] In addition, as touched on above, if I hear of that which is greater than all those things that can be thought (which, it is said, can be nothing other than God Himself), I can no more think of it nor have it in the understanding in the manner of something known to me under the categories of species or possum; qua[m] nec ipsum d[eu]m, que[m] utiq[ue] obhoc ipsum etia[m] n[on] e[ss]e cogitare possum.

[4.2] Neq[ue] eni[m] aut rem ipsa[m] novi, aut exalia possum conicere simili; quandoquide[m] & tu talem asseris illa[m] ut e[ss]e non possit simile quicqua[m].

[4.3] Na[m] si dehomine aliquo m[ihi] p[ro]rsus ignoto, que[m] etia[m] e[ss]e nescire[m], dici tamen aliquid audire[m]; p[er]illam specialem generalemve noticia[m] q[ua] quid sit homo v[e]l homines novi, de illo quoq[ue] s[e]c[un]d[u]m rem ipsa[m] qu[a]e est homo cogitare possem.

[4.4] & tamen fieri posset, ut mentiente illo qui diceret, ipse que[m] cogitare[m] homo n[on] e[ss]et, cu tamen ego de illo s[e]c[un]d[u]m vera[m] nichilominus rem non qu[a]e e[ss]et ille homo, sed qu[a]e est homo quilibet cogitarem.

[4.5] Nec sic [i]g[itur] ut habere[m] falsum istud incogitatione vel inintellectu, habere possum illud cu[m] audio dici d[eu]s, aut aliquid om[n]ib[us] maius, cu[m] quando illud s[e]c[un]d[u]m rem vera[m] m[ihi]q[ue] nota[m] cogitare possem, istud om[n]ino nequea[m] n[isi] tantu[m] s[e]c[un]d[u]m vocem s[e]c[un]d[u]m qua[m] sola[m] aut vix aut nunqua[m] potest ullu[m] cogitari verum, siq[ui]dem cu[m] ita cogitatur n[on] ta[m] vox ipsa qu[a]e res e[st] utiq[ue] vera hoc e[st] litteraru[m] sonus v[e]l syllabaru[m], qua[m] vocis audit[a]e significatio cogitetur, sed n[on] ita ut abillo qui novit quid ea soleat voce significari aquo scilicet cogitatur s[e]c[un]d[u]m rem vel insola cogitatione veram; veru[m] ut abeo qui illud non novit & solum m[odo] cogitat s[e]c[un]d[u]m animi

genus, than I can think of or understand God Himself, whom for this reason I can certainly think not to exist.

[4.2] For I have neither known this thing itself nor can I construct it from something similar, seeing that you also assert of such a thing as this, that there cannot be anything similar to it.

[4.3] For if I were to hear something said about some man utterly unknown to me, whom I did not even know to exist, I could think of him in terms of what a man is, through that notion of species or genus by which I know what a man is or men are.

[4.4] And yet it could happen that the speaker might be lying and the man of whom I was thinking might not exist, even though I thought of him in terms of something true, which is not this particular man, but man in general.

[4.5] Therefore, when I hear [the words] 'God' or 'something greater than everything' spoken, I cannot possess that notion in the same way as I possess this false thing in my thought or in my understanding. For although I could think of the latter in terms of something true and known to me, I can only think of the former by means of a word. And no true thing can scarcely or ever be thought by reference to a word alone. If it is thought in this way, it is not so much the word itself that is thought (which is certainly a true thing – that is, the sound of letters or syllables), but rather the meaning of the word which was heard. However, it is not thought of in the way that someone who knows what is customarily signified by the word thinks of something, who at least thinks of it in terms of something true in thought alone. Rather, it is thought of in the way of someone who motu[m] illius auditu vocis effectu[m] significatione[m]q[ue] p[er]cept[a]e vocis conantem effingere sibi.

does not know that thing and only thinks of it in terms of an activity in his soul, which is produced by hearing the sound of the word and who tries to represent to himself the meaning of the word he has perceived in this way.

[4.6] Q[uo]d miru[m] e[st], si unqua[m] rei veritate potuerit.

[4.6] It would be amazing, if he could ever arrive at the truth of something in this way.

[4.7] Ita [er]g[o] nec p[ro]rsus aliter adhuc in intellectu meo constat illud haberi, cum audio intelligoq[ue] dicente[m] e[ss]e aliq[ui]d maius om[n]ib[us] qu[a]e valeant cogitari.

[4.7] Therefore, it is clear that when I hear and understand someone saying that there exists something greater than all the things that can be thought, it is possessed in my understanding in this and absolutely no other way.

[4.8] H[a]ec deeo quod su[m]ma illa natura iam e[ss]e dicitur in intellectu meo.

[4.8] These words were written in response to the assertion that the supreme nature is said to be in my understanding already.

[5.1] Quod aute[m] & inre necessario e[ss]e inde m[ihi] p[ro]batur, quia n[isi] fuerit, quicquid est inre maius illa erit, ac p[er]hoc n[on] erit illud maius om[n]ib[us] q[uo]d utiq[ue] iam e[ss]e probatum est inintellectu; adhoc respondeo,

[5.1] Furthermore, it is then also proved to me that this necessarily exists in reality, because unless it existed, whatever exists in reality will be greater than it, and for this reason it will not be that which is greater than everything, which has undoubtedly been proved to exist already in my understanding. To this I reply:

[5.2] Si e[ss]e dicendu[m] e[st] in intellectu, q[uo]d s[e]c[un]d[u]m veritate[m] cuiusqua[m] rei nequit saltem cogitari; & hoc inmeo sic e[ss]e non denego.

[5.2] If one says that there exists in the understanding what cannot at all be thought true of anything, I do not deny that it also exists in my understanding in this sense.

[5.3] Sed quia p[er] hoc e[ss]e quoq[ue] inre non potest ullatenus obtinere; illud ei e[ss]e adhuc penitus n[on] concedo, quousq[ue] m[ihi] argumento p[ro]bet[ur] indubio.

[5.3] But since by this argument he can in no way demonstrate that it also exists in reality, I absolutely do not concede its existence to him, until it is proved to me by an indubitable argument.

[5.4] Q[uo]d qui e[ss]e dicit hoc quod maius om[n]ib[us] aliter non erit om[n]ibus maius; non satis attendit cui loq[ua]tur.

[5.4] For he who says that that which is greater than everything exists, since otherwise it will not be greater than everything, does not pay sufficient attention to whom he speaks.

[5.5] Ego eni[m] n[on]dum dico, immo etia[m] nego vel dubito ulla re vera e[ss]e

[5.5] For I do not admit, but deny or doubt, that it is greater than any true thing. Nor maius illud, nec aliud ei e[ss]e concedo qua[m] illud si dicendum e[st] e[ss]e cu[m] s[e]c[un]d[u]m voce[m] tantu[m] auditam: rem p[ro]rsus ignota[m] sibi conatur animus effingere.

do I concede to it any existence other than the kind – if it is to be spoken of as existence – that is signified when the soul attempts to represent something, which, apart from the sound of the word, is completely unknown to it.

[5.6] Quom[odo] [i]g[itur] inde m[ihi] p[ro]batur maius illud rei veritate subsistere, quia constet illud mai[us] om[n]ib[us] e[ss]e, cu[m] id ego eo usq[ue] negem ad huc dubitemve constare, ut ne inintellectu quidem vel cogitatione mea eo saltem m[odo] maius ipsum e[ss]e dicam quo dubia etia[m] multa sunt & incerta?

[5.6] So how is it proved to me that this greater thing truly subsists in reality, because it is established that it is greater than everything, when I continue to deny or doubt that this is the case, when in fact I say that this greater thing itself does not exist in my understanding or thought in the way that even many doubtful and uncertain things do?

[5.7] Prius eni[m] certu[m] m[ihi] necesse est fiat, re vera e[ss]e alicubi maius ipsum, & tum demu[m] exeo q[uo]d maius e[st] om[n]ibus inse ipso quoq[ue] subsistere non erit ambiguum.

[5.7] For first of all it is necessary that I am shown that that which is greater than any true thing exists somewhere, and only then, from the fact that it is that which is greater than everything, will it be established that it also subsists in itself.

[6.1] Exempli gra[tia]. Aiunt quidam alicubi oceani e[ss]e insulam, quam exdifficultate vel potius impossibilitate inveniendi q[uo]d non est cognominant aliqui p[er]ditam, qua[m]q[ue] fabulantur multo amplius qua[m] de fortunatis insulis fertur: divitiaru[m] deliciaru[m]q[ue] omniu[m] inaestimabili ubertate pollere, nulloq[ue] possessore aut habitatore universis aliis quas incolunt homines terris possidendor[um] redundantia usq[ue]quaq[ue] pr[a]estare.

[6.1] For example, certain people say that somewhere in the ocean there is an island, which because of the difficulty or, rather, the impossibility of discovering what does not exist, some call 'lost'. And they say that it possesses an inestimable abundance of riches and delights, much greater than the Fortunate Isles, and that, with no owner or inhabitant, the surfeit of things to be possessed always excels that of all the lands which men occupy.

[6.2] Hoc ita e[ss]e dicat m[ihi] quispiam, & ego facile dictu[m] inquo nichil e[st] difficultatis intelligam.

[6.2] Should someone say to me that this is the case, I would easily understand what was said, since it contains nothing difficult to understand.

[6.3] At si tunc velut consequenter adiungat ac dicat, n[on] potes ultra dubitare insula[m] illa[m] terris om[n]ibus pr[a]estantiore[m] vere e[ss]e alicubi inre, qua[m] & inintellectu tuo non ambigis e[ss]e, & quia pr[a]estantius

[6.3] But if he should then add as a consequence: 'You can no more doubt that that island, which is more excellent than all lands, truly exists somewhere in reality, than you can doubt that it also exists in your understanding. And e[st] n[on] inintellectu solo sed etia[m] e[ss]e inre, id[e]o sic eam necesse est e[ss]e quia n[isi] fuerit, qu[a]ecunq[ue] alia inre est terra pr[a]estantior illa erit, ac sic ipsa iam a te pr[a]estantior intellecta pr[a]estantior non erit, si inqua[m] p[er]h[a]ec ille m[ihi] velit astruere de insula illa q[uo]d vere sit ambigendu[m] ultra n[on] e[ss]e; aut iocari illum credam, aut nescio que[m] stultiore[m] debeam reputare, utru[m] me si ei concedam, an illu[m] si se putet aliqua certitudine insul[a]e illius essentiam astruxisse; n[isi] prius ipsa[m] pr[a]estantiam eius solu[m]m[odo] sicut rem vere atq[ue] indubie existente[m], nec ullatenus sicut falsum aut incertu[m] aliquid inintellectu meo e[ss]e docuerit.

since it is more excellent to exist, not in the understanding alone, but also in reality, therefore it is necessary that it exists in this way, because unless it should exist, whatever other land exists in reality will be more excellent than it, and the island itself already understood by you to be more excellent will not be more excellent.' – If, I say, through these arguments he should want to demonstrate to me that it is to be no longer doubted that the island truly exists, I would either believe him to be joking, or not know whom I might consider more stupid, myself, if I should concede the point to him, or him, if he should think that he had established the existence of that island with some kind of certainty, unless he shall first have established that its very excellence is in my understanding as something which truly and indubitably exists and not as something which is in any way false or uncertain.

[7.1] H[a]ec interim adobiecta insipiens ille responderit.

[7.1] [This is how] the fool would have answered these objections so far.

[7.2] Cui cum deinceps asseritur tale e[ss]e maius illud, ut nec sola cogitatione valeat non e[ss]e, & hoc rursus non aliunde p[ro]batur, qua[m] eo ipso quod aliter n[on] erit om[n]ib[us] maius; ide[m] ipsu[m] possit referre responsu[m] & dicere.

[7.2] If next it is asserted to him that such a greater thing exists, so that it cannot exist in thought alone, and this is proved again by no other means than from the assertion that otherwise it will not be greater than everything, he can make the same response once more and say:

[7.3] Quando eni[m] ego rei veritate e[ss]e tale aliquid, hoc e[st] maius om[n]ib[us] dixi, ut ex hox m[ihi] debeat p[ro]bari intantu[m] etia[m] re ipsa id e[ss]e, ut nec possit cogitari n[on] e[ss]e?

[7.3] 'But when did I say that there truly exists in reality such a thing that is a greater than everything, so that from this it might also be proved to me that it so exists in reality that it cannot be thought not to exist?'

[7.4] Quap[ro]pter certissimo primitus aliquo p[ro]bandum e[st] argumento, aliqua[m] sup[er]iore[m] hoc e[st] maiorem ac meliorem omniu[m] qu[a]e sunt e[ss]e natura[m]; ut ex hoc alia

[7.4] Therefore, it must first be proved by some argument with absolute certainty that there is a superior nature, greater and better than everything that exists, so that from this we can then prove all the iam possimus om[n]ia co[m]probare, quib[us] necesse est illud q[uo]d mai[us] ac melius e[st] om[n]ib[us] non carere.

other [attributes], which it is necessary that that which is greater and better than everything does not lack.

[7.5] Cum aute[m] dicitur quod su[m]ma res ista n[on] e[ss]e nequeat cogitari; melius fortasse diceretur, q[uo]d non e[ss]e aut etia[m] posse n[on] e[ss]e non possit intelligi.

[7.5] But when it is said that this supreme object cannot be thought not to exist, it would perhaps be better said, that it cannot be understood not to exist or even to be able not to exist.

[7.6] Na[m] s[e]c[un]d[u]m p[ro]prietatem verbi istius falsa nequeunt intelligi; qu[a]e possunt utiq[ue] eomodo cogitari, quo d[eu]m n[on] e[ss]e insipiens cogitavit.

[7.6] For according to the proper meaning of this word, false things cannot be understood, although they can undoubtedly be thought in the [same] way that the fool thought that there is no God.

[7.7] Et me quoq[ue] e[ss]e certissime scio, sed & posse non e[ss]e nichilominus scio.

[7.7] And I know with absolute certainty that I exist. Nevertheless, I also know that I am able not to exist.

[7.8] Su[m]mu[m] v[ero] illud quod est scilicet d[eu]s, & e[ss]e & non e[ss]e non posse indubitanter intelligo.

[7.8] I understand indubitably that that which is supreme, namely God, truly both exists and cannot not exist.

[7.9] Cogitare aute[m] me non e[ss]e qua[m] diu e[ss]e certissime scio; nescio utrum possim.

[7.9] However, I do not know whether I can think that I do not exist whilst I know with absolute certainty that I do exist.

[7.10] Sed si possum; cur n[on] et quicquid aliud eadem certitudine scio?

[7.10] If I can think I do not exist, why can I not also think this of something else I know with the same degree of certainty?

[7.11] Si aute[m] n[on] possum; n[on] erit ia[m] istud p[ro]prium deo.

[7.11] But if I cannot think I do not exist, this will not then be a property peculiar to God.

[8.1] C[a]etera libelli illius tam veraciter & ta[m] pr[a]eclare sunt magnificeq[ue] disserta, tanta deniq[ue] referta utilitate, & pii ac s[an]c[t]i affectus intimo quoda[m] odore fragrantia; ut nullom[odo] p[ro]pt[er] illa qu[a]e ininitiis recte quidem sensa, sed minus firmiter argumentata sunt, ista sint conte[m]nenda; sed illa potius argumentanda robustius, ac si[c] om[n]ia cu[m] ingenti veneratione & laude suscipienda.

[8.1] The remainder of this little book is argued so truthfully and so clearly and magnificently. It is filled with such usefulness and with what one might call a profound, fragrant odour of pious and holy feeling, that in no way should it be condemned on account of those assertions at the beginning, which are well meant, but less strongly argued. Rather, these assertions must be argued more robustly, so that the whole work may be accepted with veneration and praise.

3. RESPONSIO

QUID ADH[A]EC RESPONDEAT EDITOR IPSIUS LIBELLI.

[1.1] Quoniam non me reprehendit inhis dictis ille insipiens contra que[m] sum locutus inmeo opusculo, sed quidam n[on] insipiens & catholicus p[ro]insipiente; sufficere m[ihi] potest respondere catholico.

[1.2] Dicis q[ui]dem quicu[n]q[ue] es qui dicis h[a]ec posse dicere insipiente[m], quia n[on] est in intellectu aliquid quo maius cogitari n[on] possit, aliter qua[m] q[uo]d s[e]c[un]d[u]m veritate[m] cui[us]q[uam] rei nequit saltem cogitari, & quia non magis consequitur hoc quod dico quo maius cogitari n[on] possit, exeo quia est inintellectu e[ss]e & inre, qua[m] p[er]dita[m] insulam certissime existere exeo quia cum describitur verbis, audiens ea[m] n[on] ambigit inintellectu suo e[ss]e.

[1.3] Ego v[ero] dico, Si quo mai[us] cogitari n[on] potest, non intelligit[ur] vel cogitatur, nec est inintellectu vel cogitatione; p[ro]fecto d[eu]s aut n[on] [est] quo maius cogitari n[on] possit, aut non intelligit[ur] v[e]l cogitatur, & n[on] est inintellectu v[e]l cogitatione.

[1.4] Q[uo]d q[ua]m falsum sit; fide & conscientia tua p[ro]firmissimo utor argumento.

[1.5] Ergo quo maius cogitari n[on] potest vere intelligitur, & cogitatur, & est inintellectu & cogitatione.

[1.6] Quare aut vera non sunt quib[us] contra conaris p[ro]bare; aut exeis non

HOW THE AUTHOR OF [THAT] SAME SMALL BOOK MIGHT REPLY TO THESE [OBJECTIONS].

[1.1] Since it is not the fool, against whom I spoke in my little work, who criticises me with these words, but someone who is no fool, but a Catholic speaking on behalf of the fool, may it suffice for me to reply to the Catholic.

[1.2] Indeed you say – whoever you are who say that the fool can say these things – that that something than which a greater cannot be thought is not in the understanding any differently to what cannot even be thought to be true of something. [You] also [state] that [the existence] in reality of what I call '[something] than which a greater cannot be thought' no more follows from [its existence] in the understanding, than it follows that a lost island most certainly exists from the fact that when it is described in words, the hearer does not doubt that it is in his understanding.

[1.3] However, I say: 'If [something] than which a greater cannot be thought is not understood or thought, nor exists in the understanding or in thought, then, either God is not [something] than which a greater cannot be thought, or He is not understood or thought and does not exist in the understanding or in thought.'

[1.4] I employ your faith and conscience as the most powerful argument that this is false.

[1.5] Therefore, [something] than which a greater cannot be thought is truly understood and thought and exists in the understanding and in thought.

[1.6] Therefore, those statements by which you try to prove the contrary are either not true, or what you suppose you consequitur q[uo]d te consequenter opinaris concludere.

demonstrate logically does not follow from them.

[1.7] Q[uo]d aute[m] putas exeo quia intelligitur aliquid quo maius cogitari nequit, non consequi illud e[ss]e in intellectu, nec si est inintellectu ideo e[ss]e inre; certe ego dico, si v[e]l cogitari potest e[ss]e, necesse est illud e[ss]e.

[1.7] But you think that it does not follow from the fact that something than which a greater cannot be thought is understood, that it is in the understanding, nor if it is in the understanding that therefore it exists in reality. I say with certainty that, if it can even be thought to exist, it is necessary that it exists.

[1.8] Nam quo maius cogitari nequit; non potest cogitari esse n[isi] sine initio.

[1.8] For [something] than which a greater cannot be thought can only be thought to exist without a beginning.

[1.9] Quicquid aute[m] potest cogitari e[ss]e & n[on] e[st]; p[er] initium potest cogitari e[ss]e.

[1.9] But whatever can be thought to exist and does not exist, can be thought to exist with a beginning.

[1.10] Non [er]g[o] quo maius cogitari nequit, cogitari potest e[ss]e & non est.

[1.10] Therefore it is not [the case that something] than which a greater cannot be thought can be thought to exist and [yet] not exist.

[1.11] Si [er]g[o] cogitari potest e[ss]e; ex necessitate est.

[1.11] If therefore it can be thought to exist, it exists out of necessity.

[1.12] Amplius. Si utiq[ue] v[e]l cogitari potest; necesse est illud e[ss]e.

[1.12] Furthermore, if it can be thought at all, it is necessary that it exists.

[1.13] Nullus eni[m] negans aut dubitans e[ss]e aliquid quo maius cogitari non possit; negat v[e]l dubitat quia si e[ss]et, nec actu nec intellectu posset non e[ss]e.

[1.13] For no one denying or doubting that something than which a greater cannot be thought exists, denies or doubts that, if it were to exist, it would not be able not to exist either in actuality or in the understanding.

[1.14] Aliter namq[ue] n[on] e[ss]et; quo maius cogitari non posset.

[1.14] For otherwise it would not be [something] than which a greater cannot be thought.

[1.15] Sed quicquid cogitari potest, & n[on] [est]; si e[ss]et posset v[e]l actu v[e]l intellectu non e[ss]e.

[1.15] But whatever can be thought and does not exist, if it were to exist, would be able not to exist either in actuality or in the understanding.

[1.16] Quare si v[e]l cogitari potest; n[on] potest non e[ss]e quo maius cogitari nequit.

[1.16] Therefore, if it can even be thought, [something] than which a greater cannot be thought cannot not exist.

[1.17] Sed ponamus non e[ss]e, si v[e]l cogitari valet.

[1.17] But let us assume that it does not exist, even if it can be thought.

[1.18] At quicq[ui]d cogitari potest & non est; si e[ss]et, n[on] e[ss]et quo maius cogitari non possit.

[1.18] Whatever can be thought and does not exist, if it were to exist, would not be [something] than which a greater cannot be thought.

[1.19] Si [er]g[o] e[ss]et quo maius cogitari non possit; n[on] e[ss]et quo maius cogitari non possit, q[uo]d nimis e[st] absurdu[m].

[1.19] If therefore [something] than which a greater cannot be thought were to exist, it would not be [something] than which a greater cannot be thought. This is absurd.

[1.20] Falsum e[st] [i]g[itur] n[on] e[ss]e aliquid q[uo] maius cogitari n[on] possit, si v[e]l cogitari potest.

[1.20] Therefore it is false that something than which a greater cannot be thought does not exist, if it can even be thought.

[1.21] Multo itaq[ue] magis; si intelligi & inintellectu e[ss]e potest.

[1.21] And all the more so, if it can be understood and exist in the understanding.

[1.22] Plus aliquid dica[m].

[1.22] I should say something further here.

[1.23] P[ro]culdubio quicq[ui]d alicubi aut aliquando n[on] e[st]; etia[m] si e[st] alicubi aut aliquando, potest tamen cogitari nunqua[m] & nusqua[m] e[ss]e, sicut n[on] e[st] alicubi aut aliquando[.]

[1.23] Without doubt whatever does not exist in some place or at some time, even if it exists in some other place and at some other time, can yet be thought to exist in no place and at no time, just as it does not exist in some place and at some time.

[1.24] Nam q[uo]d heri n[on] fuit & hodie est; sicut heri n[on] fuisse intelligitur, ita nunqua[m] e[ss]e sub intelligi potest.

[1.24] For what did not exist yesterday and does exist today can be understood as never existing, just as it is understood that it did not exist yesterday.

[1.25] & q[uo]d hic non e[st] & alibi est; sicut non est hic, ita potest cogitari nusq[uam] e[ss]e.

[1.25] And what is not here but is elsewhere, in so far as it is not here, can be thought as existing nowhere.

[1.26] Similiter cuius partes singul[a]e non sunt, ubi aut quando sunt ali[a]e partes; eius om[ne]s partes, & id[e]o ipsu[m] totum possunt cogitari nunqua[m] aut nusqua[m] e[ss]e.

[1.26] Similarly, in the case of an object whose separate parts do not exist where and when the other parts exist, all its parts and therefore its whole self can be thought as existing at no time and nowhere.

[1.27] Nam & si dicatur temp[us] semp[er] e[ss]e & mundus ubiq[ue]; non tamen illud totu[m] semp[er], aut iste totus e[st] ubiq[ue].

[1.27] For even if it should be said that time always exists and the world exists everywhere, yet the former does not always exist in its entirety nor is the latter everywhere in its entirety.

[1.28] Et sicut singul[a]e partes temporis non sunt quando ali[a]e sunt; ita possunt nuq[ua]m e[ss]e cogitari.

[1.28] And just as the separate parts of time do not exist when the others exist, so they can be thought of as existing at no time.

[1.29] & singul[a]e mundi partes sicut non sunt ubi ali[a]e sunt; ita subintelligi possunt nusqua[m] e[ss]e.

[1.29] And so separate parts of the world, just as they do not exist where the others exist, can be understood as existing nowhere.

[1.30] Sed & q[uo]d partibus coniunctu[m] e[st]; cogitatione dissolvi & n[on] e[ss]e potest.

[1.30] And, moreover, what is made up of parts can be dissolved by thought and not exist.

[1.31] Quare quicq[ui]d alicubi aut aliquando totu[m] non e[st]; etia[m] si est, potest cogitari n[on] e[ss]e.

[1.31] Therefore whatever is not somewhere or at some time in its entirety can be thought not to exist, even if it does exist.

[1.32] At quo maius nequit cogitari; si est non potest cogitari non e[ss]e.

[1.32] But [something] than which a greater cannot be thought cannot be thought not to exist, if it exists.

[1.33] Alioq[ui]n si est; n[on] e[st] quo maius cogitari n[on] possit, q[uo]d non convenit.

[1.33] Otherwise, if it exists, it is not [something] than which a greater cannot be thought, which is not logically consistent.

[1.34] Nullatenus [er]g[o] alicubi aut aliquando totu[m] n[on] est; sed semp[er] & ubiq[ue] totu[m] est.

[1.34] Therefore, in no way does it not exist in its entirety somewhere and at some time, but it exists always and everywhere in its entirety.

[1.35] Putasne aliquatenus posse cogitari vel intelligi, aut e[ss]e incogitatione vel intellectu, dequo h[a]ec intelliguntur?

[1.35] Do you not think that that, about which these things are understood, can to some extent be thought or understood or exist in thought or the understanding?

[1.36] Si eni[m] non potest; n[on] de eo possunt h[a]ec intelligi.

[1.36] For if it cannot, then these things concerning it cannot be understood.

[1.37] Q[uo]d si dicis non intelligi & n[on] e[ss]e inintellectu q[uo]d n[on] penitus intelligit[ur]; dic quia qui non potest intueri purissima[m] luce[m] solis, non videt luce[m] diei, qu[a]e n[on] e[st] n[isi] lux solis.

[1.37] If you say that this is not understood and is not in the understanding, because it is not completely understood, you might as well say that he who cannot look at the pure light of the sun does not see daylight, which is nothing other than the light of the sun.

[1.38] Certe v[e]l hactenus intelligitur & est inintellectu, quo maius cogitari nequit; ut h[a]ec de eo intelligantur.

[1.38] But certainly [something] than which a greater cannot be thought is understood and is in the understanding, in so far as these things are understood concerning it.

[2.1] Dixi itaq[ue] inargumentatione qua[m] reprehendis quia cu[m] insipiens

[2.1] I said then, in the argument which you criticised, that when the fool hears the expression '[something] than audit p[ro]ferri quo maius cogitari non potest; intelligit, q[uo]d audit.

which a greater cannot be thought', he understands what he hears.

[2.2] Utiq[ue] qui non intelligit si nota lingua dicitur; aut nullu[m] aut nimis obrutum habet intellectum.

[2.2] Indeed, anyone who does not understand this, if it is said in a language he knows, has either no understanding or an extremely well concealed one.

[2.3] De inde dixi, quia si intelligitur; e[st] inintellectu.

[2.3] Next, I said that if it is understood, it exists in the understanding.

[2.4] An est innullo intellectu, q[uo]d necessario inrei veritate e[ss]e monstratu[m] est?

[2.4] Or does what has been shown to exist necessarily in true reality exist in no understanding?

[2.5] Sed dices quia & si est inintellectu, non tamen consequetur quia intelligitur.

[2.5] But you say that even if it exists in the understanding, it does not then follow that it is understood.

[2.6] Vide quia conseq[ui]tur e[ss]e in intellectu, exeo quia intelligitur.

[2.6] Believe me, that it exists in the understanding follows logically from the fact that it is understood.

[2.7] Sicut eni[m] q[uo]d cogitatur cogitatione cogitatur, & q[uo]d cogitatione cogitat[ur], sicut cogitatur sic e[st] incogitatione; ita q[uo]d intelligitur intellectu intelligitur, & q[uo]d intellectu intelligitur, sicut intelligitur ita e[st] inintellectu.

[2.7] For just as what is thought is thought by thought, and what is thought by thought, in so far as it is thought exists in thought, so what is understood is understood by the understanding, and what is understood by the understanding, in so far as it is understood exists in the understanding.

[2.8] Quid hoc planius?

[2.8] What could be more obvious than this?

[2.9] Postea dixi quia si est v[e]l insolo intellectu; potest cogitari e[ss]e & inre, q[uo]d maius e[st].

[2.9] After that, I said that if it is even in the understanding alone, it can also be thought to exist in reality, which is greater.

[2.10] Si [er]g[o] in solo e[st] intellectu; idipsum scilicet q[uo] maius non potest cogitari, est quo maius cogitari potest.

[2.10] Therefore, if it exists in the understanding alone, this same thing, namely [that] than which a greater cannot be thought, is [something] than which a greater can be thought.

[2.11] Rogo quid consequentius?

[2.11] I ask, what follows more logically?

[2.12] An eni[m] si e[st] v[e]l insolo intellectu, non potest cogitari e[ss]e & inre?

[2.12] For even if it exists in the understanding alone, can it not also be thought to exist in reality?

[2.13] Aut si potest, nonne qui hoc cogitat, aliquid cogitat maius eo si [est] insolo intellectu?

[2.13] And if it can, does not the one who thinks this, think something greater than it, if it exists in the understanding alone?

[2.14] Quid [i]g[itur] consequentius, qua[m] si quo maius cogitari neq[ui]t e[st] insolo intellectu, idem e[ss]e q[uo] maius cogitari possit?

[2.14] What then follows more logically than this: that if [something] than which a greater cannot be thought exists in the understanding alone, it is also [something] than which a greater can be thought?

[2.15] Sed utiq[ue] quo mai[us] cogitari potest, innullo intellectu e[st] quo maius cogitari non possit.

[2.15] But clearly no one understands [something] than which a greater can be thought to be [something] than which a greater cannot be thought.

[2.16] An [er]g[o] n[on] consequitur quo maius cogitari nequit, si e[st] inullo intellectu, n[on] e[ss]e insolo intellectu?

[2.16] Therefore does it not follow that [something] than which a greater cannot be thought, if it is in any understanding, does not exist in the understanding alone?

[2.17] Si eni[m] e[st] insolo intellectu; est quo maius cogitari potest, q[uo]d non convenit.

[2.17] For if it is in the understanding alone, it is [something] than which a greater can be thought, which is a logical contradiction.

[3.1] Sed tale est inquis, ac si aliquis insulam oceani om[ne]s terras sua fertilitate vincente[m], qu[a]e difficultate immo impossibilitate inveniendi q[uo]d n[on] e[st] p[er]dita nominatur, dicat iccirco n[on] posse dubitari vere e[ss]e inre, quia verbis descriptam facile quis intelligit.

[3.1] But you say the following: it is as if a person should say that, because someone easily understands what the words describe, it cannot be doubted that there truly exists in reality an island in the ocean surpassing all lands in its fertility, which, because of the difficulty or rather the impossibility of discovering what does not exist, is called 'lost'.

[3.2] Fidens loquor, quia siquis invenerit m[ihi] aut re ipsa, aut sola cogitatione existens pr[a]eter quo maius cogitari non possit, cui aptare valeat connexionem huius me[a]e argumentationis; invenia[m] & dabo illi p[er]ditam insulam amplius non p[er]denda[m].

[3.2] I say confidently that if anyone should discover for me [an object] that exists either in reality itself or in thought alone in addition to [something] than which a greater cannot be thought, to which he could apply the logic of this argument, I shall discover [that] lost island and give [it] to him, to be lost no more.

[3.3] Palam aute[m] iam videtur quo n[on] valet cogitari maius, non posse cogitari n[on] e[ss]e; q[uo]d tam certa ratione veritatis existit.

[3.3] Moreover, it has already clearly been seen that [something] than which a greater cannot be thought, which exists by such certain logic and truth, cannot be thought not to exist.

[3.4] Aliter eni[m] nullatenus existeret.

[3.4] For otherwise it would in no way exist.

[3.5] Deniq[ue] siquis dicit se cogitare illud n[on] e[ss]e, dico quia cu[m] hoc cogitat, aut cogitat aliquid quo maius cogitari n[on] possit; aut n[on] cogitat.

[3.5] Finally, if someone says that he thinks that it does not exist, I say that when he thinks this, he either thinks or does not think something than which a greater cannot be thought.

[3.6] Si non cogitat; non cogitat n[on] e[ss]e q[uo]d n[on] cogitat.

[3.6] If he does not think it, he does not think that what he does not think does not exist.

[3.7] Si vero cogitat; utiq[ue] cogitat aliq[ui]d q[uo]d nec cogitari possit non e[ss]e.

[3.7] But if he does think it, he undoubtedly thinks something that cannot be thought not to exist.

[3.8] Si enim posset cogitari n[on] e[ss]e; cogitari posset habere principiu[m] & finem.

[3.8] For if it could be thought not to exist, it could be thought to have a beginning and an end.

[3.9] Sed hoc non potest.

[3.9] But this is not possible.

[3.10] Qui [er]g[o] illud cogitat; aliquid cogitat q[uo]d nec cogitari non e[ss]e possit.

[3.10] Therefore, he who thinks this, thinks something which cannot be thought not to exist.

[3.11] Hoc v[ero] qui cogitat; n[on] cogitat idipsum non e[ss]e.

[3.11] Clearly, he who thinks this, does not think that this very thing does not exist.

[3.12] Alioquin cogitat q[uo]d cogitari non potest.

[3.12] Otherwise he is thinking what cannot be thought.

[3.13] Non [i]g[itur] potest cogitari non e[ss]e quo mai[us] nequit cogitari.

[3.13] Therefore, [something] than which a greater cannot be thought cannot be thought not to exist.

[4.1] Quod aute[m] dicis, quia cu[m] dicitur q[uo]d su[m]ma res ista n[on] e[ss]e nequeat cogitari, melius fortasse diceretur quod n[on] e[ss]e aut etia[m] posse non e[ss]e non possit intelligi; potius dicendum fuit n[on] posse cogitari.

[4.1] You say, that when it is said that this supreme reality cannot be thought not to exist, it would perhaps be better to say that it cannot be understood not to exist or to be able not to exist. However, it would be preferable to say 'not to be able to be thought [not to exist]'.

[4.2] Si enim dixissem rem ipsam non posse intelligi n[on] e[ss]e; fortasse tu ipse qui dici[s] quia s[e]c[un]d[u]m p[ro]p[ri]etatem verbi istius falsa nequeunt intelligi, obiceres nichil q[uo]d est posse intelligi non e[ss]e.

[4.2] If I had said that the thing itself could not be understood not to exist, perhaps you would object that nothing that exists can be understood not to exist, since you say that, according to the proper meaning of the word, false things cannot be understood.

[4.3] Falsum e[st] enim n[on] e[ss]e q[uo]d e[st].

[4.3] For it is false that what exists does not exist.

[4.4] Quare non e[ss]e p[ro]p[ri]um d[e]o, n[on] posse intelligi non e[ss]e.

[4.4] Therefore, it is not a unique property of God that He cannot be understood not to exist.

[4.5] Quod si aliquid eor[um] qu[a]e certissime sunt potest intelligi n[on] e[ss]e; similiter & alia certa n[on] e[ss]e posse intelligi.

[4.5] For if some of those things that most certainly exist can be understood not to exist, then in a similar way other certain things can be understood not to exist.

[4.6] Sed hoc utiq[ue] non potest obici decogitatione; si bene consideretur.

[4.6] But clearly this objection cannot be raised against thought, if it is considered properly.

[4.7] Nam & sinulla qu[a]e sunt possint intelligi non e[ss]e; om[n]ia tam[en] possunt cogitari n[on] e[ss]e, pr[a]eter id q[uo]d su[m]me est.

[4.7] For even if nothing that exists can be understood not to exist, yet all things can be thought not to exist, except that which is supreme.

[4.8] Illa quippe om[n]ia & sola possunt cogitari non e[ss]e; qu[a]e initium aut fine[m] aut partiu[m] habent coniunctionem, & sicut iam dixi, quicquid alicubi aut aliquando totu[m] non est.

[4.8] Indeed all those things, and only they, which have a beginning or an end or are a conjunction of parts – as I have already said, whatever does not exist somewhere and at some time in its entirety – can be thought not to exist.

[4.9] Illud v[ero] solum n[on] potest cogitari n[on] e[ss]e; inquo nec initiu[m] nec finem nec partium coniunctione[m], & q[uo]d non n[isi] semp[er] & ubiq[ue] totu[m] ulla invenit cogitatio.

[4.9] Rather, that alone cannot be thought not to exist, in which thought finds neither beginning nor end nor a conjunction of parts, but which it finds always and everywhere in its entirety.

[4.10] Scito [i]g[itur] quia potes cogitare te n[on] e[ss]e qua[m] diu e[ss]e certissime scis; quod te miror dixisse nescire.

[4.10] Therefore, I reply that you can think that you do not exist, even while you know that you most certainly do exist. I am amazed that you said you did not know this.

[4.11] Multa nanq[ue] cogitamus n[on] e[ss]e qu[a]e scimus e[ss]e, & multa e[ss]e qu[a]e n[on] e[ss]e scimus, n[on] existimando sed fingendo ita e[ss]e ut cogitam[us].

[4.11] For we think that many things do not exist which we know to exist, and that many things do exist which we know not to exist, not by judging, but by imagining that [things] are as we think.

[4.12] Et quidem possumus cogitare aliq[ui]d non e[ss]e qua[m] diu scimus e[ss]e; quia simul & illud possumus, & istud scimus.

[4.12] On the one hand, we can think that something does not exist, while we know that it does exist, because we can think the former and know the latter at the same time.

[4.13] & non possumus cogitare n[on] e[ss]e, qua[m] diu scimus e[ss]e; quia

[4.13] On the other, we cannot think that it does not exist, while we know that it does exist, because we cannot n[on] possumus cogitare e[ss]e simul & n[on] e[ss]e.

think that it exists and does not exist at the same time.

[4.14] Siquis [i]g[itur] sic distinguat huius p[ro]lationis has duas sententias; intelliget nichil qua[m]diu e[ss]e scitur, posse cogitari n[on] e[ss]e, & q[ui]cq[ui]d e[st] pr[a]eter id quo maius cogitari neq[ui]t, etia[m] cu[m] scitur e[ss]e posse n[on] e[ss]e cogitari.

[4.14] Therefore, if anyone should make this distinction between the two meanings of this statement, he will understand that nothing can be thought not to exist, whilst it is known to exist, and that whatever exists, except for that than which a greater cannot be thought, even while it is known to exist, can be thought not to exist.

[4.15] Sic [i]g[itur] & p[ro]p[ri]um e[st] d[e]o n[on] posse cogitari n[on] esse, & tamen multa n[on] possunt cogitari qua[m] diu sunt n[on] e[ss]e.

[4.15] In this way, therefore, it is both a distinguishing property of God not to be able to be thought not to exist, and nevertheless many things cannot be thought not to exist, whilst they exist.

[4.16] Quom[odo] tamen dicat[ur] cogitari d[eu]s n[on] e[ss]e; inipso libello puto sufficienter e[ss]e dictum.

[4.16] And how God is said to be thought not to exist has, I think, been sufficiently expressed in that little book itself.

[5.1] Qualia v[ero] sint & alia qu[a]e m[ihi] obicis p[ro]insipiente; facile e[st] deprehendere v[e]l parum sapienti, & id[e]o id ostendere sup[er[sedendu[m] existimavera[m].

[5.1] In fact the other objections that you raised against me on behalf of the fool, are easily addressed, even by someone who is not at all wise, and therefore I decided to omit to show this.

[5.2] Sed q[uonia]m audio quibusdam ea legentibus aliquid contra me valere videri; paucis de illis co[m]memorabo.

[5.2] But since I hear that to certain readers some of the objections against my position appear to be valid, I will make a few comments about them.

[5.3] Primu[m] q[uo]d sepe repetis me dicere, quiaq[uo]d est maius om[n]ib[us] e[st] inintellectu, si e[st] inintellectu est & inre, aliter eni[m] om[n]ibus maius non e[ss]et om[n]ib[us] maius; nusqua[m] inomnib[us] dictis meis invenitur talis p[ro]batio.

[5.3] Firstly, nowhere in all my utterances is there the kind of proof that you frequently repeat that I put forward, that what is greater than everything exists in the understanding, and that if it exists in the understanding it also exists in reality, for otherwise the greater than everything would not be greater than everything.

[5.4] Non eni[m] idem valet q[uo]d dicit[ur] maius om[n]ib[us], & quo maius cogitari nequit, adp[ro]bandum quia e[st] inre quod dicitur.

[5.4] For [the phrase], 'greater than everything', does not have the same force for the purposes of proving that what is spoken of exists in reality as [the phrase], 'than which a greater cannot be thought'.

[5.5] Siquis eni[m] dicat quo maius cogitari non possit n[on] e[ss]e aliquid

[5.5] For if someone should say that [something] than which a greater inre, aut posse n[on] e[ss]e aut v[e]l n[on] e[ss]e posse cogitari; facile refelli potest.

cannot be thought is not something in reality or is able not to exist or even can be thought not to exist, he can easily be refuted.

[5.6] Nam q[uo]d n[on] e[st]; potest non e[ss]e, & quod non e[ss]e potest; cogitari potest non e[ss]e.

[5.6] For what does not exist is able not to exist, and what is able not to exist can be thought not to exist.

[5.7] Quicquid aut[em] cogitari potest non e[ss]e; si e[st] non e[st] q[uo] maius cogitari non possit.

[5.7] But whatever can be thought not to exist, even if it exists, is not [something] than which a greater cannot be thought.

[5.8] Q[uo]d si n[on] e[st]; utiq[ue] si e[ss]et, non e[ss]et quo maius non possit cogitari.

[5.8] If it does not exist, then even if it were to exist, it would not be [something] than which a greater cannot be thought.

[5.9] Sed dici non potest, quia quo maius non possit cogitari si est non e[st] quo maius cogitari n[on] possit, aut si e[ss]et non e[ss]et quod n[on] possit cogitari maius.

[5.9] But it cannot be said that, if [something] than which a greater cannot be thought exists, it is not [something] than which a greater cannot be thought, or that if it were to exist, it would not be what cannot be thought [to be] greater.

[5.10] Patet [er]g[o] quia nec non e[st], nec potest n[on] e[ss]e aut cogitari non e[ss]e.

[5.10] Therefore it is evident that neither does it not exist, nor is it able not to exist or to be thought not to exist.

[5.11] Alit[er] enim si est n[on] e[st] quod dicitur, & si e[ss]et non e[ss]et.

[5.11] Otherwise, if it does exist, it is not what it is said to be, and if it were to exist, it would not exist.

[5.12] Hoc aute[m] n[on] tam facile p[ro]bari posse videtur de eo quod maius dicit[ur] omnib[us].

[5.12] However, this does not appear to be so easily proved in the case of that which is said to be greater than everything

[5.13] Non enim ita patet quia q[uo]d non e[ss]e cogitari potest, n[on] e[st] maius om[n]ib[us] qu[a]e sunt; sicut quia n[on] e[st] quo mai[us] cogitari n[on] possit, nec sic e[st] indubitabile quia si e[st] aliquid maius om[n]ib[us], n[on] e[st] aliud qua[m] quo maius n[on] possit cogitari, aut si esset n[on] e[ss]et similiter aliud; quom[odo] certu[m] [est] de eo quod dicitur quo maius cogitari nequit.

[5.13] For it is less obviously the case that what can be thought not to exist is not greater than everything that exists than that it is not [something] than which a greater cannot be thought. Nor is it certain that, if something is greater than everything, it is the same as [something] than which a greater cannot be thought. Nor [is it obvious that], if it were to exist, something similar [to it] would not [also] exist, as is [established as] certain in the case of what is called '[something] than which a greater cannot be thought'.

[5.14] Quid eni[m] siquis dicat e[ss]e aliquid maius om[n]ib[us] qu[a]e sunt, & id ipsu[m] tamen posse cogitari non e[ss]e, & aliq[ui]d maius eo etiam si n[on] sit, posse tamen cogitari?	[5.14] And what if someone should say that there exists something greater than everything that is, [but] that this same thing can be thought not to exist, and that something greater than it, even if it does not exist, can still be thought?
[5.15] An hic sic ap[er]te inferri potest; non e[st] [er]g[o] maius om[n]ib[us] qu[a]e sunt, sicut ibi apertissime diceretur, [er]g[o] n[on] e[st] quo maius cogitari nequit?	[5.15] Can it be as clearly inferred [in your work], that therefore it is not greater than everything that exists, as it was most clearly argued [in the Proslogion], [that] therefore it is not [something] than which a greater cannot be thought?
[5.16] Illud nanq[ue] alio indiget argumento qua[m] hoc quod dicitur om[n]ib[us] maius; inisto v[ero] n[on] e[st] op[us] alio qua[m] hoc ipso quod sonat, quo maius cogitari non possit.	[5.16] For the former [work] requires an additional argument to that which is identified [under the heading of] 'greater than everything'. But, in the latter, there is no need for an [argument] other than the one itself which is identified [under the heading] 'than which a greater cannot be thought'.
[5.17] Ergo si n[on] similiter potest p[ro]bari de eo quod mai[us] om[n]ib[us] dicitur, q[uo]d de se p[er]se ipsum p[ro]bat quo maius nequit cogitari; iniuste me reprehendisti dixisse quod n[on] dixi, cu[m] tantu[m] differat ab eo q[uo]d dixi.	[5.17] Therefore, if it is not possible to prove, concerning that which is called greater than everything, anything similar to what [something] than which a greater cannot be thought proves about itself through itself, you have unjustly rebuked me for having said what I did not say, since it differs so much from what I did say.
[5.18] Si v[ero] v[e]l post aliud argumentu[m] potest; nec sic me debuisti reprehendere dixisse q[uo]d p[ro]bari potest.	[5.18] However, if, after further argument, it does turn out to be possible [to prove that something greater than everything exists], you ought not to have rebuked me in this way for saying what can be proved.
[5.19] Utrum aute[m] possit facile p[er]pendit, qui hoc posse quo mai[us] cogitari nequit cognoscit.	[5.19] And whether it is possible is easily grasped by the person, who knows that [something] than which a greater cannot be thought can [be proved to exist].
[5.20] Nullaten[us] enim potest intelligi quo maius cogitari non possit; n[isi] id q[uo]d solum om[n]ib[us] est maius.	[5.20] For in no way can [something] than which a greater cannot be thought be understood unless it alone is that which is greater than everything.

[5.21] Sicut [er]g[o] quo maius cogitari nequit intelligitur & est inintellectu, & ideo e[ss]e inrei veritate asseritur; sic q[uo]d maius dicitur om[n]ib[us] intelligi & e[ss]e in intellectu, & iccirco re ipsa e[ss]e exnecessitate concluditur.

[5.21] Therefore just as [something] than which a greater cannot be thought is understood and exists in the understanding, and therefore is asserted to exist in actual reality, so what is called greater than everything is understood and exists in the understanding, and for that reason it is demonstrated that it necessarily exists in reality itself.

[5.22] Vides [er]g[o] qua[m] recte me comparasti stulto illi qui hoc solo q[uo]d descripta intelligeretur, p[er]dita[m] insula[m] esse vellet asserere?

[5.22] Do you now see whether you were right to compare me to that idiot, who wanted to assert that the lost island existed solely because he understood what the term described?

[6.1] Q[uo]d aute[m] obicis qu[a]elibet falsa v[e]l dubia similiter posse intelligi & e[ss]e inintellectu, que[m]admodum illud q[uo]d dicebam; miror q[ui]d hic sensisti contra me dubiu[m] p[ro]bare volente[m], cui p[ri]mu[m] hoc sat erat, ut quolibet m[odo] illud intelligi & e[ss]e inintellectu ostenderem, q[ua]tinus consequenter consideraretur, utru[m] e[ss]et insolo intellectu, vel ut falsa.

[6.1] Moreover you object that any false or doubtful thing can be understood and exist in the understanding in a way similar to that which I spoke of. I am amazed that you have judged against me here. I wanted to prove something in doubt. For this purpose it was enough that I should first show that it is understood and exists in the understanding in some way, in order that as a consequence it might be considered whether it exists in the understanding alone, as something false.

[6.2] An et in re, ut vera.

[6.2] Or in reality as well, as something true.

[6.3] Nam si falsa & dubia hoc m[odo] intelliguntur & sunt inintellectu, quia cu[m] dicuntur, audiens intelligit quid dicens significet; nichil p[ro]hibet q[uo]d dixi intelligi & esse inintellectu.

[6.3] For nothing prevents what I have said from being understood and existing in the understanding, if [the words] 'false and doubtful things are understood and exist in the understanding in this way' mean that when they are spoken, the hearer understands what the speaker says.

[6.4] Quom[odo] aute[m] sibi conveniant, q[uo]d dicis quia falsa dicente aliquo qu[a]ecunq[ue] ille diceret intelligeres, & quia illud q[uo]d n[on] eo m[odo] quo etia[m] falsa habetur in cogitatione n[on] diceris auditu[m] cogitare, aut incogitatione

[6.4] But how are [these statements] logically consistent with each other? [i] You would understand someone saying false things, whatever he said. [ii] With reference to what is not had in thought in the manner of false things, you are not said to think or to have in thought what habere, sed intelligere & inintellectu habere, quia scilicet non possis hoc alit[er] cogitare n[isi] intelligendo, id est scientia comprehendendo re ipsa illud existere, quom[odo] inqua[m] conveniant & falsa intelligi & intelligere e[ss]e scientia comprehendere existere aliq[ui]d; nil adme tu videris.

you have heard, but are said to understand it and have it in the understanding, because apparently you could not think it other than by understanding it, that is by comprehending by means of knowledge that it exists in reality itself. How, I ask, are the statements, that false things are understood and that to understand is to comprehend by means of knowledge, logically consistent. This is an not issue for me to sort out, you may see to it yourself.

[6.5] Q[uo]d si & falsa aliquom[odo] intelliguntur, & n[on] om[n]is sed cuiusdam intellectus e[st] h[a]ec diffinitio; non debui reprehendi, q[ui]a dixi quo maius cogitari n[on] possit intelligi & inintellectu e[ss]e etia[m] ante qua[m] certu[m] e[ss]et re ipsa illud existere.

[6.5] But if false things are also understood in some way, and this is a definition of some but not all understanding, you ought not to have objected that I said that [something] than which a greater cannot be thought is understood and exists in the understanding, even before it was certain that it existed in reality itself.

[7.1] De inde q[uo]d dicis vix unqua[m] posse e[ss]e credibile cu[m] dictu[m] & auditu[m] fuerit istud n[on] eom[odo] posse cogitari n[on] e[ss]e q[uo] etiam potest cogitari non e[ss]e d[eu]s; respondeant p[ro]me qui v[e]l parva[m] scientia[m] disputandi argumentandiq[ue] attigerunt.

[7.1] Next you say that it is scarcely credible that, once it has been spoken and heard, it cannot be thought not to exist in the same way that God can be thought not to exist. Those who have attained even a little knowledge of disputation and argument might reply on my behalf.

[7.2] An eni[m] rationabile e[st] ut iccirco neget aliquis q[uo]d intelligit, q[ui]a e[ss]e dicitur id quod id[e]o negat quia non intelligit?

[7.2] For is it reasonable that someone should deny what he understands because it is said to be that which he denies, since he does not understand it?

[7.3] Aut si aliquando negatur q[uo]d aliquatenus intelligitur, & idem e[st] illi q[uo]d nullatenus intelligitur, nonne facilius p[ro]batur q[uo]d dubium e[st] de illo q[uo]d inaliquo, qua[m] de eo q[uo]d innullo e[st] intellectu?

[7.3] Or, if what is understood to some extent is denied at any time and is the same as that which is in no way understood, is not what is in doubt more easily proved concerning that which is partly understood, than what is not understood?

[7.4] Quare nec credibile potest e[ss]e iccirco quenlibet negare quo maius cogitari nequit, q[uo]d auditum

[7.4] Therefore it cannot be credible that someone denies [something] than which a greater cannot be thought, which he understands in some way, when he aliquatenus intelligit; quia negat d[eu]m cuius sensu[m] nullom[odo] cogitat.

hears it, because he denies God, whose meaning he does not think in any way.

[7.5] Aut si & illud quia n[on] om[n]ino intelligitur negatur, nonne tamen facilius id q[uo]d aliquom[odo] qua[m] id quod nullo m[odo] intelligitur p[ro]batur?

[7.5] Or, if the former is denied, because it is not completely understood, is it not the case that that which is understood in some way is more easily proved than that which is in no way understood?

[7.6] Non [er]g[o] irrationabiliter contra insipiente[m] adp[ro]bandum d[eu]m e[ss]e attuli quo maius cogitari n[on] possit; cu[m] illud nullo m[odo], istud aliquo m[odo] intelligeret.

[7.6] Therefore, I did not ureasonably put forward [something] than which a greater cannot be thought against the fool to prove that God exists, since whilst there was no way in which he understood the latter, he did understand the former in some way.

[8.1] Quod v[ero] tam studiose p[ro]bas, quo maius cogitari nequit, non tale e[ss]e qualis non dum facta pictura inintellectu pictoris; sine causa fit.

[8.1] In fact, what you so earnestly proved, that [something] than which a greater cannot be thought is not the same kind of thing as the yet to be created picture in the understanding of the painter, served no purpose.

[8.2] Non eni[m] ad hoc p[ro]tuli picturam pr[a]ecogitata[m], ut tale illud dequo agebatur vellem asserere; sed tantu[m] ut aliquid e[ss]e inintellectu, q[uo]d e[ss]e n[on] intelligeretur, possem ostend[er]e.

[8.2] For I did not put forward the preconception of the picture, because I wanted to assert this kind of thing about the matter in question, but only so that I could show that something exists in the understanding, which is not understood to exist.

[8.3] Item q[uo]d dicis quo maius cogitari nequit, s[e]c[un]d[u]m rem vel exgenere t[ibi] v[e]l ex specie notam te cogitare auditu[m] v[e]l inintellectu habere n[on] posse, q[uonia]m nec ipsam rem nosti, nec ea[m] exalia simili potes conicere; palam e[st] rem aliter sese habere.

[8.3] Likewise, you say that you cannot think or have in the understanding what you have heard, [i.e. something] than which a greater cannot be thought, as something known to you under the categories of genus or species, since you did not know the thing itself, nor can conceive it from something similar. The matter is clearly quite different.

[8.4] Q[uonia]m nanq[ue] om[n]e minus bonum intantu[m] e[st] simile maiori bono inquantu[m] e[st] bonu[m]; patet cuilibet rationabili menti quia debonis minorib[us] ad maiora conscendendo, exiis quib[us] aliquid maius cogitari potest, multu[m] possumus conicere illud quo nichil potest maius cogitari.

[8.4] For since every lesser good is good in so far as it is similar to a greater good, it is clear to any rational mind that in ascending from lesser goods to greater goods, we can conceive that than which nothing greater can be thought from those things than which something greater can be thought.

[8.5] Quis eni[m] verbi gra[tia] v[e]l hoc cogitare non potest etia[m] si n[on] credat inre e[ss]e quod cogitat, scilicet si bonum e[st] aliquid q[uo]d initiu[m] & finem habet, multo meli[us] e[ss]e bonu[m], quodlicet incipiat non tamen desinit, & sicut istud illo melius e[st] ita isto e[ss]e melius illud q[uo]d nec finem habet nec initium, etiam si semp[er] depr[a]eterito p[er]pr[a]esens transeat adfuturum, & sive sit inre aliquid huiusmodi sive non sit, valde tamen eo melius e[ss]e id quod nullom[odo] indiget v[e]l cogitur mutari v[e]l moveri?

[8.5] Indeed, who for example – even if he should not believe that what he thinks of exists in reality – cannot think that, if something which has a beginning and an end is good, there is a much better good, which although it begins, nevertheless does not cease; and just as the latter is better than the former, so that which does not have an end or a beginning is better than the latter, even if it should pass from the past through the present to the future; and whether or not something of this kind exists in reality, that which is in no way lacking nor is thought to change or to be in motion is very much better than it?

[8.6] An hoc cogitari non potest, aut aliq[ui]d hoc maius cogitari potest?

[8.6] Can this not be thought, or can something greater than this be thought?

[8.7] Aut n[on] est hoc exiis quib[us] maius cogitari valet conicere, id quo maius cogitari nequit?

[8.7] Or is this not to conceive that than which a greater cannot be thought from those things than which a greater can be thought?

[8.8] Est [i]g[itur] unde possit conici quo maius cogitari nequeat.

[8.8] It is in this way, then, that [something] than which a greater cannot be thought can be conceived.

[8.9] Sic itaq[ue] facile refelli potest insipiens qui sacram auctoritate[m] non recipit; si negat quo maius cogitari non valet exaliis reb[us] conici posse.

[8.9] Thus, the fool, who does not accept sacred authority, can easily be refuted, if he denies that [something] than which a greater cannot be thought can be conceived from other things.

[8.10] At siquis catholicus hoc neget; meminerit quia invisibilia d[e]i a creatura mundi p[er]ea qu[a]e facta sunt intellecta conspiciuntur, sempit[er]na quoq[ue] eius virtus & divinitas.

[8.10] But if any Catholic should deny this, let him remember that the invisible things of God and His eternal power and divinity are observed from the created things of the world, being understood by means of those things which have been made.

[9.1] Sed & si veru[m] e[ss]et, non posse cogitari v[e]l intelligi illud quo maius nequit cogitari; n[on] tamen falsum e[ss]et, quo maius cogitari neq[ui]t cogitari posse & intelligi.

[9.1] But even if it were true that that than which a greater cannot be thought cannot be thought or understood, it would still not be false that [the phrase], ‘than which a greater cannot be thought’, can be thought and understood.

[9.2] Sicut eni[m] nil p[ro]hibet dici ineffabile, licet illud dici non

[9.2] For nothing prohibits [the word], ‘ineffable’, being said, although that possit q[uo]d ineffabile dicitur, & que[m]admodu[m] cogitari potest n[on] cogitabile, quanvis illud cogitari n[on] possit cui convenit non cogitabile dici; ita cu[m] dicitur quo nil maius valet cogitari, p[ro]culdubio q[uo]d auditur cogitari & intelligi potest; etiam si res illa cogitari n[on] valeat aut intelligi, qua maius cogitari nequit.

thing which is called ineffable cannot be spoken of. And, the phrase, 'not thinkable', can be thought, although that [object], to which [the phrase], 'not thinkable', refers, cannot be thought. Thus, when [the phrase] 'than which nothing greater can be thought' is spoken, what is heard can undoubtedly be thought and understood, even if the object, than which a greater cannot be thought, cannot be thought or understood.

[9.3] Nam & siquisqua[m] e[st] tam insipiens, ut dicat non e[ss]e aliquid quo maius non possit cogitari; n[on] tamen ita erit impudens ut dicat se non posse intelligere aut cogitare quid dicat.

[9.3] For even if someone is so foolish, that he should say that something than which a greater cannot be thought does not exist, still he will not be so shameless as to say that he could not understand or think what he said.

[9.4] Aut siquis talis invenitur; non m[odo] sermo eius e[st] respuendus, sed & ipse conspuendus.

[9.4] If such a person is discovered, both he and what he says are to be reviled.

[9.5] Quisquis [i]g[itur] negat aliquid e[ss]e q[uo] maius nequeat cogitari; utiq[ue] intelligit & cogitat negatione[m] qua[m] facit.

[9.5] Whoever denies that something than which a greater cannot be thought exists undoubtedly understands and thinks the denial that he makes.

[9.6] Qua[m] negatione[m] intelligere aut cogitare n[on] potest; sine partib[us] eius.

[9.6] He cannot understand or think this denial without its parts.

[9.7] Pars aute[m] eius est quo maius cogitari n[on] potest.

[9.7] But one of its parts is [the phrase], 'than which a greater cannot be thought'.

[9.8] Quicu[n]q[ue] [i]g[itur] hoc negat; intelligit & cogitat quo maius cogitari nequit.

[9.8] Therefore, whoever denies this, understands and thinks [the phrase], 'than which a greater cannot be thought'.

[9.9] Palam aute[m] e[st] quia similiter potest cogitari & intelligi, q[uo]d non potest n[on] e[ss]e.

[9.9] Indeed, it is clear that what cannot not exist can similarly be thought and understood.

[9.10] Maius v[ero] cogitat qui hoc cogitat; qua[m] qui cogitat q[uo]d possit n[on] e[ss]e.

[9.10] Truly, he who thinks this thinks of something greater than he who thinks of what is able not to exist.

[9.11] Dum [er]g[o] cogitatur quo maius non possit cogitari; si cogitat[ur] q[uo]d possit non e[ss]e, n[on] cogitatur q[uo] non possit cogitari maius.

[9.11] If, when 'than which a greater cannot be thought' is thought, what is able not to exist is thought, then 'than which a greater cannot be thought' is not thought.

[9.12] Sed nequit idem simul cogitari & non cogitari.

[9.12] But the same thing cannot be thought and not thought at the same time.

[9.13] Quare qui cogitat quo maius n[on] possit cogitari; non cogitat q[uo]d possit, sed q[uo]d n[on] possit n[on] e[ss]e.

[9.13] Therefore, he who thinks 'than which a greater cannot be thought', thinks not what is able, but rather what is not able, not to exist.

[9.14] Qua p[ro]pter necesse e[st] e[ss]e q[uo]d cogitat; quia quicq[ui]d non e[ss]e potest, n[on] e[st] q[uo]d cogitat.

[9.14] Therefore, it is necessary that what he thinks exists, because whatever is able not to exist, is not what he thinks.

[10.1] Puto quia monstravi me n[on] infirma sed satis necessaria argum[en]tatione p[ro]basse in pr[a]efato libello re ipsa existere aliquid quo maius cogitari n[on] possit, n[ec] eam alicuius obiectionis infirmari firmitate.

[10.1] I think that I have shown that I proved in the aforementioned little book, not by unsound but by sufficiently necessary argumentation, that there exists in actual reality something than which a greater cannot be thought, and that [the argumentation] was not undermined by any sound objection.

[10.2] Tanta[m] eni[m] vim huius p[ro]lationis inse continet significatio; ut hoc ipsu[m] quod dicit[ur], ex necessitate eo ipso q[uo]d intelligit[ur] v[e]l cogitatur, & revera p[ro]betur existere & id ipsum e[ss]e quicquid de divina substantia oportet credere.

[10.2] For the meaning of this phrase contains such force in itself, that this very thing which is spoken of, which is of necessity understood and thought of by itself, is also proved to be that very thing, which is whatever it is necessary to believe about the divine substance.

[10.3] Credimus na[n]q[ue] de divina substantia quicq[ui]d absolute cogitari potest melius e[ss]e qua[m] n[on] e[ss]e.

[10.3] For, indeed, we believe of the divine substance whatever can be thought to be absolutely better to be than not to be.

[10.4] Verbi gra[tia], melius e[st] e[ss]e [a]eternu[m] qua[m] n[on] [a]et[er]num, bonu[m] qua[m] n[on] bonum, immo bonitate[m] ipsam qua[m] n[on] ipsam bonitate[m].

[10.4] For example, it is better to be eternal than not eternal, good than not good, indeed goodness itself than not goodness itself.

[10.5] Nichil aute[m] huiusmodi n[on] e[ss]e potest, quo maius aliq[ui]d cogitari non potest.

[10.5] But nothing of this sort, than which something greater cannot be thought, is able not to exist.

[10.6] Necesse [i]g[itur] e[st] quo maius cogitari n[on] potest e[ss]e quicq[ui]d de divina e[ss]entia credi oportet.

[10.6] Therefore it is necessary that [something] than which a greater cannot be thought is whatever must be believed concerning the divine essence.

[10.7] Gra[tia]s ago benignitati tu[a]e, et inreprehensione & inlaude mei opusculi.

[10.8] Cu[m] enim ea qu[a]e t[ibi] digna susceptione videntur, tanta laude extulisti; satis apparet quia qu[a]e t[ibi] infirma visa s[un]t, benivolentia n[on] malivolentia reprehendisti.

[10.7] I thank you for your kindness both in your criticism and in your praise of my little work.

[10.8] For since you extolled with such great praise those things which seemed to you worthy of acceptance, it is apparent enough that you criticised those things which appeared to you unsound through good will and not through malice.

Chapter 4
Commentary on the *Proslogion*

The Title of the *Proslogion*

The title is usually taken simply to refer to the fact that this work is in the form of an address to God. In *E*109 Anselm asked Hugh, Archbishop of Lyons, to change the titles of the works he had sent him to *Monologion* (from *Monoloquium de Ratione Fidei*) and *Proslogion* (from *Alloquium*[1]), but chose not to explain his reasons for these changes or for his use of the Greek forms. A clue to what Anselm was doing in renaming the work from *Alloquium* to *Proslogion* is to be found in Anselm's dialectical background. The term '*proslogion*' appears in its Latinate form '*proloquium*' in Augustine's *De Dialectica*, IV.[2] The meaning of the term in Augustine is 'statement' or 'proposition'. Augustine uses the heading '*de proloquiorum summa*' to refer to the conclusions of combinations of *proloquia* (i.e. it is the heading under which he places syllogisms). The term '*proloquium*' derives from Stoic logic and, according to Aulus Gellius, was employed by Varro in his *De Lingua Latina* to translate the Greek term αξίωμα [*axioma* = proposition].[3] Varro defined *proloquium* as a statement in which there is nothing lacking. Since Anselm did not explain this title further, it is impossible to confirm that he had the dialectical term '*proloquium*' in mind. He would not have had firsthand knowledge of Stoic doctrine.[4] However, his acquaintance with Augustine and almost certainly with Martianus Capella suggests that he was familiar with this usage.

The Preface

§0.1 In the Preface Anselm gives a brief account of how and why the *Proslogion* came to be written. After completing the *Monologion* (his first major work written a year or two previously), he began to search for a single argument that could achieve what the series of arguments in the *Monologion* had.

---

1 The original title of what Anselm called *Alloquium* and then *Proslogion* had been *Fides Quaerens Intellectum*.

2 See also Martianus Capella, *De Nuptiis Philologiae et Mercurii*, Book 4, *De Arte Dialectici*.

3 See Aulus Gellius, *Noctes Atticae*, XVI, 8, 2–6 (*The Attic Nights of Aulus Gellius*, vol. 2, translated by J.C. Rolfe, Cambridge Mass. 1952, p. 158f.).

4 M. Lapidge, 'The Stoic Inheritance', in P. Dronke (ed.), *A History of Twelfth-Century Western Philosophy*, pp. 81–112, p. 83.

§0.2 *opusculum quoddam* – i.e. the *Monologion.*
exemplum meditandi – Although written fifty years after Anselm's death, John of Salisbury's *Metalogicon* provides an indication of what Anselm means when he talks of *meditatio* in the *Proslogion.* The exercise of philosophy and of virtue require 'reading, learning, meditation and constant effort'.[5] Meditation is that which 'reaches out to the unknown and raises itself frequently as far as the incomprehensible, exploring matters that are hidden as well as those that are visible'. With reading and learning it produces knowledge. Anselm describes his understanding of meditation in a similar way, as a silent investigation of the unknown.
de ratione fidei – It is the rational basis or reasonableness of the Catholic faith on which Anselm meditates. Lacking a definite article Latin does not distinguish between 'faith' and 'the faith'.
multorum concatenatione contextum argumentorum – According to Aristotle, employing more steps than is necessary is a fault in deduction.[6]
inveniri – The topics constitute 'the science of finding arguments'.[7]
unum argumentum – According to Boethius, an argument (*argumentum*) is a reason (*ratio*) that produces faith or belief (*fides*).[8] The argument of the *Proslogion* addresses something that is the subject of doubt. Anselm sets out as a dialectician to present such an argument. He is looking for a single argument, with a single middle term. Given what Anselm proposes to do with his *unum argumentum*, we should beware of thinking that any one chapter of the *Proslogion* represents the whole of it.
ad se probandum – Anselm seeks to address the doubt by means of an argument intended as a proof.
deus vere est – Anselm seeks to establish that God truly exists. This has been taken to mean that he is concerned with the manner of God's existence (i.e. as 'truly-existing') rather than the fact of God's existence.[9] But Anselm is clear that He wishes to establish that God exists (which is after all something that Catholics believe about God). Even if one were unnecessarily to take 'truly exists' to refer to the manner of God's existence, it would still be the case for Anselm that the manner of God's existence entailed the fact of God's existence.

---

[5] John of Salisbury, *Metalogicon*, I, 23 [*PL*199 col. 853AB].

[6] Aristotle, *Topics*, VIII, 162a 24–6.

[7] Boethius, *In Ciceronis Topica*: '*scientia inveniendorum argumentorum*' [*PL*64 col. 1043A].

[8] Ibid.: '*Argumentum autem ratio est quae rei dubiae faciat fidem*' [*PL*64 col. 1048A].

[9] A. Stolz, '"Vere esse" im *Proslogion* des hl. Anselm', in *Scholastik*, 9 (1934) 400–409; and 'Anselm's Theology in the *Proslogion*', in J. Hick and A.C. McGill (eds), *The many-faced argument: recent studies on the ontological argument for the existence of God*, London 1968, pp. 183–206.

summum bonum – The argument is more than a proof of existence, since to simply prove that something exists does not tell us what it is. In the case of God, we must be able to show that what we are setting out to prove is God. This is to be done by developing an argument that establishes the identity of that which is proved to exist with God.
et quaecumque de divina credimus substantia – Anselm also wishes to ensure that this God is to be identified with the God of Catholic belief, and so intends to exhibit this identity.
The structure of the *Proslogion* reflects Anselm's aims as set out in the Preface:
P1 – A preparatory *excitatio*
P2–4 – God's existence and the inconceivability of His non-existence
P5–22 – God's goodness; the attributes of God and their coherence; God's unity and uniqueness
P23 – The specifically Catholic belief about God as Trinity
P24 – A second *excitatio*
P25–26 – A scriptural reflection on the significance of what Anselm has achieved in the *Proslogion*.
§0.3 *mentis aciem* – More literally 'the acute gaze of the mind'.
At this point in his investigation Anselm had considered that dialectic would not be able to supply him with the middle term for his argument.
mentem meam frustra occupando – Eadmer provides an account of this struggle, the source for which is certainly Anselm.[10]
§0.4 Note the fate of the wax tablets on which Anselm first drafted his argument – the first copy disappeared and the second was smashed – an indication perhaps that not all of the brethren shared his enthusiasm for his 'discovery'.[11]
§0.5 *de hoc ipso et de quibusdam aliis* – *Hoc* refers to the proof of God's existence and whatever we believe about Him; *aliis* to the other questions dealt with throughout the *Proslogion*.
sub persona – Anselm decides to write his argument down, and to present it in the literary form of a prayer and meditation.
quaerentis intelligere quod credit – Anselm's first reference to the Augustinian principle of '*fides quaerens intellectum*'. This is a rational enquiry into matters of faith.
§0.6 *istud* = the *Proslogion*; *illud* = the *Monologion*.
Fides/credere precedes *intellectus/intelligere*. The discovery of 'theological' or 'philosophical' truths about God requires faith. That is not the same thing as saying that one needs faith in order to understand the argument.
'*exemplum meditandi de ratione fidei*' and '*fides quaerens intellectum*' – Anselm never fully explains why he changes the titles of these works. The earlier work is an example of meditating, of silent reasoning, in which Anselm draws on his own

10 Eadmer, *Life*, pp. 29f.

11 Ibid., pp. 30f.

intellectual power with little reference to God. The *Proslogion* is different in that it takes the form of an address to God.
§0.7 *a pluribus* – Among those who requested copies was Archbishop Hugh (see *E*100, written c. 1083/1084). When Anselm sent Hugh these works they already bore his name and the title of Abbot.
plures – See *E*109 (written c. 1085) where Anselm writes to Archbishop Hugh telling him of the new titles.
hugo – Hugh, Bishop of Die from 1073, apostolic legate from 1074/75 and Archbishop of Lyons from 1083. Excommunicated by Pope Victor III in 1087 and reconciled under Pope Urban II. Died 1106.
§0.8 *ut aptius fieret* – More fitting perhaps because each of the original titles could be applied to either book.

The Chapter Headings

In B and the earliest manuscripts, the chapter headings were placed at the beginning of the *Proslogion*, the individual chapters being merely noted by numbers in the margin, the text running continuously. It would appear that the later divisions in the text are an afterthought and somewhat intrusive of its unity. Too much should not be made of the titles themselves as exact descriptions of all that is to follow in the chapter. Although it is clear from the text of *P*2 that Anselm does not there reach the conclusion that God exists, he nevertheless chooses to entitle this chapter: '*Quod vere sit deus*'. The use of the subjunctive in the chapter headings indicates that these are matters in doubt and to be investigated, not simply assumed.

The Text

§1.1 The 's' of *Proslogion* was originally omitted in B and later inserted over text by a corrector. The omission may have been as a result of the scribe's familiarity with the Latin form, *Proloquium*.
§1.2 The rhetorical style in which this chapter is written can mislead us into believing that it possesses little or no philosophical content. However, what we find in this chapter are several important themes that re-emerge throughout the text: man's littleness and God's inaccessibility; God as dwelling in inaccessible light; man as made to see God but having lost this vision through Adam's fall; God as the one who enlightens men's eyes; man as made in God's image, which, though obscured, allows him to remember God.
excitatio – A rhetorical device intended to rouse someone out of a stupor or into action.
ad contemplandum deum – Anselm has already stated in the Preface that he is presenting his argument in the guise of someone contemplating God. This chapter creates the literary and rhetorical ambiance in which the argument is presented.

§1.3 There appears to be a biographical element to this literary device, if one recalls Anselm's distractions and the difficulties he experienced when he tried to give up the pursuit of the argument.
§1.4 *Matthew* 6:6.
quaere eum – The theme of seeking God recurs throughout the *Proslogion* as Anselm comes to an understanding of the relationship between seeking and finding God.
§1.5 *Psalm* 26:8. (All references to the *Psalms* follow the Vulgate numbering.) Anselm seeks 'real' knowledge of God, something that dialectic and the discovery of arguments cannot give him.
§1.6 By his own power, Anselm has been unable to find God. The techniques he employed were not sufficient. He needs God to show him how to go about finding Him.
§1.7 *absentem/praesentem* – God is either absent (in which case He cannot be found) or present, but hidden (in which case the point is to possess a way of 'seeing' Him). Part of Anselm's distress arises from the possibility that his failure to capture God may be an indication of God's absence.
§1.8 This recurring theme from *1 Timothy* 6:16 plays an important role in the *Proslogion*. It provides an explanation of God's presence (light) and his absence (inaccessibility), and of how God can both be and not be understood/known.
§1.9 *facies* – Anselm has not seen God. The argument of the *Monologion* did not provide him with this vision or glimpse of God.
§1.10 *Psalm* 50:13: *'ne proiicias me a facie tua'*. Anselm stresses his experience of God's absence, which he seeks to overcome.
§1.11 Anselm wishes to have a direct experience of God, an experience that is both spiritual and intellectual. In neither case can he achieve this by himself. God's assistance is required to attain and maintain any such experience.
§1.12 In spite of the fact that Anselm has faith, he has not seen or known God, even though he was created for this purpose, and has received the grace of baptism.
§1.13 It is not that man never possessed that for which he was made. He has lost it. He does not find, but rather loses. What he finds is a loss. This is why Anselm has not been able to find God or the argument that will make Him known directly to the understanding.
§1.14 *Psalms* 77: 25 and 126:2.
filiorum adae – Adam was created without sin (*CDH*I:5). If he had not sinned Adam and his descendants, the human race, would have retained their knowledge of God (*CDH*II:8). The human race is damned through the sin of Adam and Eve (*DCV*9). Adam robbed himself of the blessings God gave him and earned for himself their opposites (*DCV*12).
§1.15 Adam's blessings are contrasted with our sufferings.
§1.16 Adam's sin has removed the light and left us in darkness.
§1.17 *a visione dei* – It is because of Adam's sin that the human race no longer enjoys the vision of God and immortality, but experiences instead blindness and death.

§1.18 For Anselm, Adam's fall represents a 'wretched transformation', rather than a 'happy fault' (*felix culpa*).
§1.19 In spite of his intentions and his apparent understanding in the *Monologion* of how to attain knowledge of God, Anselm has made no progress. His hopes of joy and enlightenment have apparently ended in despair and darkness.
§1.20 *Psalm* 121:9 and *Jeremiah* 14:19.
offendi in me – In his present state without God's assistance Anselm realises that although he seeks God, when he investigates through his rational mind, it is himself rather than God whom he attains knowledge of. He is unable to see that which he knows is present, that of which his rational mind is the image. (See *M*67.)
§1.21 *Psalms* 114:3 and 37:9.
Anselm seeks peace but finds confusion and sorrow. Yet, according to Augustine, 'Faith seeks; understanding finds'. What, then, is Anselm doing wrong? He has not placed his trust in God, not sought God's assistance. It is not enough to seek, so that he may find. He must also ask, so that he may receive.
§1.22 *Psalms* 6:4, 12:1, 4 and 79:4, 8, 20.
§1.23 Finally, Anselm asks for God's aid and enlightenment. He is no longer seeking God without God's assistance.
§1.24 Since the fall of Adam, man no longer possesses God's blessings. If Anselm is to see God, then God will have to give back to him what Adam lost.
ut bene sit – see the use of this phrase in *P*0.2. Anselm's argument addresses, as well as other points, God as that which all things need for their wellbeing.
§1.25 *Psalms* 43:26 and 78:9.
This request marks the turning point in the '*excitatio*'. Anselm is not asking for something that he should not have. He is asking for that which God invites him to ask.
§1.26 Anselm must still strive to obtain what God wants him to have and asks for God's encouragement and consolation, so that he will not give up before he has reached the goal of his investigation.
§1.27 *Job* 3:24. Anselm likens himself to Job, but asks that God will take mercy on him, feeding him and giving him what he needs.
§1.28 *Psalms* 37:5 and 68:16.
Anselm is like a man bent over who cannot look up at the sky. He asks to see God even if only from a distance. But even this distant glimpse of God requires God's help.
§1.29 Faith seeks and understanding finds, but *both* require God's help. Anselm's efforts to seek for God have been fruitless, but God will not simply show Himself, without being sought. Thus, Anselm needs to be taught how to seek God, so that God my show Himself to him.
§1.30 To seek and to find God, it is necessary to desire and love Him. God will only show Himself to one who has sought Him in this way. See the final prayer in *P*26.10.
§1.31 *Genesis* 1:27.

Anselm introduces his Augustinian belief in the image of God as the basis of human rational activity and of the ability to think of or love God at all. The image is found in the rational mind. Original sin has damaged man's will and therefore this image. Anselm had set out his position in *M*67, where he talks of *memoria, intelligentia* and *amor*. There is in the rational mind an image of God, because the mind alone can remember, understand and love itself. For Anselm the reality of this image is established even more securely by the fact that the rational mind can remember, understand and love God. Anselm's argument does not depend on this belief, but supports it. The argument can be seen as a justification of the notion that man is the *imago dei*, and consequently of the method and argument of the *Monologion*.

Tui memor – 'mindful of you' or 'remembering you'. The Latin, '*memoria*', has much wider connotations than the English, 'remembrance', including 'being mindful of', 'aware of' and 'conscious of'.

§1.32 The image is like a scratched or smoke-damaged mirror in which no reflection is visible. Unless God repairs it, the image will not be able to function in the way it was created to.

§1.33 In spite of the *imago dei*, God can only be understood '*aliquatenus*' ['to some extent']. It is God's greatness as well as man's sinfulness that prevents the direct vision of God.

§1.34 In *De Trinitate*, XV, 2, 2, Augustine writes: 'faith seeks, understanding finds: for which reason the prophet says, Unless you believe, you will not understand.' Anselm's use of the non-Vulgate version of this text suggests that he has taken it from Augustine (where it occurs frequently).

§2.1 The title of the chapter is interesting, because in it Anselm does not do what the chapter heading appears to suggest he will. He does not draw the conclusion that God exists from his argument. Certainly, in the preamble to the argument he states that he believes God exists, and that God is believed to be 'something than which nothing greater can be thought'. He also proves (or so he believes) that this 'something' exists. But he does not yet prove that this 'something' is 'God'.

§2.2 *da mihi ut quantum scis expedire intelligam* – Anselm indicates that this understanding is a gift, which possesses a fundamentally supernatural character. God determines the extent to which Anselm understands. This reflects Anselm's own experience of coming to understand. This gift of understanding is to be equated with his discovery. It is not to be equated with the act required to grasp the significance of the '*unum argumentum*', which presupposes faith neither logically (i.e. that one must accept any premises on faith) nor existentially (i.e. that one must have a faith commitment before one can understand the premises, form and conclusion of the argument).

§2.3 Anselm presents the middle term of his argument. It is not a definition of God, and could not be, since God is not susceptible of definition in the dialectical tradition in which Anselm is operating, i.e. God is not a differentiated species of a higher genus.

aliquid – In the *Philosophical Fragments* Anselm identifies the different ways in which the term '*aliquid*' is used.[12] It is used properly (*proprie*) when it is applied to that which has a name, is thought in the mind and exists in reality, e.g. a stone or a tree. Anselm believes that this term is used properly in the case of God, but it is the point of his argument to establish that this is the case.

quo nichil maius cogitari potest – I refer to this phrase and its variants as X. Other thinkers have come up with similar phrases to X; see for example Augustine, in the *Confessiones* VII, 4, 6 and *De Moribus*, II, 11, 24. As we have already seen in Chapter 2, similar language to that of Augustine and Anselm is also found in Boethius's *De Consolatione Philosophiae*, III, 10. The kind of argument put forward by Boethius may have its origins in Aristotle, who is reported by Simplicius to have come up with a proof of the existence of God in the no longer extant work, *On Philosophy*:[13] 'He [sc. Aristotle] speaks of this in his On Philosophy. In general, where there is a better there is also a best. Since, then, amongst existing things one is better than another, there is also something that is best, which will be the divine.' Another possible source of Anselm's formula 'X' is Cicero. In his *De Natura Deorum*, II, 7, 18, he writes that 'amongst all things nothing is better than the world, nothing more excellent, nothing more beautiful, and not only is there nothing better, but something better than it cannot even be thought.' Clearly Cicero's description here concerns the world and not God. Seneca, in his *Naturales Quaestiones*, I, Praefatio 13, states that God is everything, whose magnitude represents 'that than which a greater cannot be thought' ['*qua nihil maius cogitari potest*']. Here we have the closest statement to that of Anselm, and so are obliged to ask whether Anselm was aware of this text. H. Hine argues from citations in contemporary authors and from the provenance of extant manuscripts that the *Naturales Quaestiones* was rediscovered in Northern France in the early twelfth century at the latest, referring to the 'tantalising possibility' that Anselm was acquainted with it.[14] The date of authorship of the *Proslogion* would put this rediscovery into the last quarter of the eleventh century. According to M. Colish, there are 50 or more extant manuscripts containing the *Naturales Quaestiones*, none of which predates the twelfth century.[15] Thus, although there is no conclusive supporting evidence of Seneca's influence

---

12 F.S. Schmitt, *Ein neues unvollendetes Werk des hl. Anselm von Canterbury (Beiträge zur Geschichte der Theologie und Philosophie des Mittelalters*, 33/3), Münster 1936, pp. 42f.

13 See Simplicius, *Commentarius in de Caelo*, 289, 1–4 (Fragment F16R^{3,} in J. Barnes (ed.), *The Complete Works of Aristotle*, vol. 2, Princeton 1984, pp. 2392).

14 H. Hine 'Natural Questions', in L. Reynolds (ed.), *Texts and Transmission: A Survey of the Latin Classics*, Oxford 1983, pp. 376–8, p. 377.

15 M. Colish, *The Stoic Tradition from Antiquity to the Early Middle Ages*, vol. 1, Leiden 1990, p. 18. It should be noted that three copies of Seneca's *Naturales Quaestiones* are recorded in the twelfth century catalogues at Bec, and that one of them may have predated the gift of Philip Harcourt in the mid-twelfth century. See the discussion in Gasper, *Anselm of Canterbury*, p. 93.

here, nevertheless it cannot be ruled out, for of all the possible anticipations of Anselm's formula Seneca's is the closest to that of Anselm and is the only one that employs the word '*maius*' rather than '*melius*'.[16] In fact, K. Nothdurft suggests[17] that the apologetic nature of the *Proslogion* and the use of a phrase that the fool or unbeliever will accept supports the view that Anselm made use of it precisely because of its non-Christian origins and, all the more so, given that the formula was precisely not referring to the Christian God, but to the divinity of the world. In *De Doctrina Christiana*, I, 7, 7, Augustine appears to make reference to Seneca and Cicero, when he writes of thought striving after that than which nothing is better. According to Augustine, everyone believes that nothing better than God exists, whatever it is they believe God to be·. There is an understanding of God, which even the pagans, who have a different conception of God, can employ, and which is shared by Christians. Particularly important for our understanding of X is its likely origin in non-Christian thought. On hearing it, then, the fool will not assume that it refers to, or is a name of, Anselm's God.

§2.4 *aliqua talis natura* – Anselm makes it clear that the sense in which he is using '*aliquid*' in the formula '*aliquid quo nichil maius cogitari potest*' is yet to be determined. His argument can be seen as a proof that *aliquid* is being employed in the proper sense of the term.

dixit insipiens in corde suo non est deus – *Psalms* 13:1 and 52:1.

Augustine discusses *Psalm* 52 in his *Enarrationes in Psalmos*.[18] He considers that there are very few men who deny God's existence, but that those who do would not dare to say so openly and therefore they say it in their hearts. In *CDH*I:25, Anselm writes of the fool as someone who asserts that something that is necessarily the case is impossible, because he does not know how it is the case. In *DIV*6, he states that in the *Monologion* and *Proslogion*, he tried to answer those who do not want to believe what they do not understand. It is at the fool who rejects belief in what he does not understand that Anselm's argument is aimed. Anselm possesses the scriptural authority to pursue the notion that unbelief arises out of, and can be addressed as, an error of understanding. In *R*8.9, Anselm refers to the fool as someone who does not accept 'sacred authority'.

§2.5 *esse* – Can be translated as either 'to be' or 'to exist', depending on the context.

Anselm states that the fool 'understands what he hears' and that what he 'understands is in his understanding'. Anselm does not discuss the meaningfulness of X or mention the possibility that the fool might claim not to understand it. Thus, one presupposition of the *Proslogion* is that X is meaningful and, hence, understandable. Anselm has not overlooked these potential difficulties unwittingly.

---

[16] See G. Ross, 'Seneca's Philosophical Influence', in C. Costa (ed.), *Seneca*, London 1974, pp. 116–65, p. 134.

[17] K. Nothdurft, *Studien zum Einfluss Senecas auf die Philosophie und Theologie des zwölften Jahrhunderts*, Leiden 1963, pp. 194f.

[18] *PL*37 coll. 612–19. Augustine uses the term *imprudens* rather than *insipiens*.

To him it is evident that the notion of X is understandable; there is nothing in the individual words nor in the way in which they are combined that provides just cause for any objection. What he means by the language used in the formula 'X' is observable in the argument of the *Monologion*. But in this earlier work he was not able to order the language and concepts in such a way as to produce what he went on to say in the *Proslogion*. This was only achieved with his discovery of the middle term. Of course, if the fool knows at the outset that X refers to God, he may well claim that he does not understand it. This is why Anselm's argument begins with X rather than God.

§2.6 *Aliud ... aliud* .... As one would expect, given his account of the uses of '*aliquid*', Anselm makes a distinction between something existing in the understanding and understanding that something exists. The latter involves the proper use of the concept, whilst the former is consistent with both proper and improper uses. His argument will go on to show that the possession of the concept (*rem esse in intellectu*) in this instance at least is dependent on the act of judgement concerning the existence of its referent (*intelligere rem esse*).

§2.7 *pinctor* – Anselm uses the analogy of the painter to show that the terms *intelligere* and *esse in intellectu* do not equivocally introduce *esse in re* into his argument.[19]

§2.8 Anselm asserts that the fool understands X when he hears it. He does not justify this assertion, which appears to be based on the idea that there is nothing difficult concerning the words themselves nor their meaningful juxtaposition in relation to each other. The fool's understanding at this point appears to be independent of any understanding of X's existence. For the purposes of dialectical argument, Anselm only requires the fool to agree that he understands X.

§2.9 *id quo maius cogitari nequit* – Anselm substitutes the pronoun, *id*, for *aliquid* in this variant of X. (See Chapter 8 for the possible significance of this move.)

non potest esse insolo intellectu – Anselm's great claim is that given that X exists in the understanding, it cannot only exist in the understanding.

§2.10 *potest cogitari esse & inre* – Anselm appears to suggest that understandability entails the possibility of actual existence. However, the discussion of *aliquid* in the *Philosophical Fragments* does not support this interpretation, since a chimera can be understood, although it cannot exist, since it is by definition a mythical beast. Nor does Anselm mean that understanding the term 'a square circle' involves the possibility of its actual existence. Rather, Anselm's meaning is that if it is greater for X to exist in reality than only in the understanding, then 'by definition' X must exist in reality.

quod maius est – Anselm provides the basis for the claim he has made in *P*2.9. He can be understood as making the point either (i) that it is generally greater to exist in reality than in the understanding alone or (ii) that it is specifically greater for X to exist in reality than in the understanding alone. (i) The justification for

---

19 See Priscian's analogy of God as an artist in *Inst. Gramm.* XVII, in H. Keil, *Grammatici Latini*, vol. 3, 1858, p. 135.

understanding him in the former sense is that it is consistent with an Augustinian or Neo-platonic worldview concerning the goodness or greatness of being. Actual existence is 'greater' (*esse in re*) than conceptual existence (*esse in intellectu*). There is a correspondence between the intensity or levels of 'greatness' and the degrees of being. That which is higher up the ladder of being is greater than that which is lower. Consequently, the thing that exists must be greater than the mere idea of it. (ii) On the other hand, Anselm can be understood in the latter sense, since his argument does not require such a general Platonic ontology. He simply requires that in the specific case of X, the concept must contain all that is highest, most worthy and best. Thus, if it exists *in re*, it must be possessor of greatness in a sense which is clearly greater than if it exists *in intellectu* alone. This meaning is sufficient for the purposes of Anselm's argument. Consequently, I take Anselm's meaning in the second sense.

§2.11 *est quo maius cogitari potest* – Anselm subjects the proposition that X exists in the understanding alone to a *reductio* argument. Any attempt to maintain this position entails a contradiction concerning X, i.e. that both nothing greater and something greater than it can be thought.

§2.12 *Existit ergo procul dubio* – As a result of the *reductio*, Anselm is able to claim that X can only be thought of as existing in reality, since this is the only way to avoid the absurd conclusion of *P*2.11. However, it is important to remember that, in spite of the chapter heading, Anselm does not here establish that God exists. He has stated 'we' believe God to be 'something than which nothing greater can be thought'. He has, he believes, established the existence of that 'something', but has not established the identity of God and that 'something'. For Anselm the affirmation of X as existing functions as a condition for the possibility of having the correct concept of X.

§3.1 The first sentence of *P*3 ('*Quod utique ....*') refers back to and follows directly on from the '*aliquid*' of the last sentence of *P*2. At this point Anselm is talking about X. Nevertheless it seems correct to assume the masculine pronoun in the chapter heading, rather than the neuter, since the chapter headings generally refer to God, and in this chapter Anselm argues that what is true of X is true of God. This identity of God and X is at the core of the argument of the *Proslogion*.

§3.2 *sic vere* – This can also be translated as 'so truly' or 'truly ... to such an extent', which might fit better with a Neo-platonic reading of Anselm. God has a higher degree of being than anything else. However, translating '*sic vere*' as 'truly ... in such a way' leaves open the possibility of a Neo-platonic interpretation without assuming it, reflecting an ambivalence to be found in the text. It is possible, but not necessary (and may even be misleading) to read Anselm in Neo-platonic terms here. Not being able to be thought not to exist is related to the nature of God's existence, thus my preferred translation. Anselm's usage in *P*4.5 supports the translation here of '*sic*' as 'in such a way'.

§3.3 *maius* – For Anselm, something that cannot be thought not to exist [in reality] is greater than something that can be thought not to exist [in reality]. He does not seek to justify this claim here. At the end of *P*2 he had shown that X does not

exist in the understanding alone, and therefore it exists in reality. Here he seeks to show that it is not possible to think of the non-existence in reality of X. The next sentence shows why Anselm wishes to make this move.
§3.4 Anselm seeks to show that it is the manner of this something's existence that is involved in this 'inability' to be thought not to exist. However, as above '*sic* ... *vere*' can also be translated here as 'so truly' or 'truly ... to such an extent'. In which case it is the degree of existence that involves this 'inability'.
§3.5 If X exists in such a way that it cannot be thought not to exist, it shares this characteristic with God. But as we have just seen this is not simply stated here as an act of faith. Anselm has demonstrated by reason that there must exist something the non-existence of which cannot be thought. He has not as yet shown that there is only one such thing. The point now is to attach this demonstration to what is believed about God, including His uniqueness. Anselm starts out here on the path of showing the identity of God and this 'something'. It takes him much of the *Proslogion* to establish it. If we demonstrate of X everything we believe about God, then given what later in the history of philosophy is called 'the identity of indiscernibles', X is God, and what we have demonstrated of X we have demonstrated of God.
§3.6 Anselm introduces the word '*melius*', not simply as a synonym for '*maius*', but because he is seeking to establish the identity of X with the highest good (i.e. God).
ascenderet creatura sup[er] creatorem – The absurdity of the idea of the creature judging its creator lies in the gulf that man cannot bridge, given his limitedness and God's unlimitedness.
§3.7 It is a characteristic of God alone not to be able to be thought not to exist. But he has already shown this is a characteristic of X too. Thus, God and X possess the same referent.
§3.8 *Psalms* 13:1 and 52:1. The manner of God's existence as X allows us to conclude that He has existence to the greatest extent. The fool does not understand that God cannot be subject to the judgement of men in such a way that they can question His existence, if they know what they are doing. He misunderstands the relationship between the creature and its Creator. God as that which exists most fully and most greatly cannot be thought not to exist.

Anselm's argument in *P*3 raises a problem. It might appear that he moves from the experience of not being able to use language meaningfully to deny the existence of X to the statement that the actual existence of X is what underlies this experience. If it is the case that Anselm is making an untestable ontological claim based on induction, then this appears to be a serious weakness in his proof. However, Anselm is rather establishing that the affirmation of the existence of God is a condition governing the possibility of the possession of the concept of God. It is not possible to deny God in such circumstances, because that would lead to a contradiction between the act of denial and the content of the denial.
§4.1 The question remains as to how the fool can think the unthinkable.

§4.2 *quia dixit in corde, & non dixit in corde* – Anselm has to address the point that the fool has said something in his heart, i.e. thought something, since scripture says he has, whilst at the same time he cannot have said it in his heart or thought it, since Anselm's argument claims to show that it cannot be thought.
non uno tantum modo – One task of the dialectician is to clarify the various ways in which language is used, including the proper and improper uses of terms, and literal and metaphorical usage.
§4.3 *Aliter ... aliter...* – Anselm is talking here not about two equally valid ways of using words, but between a potentially improper and a proper usage. Thus, it is possible to use the word 'God' incorrectly, as in the example 'God is a species of mammal', but this needs to be distinguished from the use of the word 'God' when correctly understood. In *M*10, Anselm distinguishes four ways in which a word can be 'spoken': (1) when the word is spoken out loud; (2) when it is thought; (3) when the mind possesses an image of something; and (4) when its universal essence is grasped. Anselm is distinguishing here between the senses (2) and (4). The fool is employing words in sense (2), but not, according to Anselm, in sense (4). If one's use of a word in sense (1) or (2) does not correspond to sense (4), one is not using the word with any degree of understanding.
§4.4 *aut sine ulla aut cum aliqua extranea significatione* – Anselm argues that, even if one understands what God is, it is still possible to employ the word 'God' in sense (2) 'without any or with some extraneous meaning'. The fool can continue in his ways, even after having heard Anselm's words, because having understood X he fails to see that this is what the word 'God' signifies. Thus, Anselm provides us not only with an explanation of why the fool says that there is no God, but also why he continues to say this, even though according to Anselm in the light of his argument it is 'so obvious to a rational mind' (*P*3.8) that God exists.
§4.5 Anselm now goes on to summarise his argument so far, and sets out what needs to be done in order to prove that his argument validly applies to God. His first step is to restate the identification of God and X. It is as X that God's non-existence is shown to be unthinkable. In his next step he does not speak of God but of 'this same thing', i.e. X. Whoever really understands X understands that X exists in such a way that no act of cogitation can avoid its existence. Anselm concludes that anyone who understands that God exists in this way understands that they have to make the thought their own, recognise it as their thought. They have no choice other than to affirm God's existence. The insight is Anselm's, and initially Anselm's alone, but once someone understands his argument, they find made explicit an element of their own thought: the affirmation of God's existence as the condition governing the possibility of understanding the concept of God at all. From this Anselmian perspective, the attempt to stand back from one's situation and ask, 'I have to say that God exists, but does He really?', would involve a wilful misuse of the word 'God'.

Quod qui bene intelligit – By 'this' Anselm is referring clearly to X ('*quod*' – neuter pronoun referring back to '*id quo maius cogitari non potest*') and not to God (the masculine noun '*deus*').[20]

The question now becomes, how can we know that God exists in the same manner as X? Anselm will seek to establish that this is the case by showing the identity of the attributes of God and X.

§4.6 Anselm gives us here a strong indication as to the significance of '*fides quaerens intellectum*'. Faith is necessary for understanding, but once understanding is attained then understanding is not dependent on faith. Although, of course, for Anselm, the two are mutually supportive, so that faith is strengthened rather than replaced by understanding. As we saw in the discussion of Kretzmann's distinction between propositional faith and the way of faith in Chapter 2 above, propositional understanding supplants propositional faith, but supplements the way of faith. Thus it is that Anselm sees the importance of rational argument, rather than simply statements of faith, for unbelievers. They can understand and through their understanding approach faith.

It is worth noting at the end of *P*4 that Anselm has not argued for the necessity of God's existence. He only does that in the *Responsio*. He does not use the word 'necessary' until *P*23 and then not in relation to God's existence.

§5.1 In *P*3, Anselm introduced the term '*melius*', and started to develop the idea that God could be identified with X. He now pursues this point. In this he is following Augustine, who in *De Trinitate*, VI, 8, states that, leaving aside the issue of physical mass, to be greater is the same as to be better. Anselm also employs Augustine's principle that God's attributes are better than their negation,[21] although he expresses this in his own way.

§5.2 *quo nil maius valet cogitari* – Anselm introduces a variation on X, in applying the phrase to God here. This variation appears to be simply stylistic.

§5.3 *solum existens per se ipsum* – Anselm commenced the *Monologion* with the argument that the '*summum omnium*' exists and in *M*3–4 argues that the '*summum omnium*' exists '*per seipsum*'. He developed this idea further in *M*7, showing that the only things that can be thought to exist are the '*summum omnium*', which uniquely exists through itself, and those things that it creates, which exist through it and through nothing else.

§5.4 God's uniqueness means that He is the sole member of the class of X. All other things are 'less than can be thought', i.e. members of the class of not-X.

It is not possible to think of a greater Creator than one who creates from nothing. According to *M*7, the '*summum omnium*' creates everything from nothing and not from some kind of 'matter', and the God who creates from nothing is greater than one who creates from (pre-existing) material.

---

[20] On this point see I. Logan, '"Whoever understands this…": On translating the Proslogion', in *New Blackfriars*, 89 (2008) 560–74.

[21] *Confessiones*, VII, 4, 6.

§5.5 It is not possible to think of something greater than God according to Catholic belief. Anselm has to keep proving that it is not possible to think of God having greater attributes than Catholics believe Him to possess. If he cannot show this, then his argument cannot be made to work.
§5.6 This is a rhetorical question. Anselm is saying that there is no such absent good.
§5.7 If God is not 'whatever it is better to be than not to be', something greater than Him can be thought and He cannot be identified with X. Anselm's conclusion here is the same as that of *M*15.
§6.1 Anselm enters into detailed considerations about what has to be believed of God.
§6.2 He puts the questions that he will deal with in *P*6–8, seeking to address the obvious problems involved in ascribing to God attributes that appear to contradict each other and accordingly to render the concept of God incoherent.
§6.3 *quomodo es sensibilis* – In *P*6, Anselm attempts to show that the fact that God does not have a body is not contradicted by the fact that He is sensible.
§6.4 Anselm equates sensibility with knowing, on the basis that the senses exist for a kind of knowing and that therefore it is not inappropriate to say that knowing is a kind of sensibility. The way in which God is said to be sensible is related to, but distinct from, the way in which bodily creatures are said to be sensible. God can be called sensible, because He knows, and supremely sensible because He is omniscient.
§7.1 Anselm addresses the issue of how God can be X, if there are things He cannot do, since it would appear in that case that it is possible to think of something greater than him, i.e. that which can do anything. Henry suggests that this chapter 'represents a *prise de position*' in relation to Peter Damian's view in *De Divina Omnipotentia*, VII, that an 'inability' on the part of God to change past events would constitute a limit on His omnipotence.[22] Anselm shows that it is possible to employ the skills of a dialectician to resolve apparent problems concerning God's omnipotence, and that therefore it is not necessary to take up a position such as that of Peter Damian, which itself is based on improper usage.
§7.2 *si non potes corrumpi* – Augustine addresses the question of God's incorruptibility in *Confessiones*, VII, 4, 6, establishing that God is incorruptible, because it is better to be incorruptible than corruptible. Anselm, however, sees a problem in the outcome of the application of the principle that God is whatever it is better to be than not to be, since, as in this example and others, it appears to suggest that there are things God cannot do, and that therefore there are limits on his power.
§7.3 Anselm's argument continues to be influenced by Augustine here. Augustine argues that if God were to do certain things such as sin or lie, He would not be omnipotent.[23]

[22] D.P. Henry, *The Logic of Saint Anselm*, Oxford 1967, p. 151.

[23] *Sermo* CCXIII, 1, 1.

§7.4 It is necessary to clarify how the words which suggest God has limits on His omnipotence are operating, in order to resolve the problem. The kind of activity that Anselm undertakes in *DG* is reflected here in the distinction between language that is properly (*proprie*) and improperly (*improprie*) employed.[24]
§7.5 Anselm provides examples of improper and proper usage.
§7.6 Based on his analysis of such usage, Anselm shows how what appears to be a power (*potentia*) can in fact be a lack of power (*impotentia*). Improper usage misleads us into thinking that some *impotentiae* are *potentiae*.
§7.7 That God cannot lie etc. is an indication of His omnipotence, and not of any impotence. See here also, the argument of Boethius that the ability to do evil is not a power.[25]
§8.1 Anselm goes on to seek to show how apparently contradictory attributes can be understood of God.
§8.2 According to Anselm, mercy is to be identified with compassion. But, if God is impassible, He cannot feel compassion, and hence cannot be merciful. But if He is not merciful, how is it that we experience the consolation of His mercy?
§8.3 *secundum nos/secundum te* – Anselm's resolution of this problem is linguistic. He argues that God is merciful 'in relation to us'. We feel the effect of God's mercy, but God does not experience the feeling of mercy or compassion. For Anselm, mercy is something God shows, rather than feels.
§8.4 If being merciful means having an emotional response to someone in need of mercy, then God is not merciful. However, God can be said to be both merciful and unmerciful without contradiction and in a way that is consistent with Catholic doctrine and Anselm's understanding of the functioning of language. Proper usage would say that we experience God as merciful, not that God is merciful.
In trying to prove what we believe about God, Anselm may appear to be forcing the argument here. However, from the previous two chapters we are able to see how he can ascribe impassibility to God. In *P*6.4 Anselm argues that God is supremely sensible or perceptive, but only insofar as He knows 'all things supremely, and not in the way in which an animal knows by bodily sense'. There is no passivity or receptivity in God's sensible power. If there were, it would follow from *P*7 that God in some sense lacked power. He would be open to external influences and impotent against them. In the same way, if God were passible, He would be powerless against the influence on Him of the actions of others. Talk of God as compassionate must be understood in the same way as that which concerns God's sensibility.
§9.1 Anselm addresses another apparent contradiction in the Catholic conception of God, that He is both just and merciful.

[24] See Henry, *Logic*, p. 22: At the heart of *DG* 'are to be found the distinctions which are the key to the Anselmian attitude to language and which permeate all his works'.

[25] Boethius, *De Consolatione Philosophiae*, IV, Prosa 2.

§9.2 The question is how God can do something that is apparently unjust. Anselm continues in this chapter to attempt to unravel the linguistic usage that produces apparent contradictions.

§9.3 *incomprehensibilis* – Anselm is moving towards the conclusion that becomes explicit in *P*15, that God as X is greater than can be thought. Here he is trying to determine whether God's incomprehensibility is part of the explanation for the linguistic problems we face in understanding how His attributes can co-exist.

in luce inaccessibili – Anselm recalls the reference to *I Timothy* 6:16 in *P*1.8: the inaccessible light in which God dwells, which men cannot see, yet yearn to see, something of which can only be seen if God enlightens the eyes.

§9.4 God's goodness requires that He show mercy to the wicked, otherwise He would be less good, and therefore would not be X.

§9.5 *videtur ... et non pervidetur* – Anselm understands that it is the case that God gives good things to the wicked, but does not fully understand how this can be so, since it is hidden in God's incomprehensibility, i.e. in the inaccessible light.

§9.6 Anselm introduces another image, that of the stream and its source. The spring lies hidden, although we know that it is there, otherwise there could not be a stream. Similarly, we know that God shows mercy, and that this must be as a result of his goodness, but nevertheless the reason why lies hidden.

§9.7 It is not only by reason of God's goodness, but also by that of His justice that He wishes good for the wicked, although this is hard to understand.

§9.8 Anselm addresses God and speaks eloquently of His goodness in rewarding the just and sparing the unjust.

§9.9 Anselm reminds us that he is not simply engaged in an exercise in dialectic, but is attempting to understand the living God, with whom he lives in an intimate and profound relationship. The God of this philosopher is no god of the philosophers, but is a God who forgives and saves in this world and in this life. It is the God of Catholic belief whom Anselm addresses and whom his dialectical argument seeks to prove. He is overwhelmed by this God, who is not capable of being grasped by human concepts. Anselm's *argumentum* can only provide him with the beginnings of an understanding, not with its fullness.

§9.10 Anselm states the principle of the coherence of God's attributes. The point is not to determine whether they are coherent, but to understand how this might be the case. Their coherence it appears arises because they are identical. God is merciful because He is good. He is good, because He is just. Therefore He is merciful, because He is just. It should be noted that Anselm does not make an equivalent move to say that God punishes because He is merciful. The reason for this becomes clear in *P*10. The attribute of mercy is what we experience when the good and just God acts in relation to us; it is an effect of the other attributes.

§9.11 Anselm seeks to understand what faith teaches about God's attributes, but knows he will come up against the mystery of God's greatness and incomprehensibility, which set the absolute limits on understanding.

§9.12 Is God's mercy an effect of His justice? Anselm asks that if it is so, God will show him how.

§9.13 For Anselm there is 'justice' in the notion that nothing better or more powerful than God can be thought.
§9.14 If God's goodness is real, then it must be the case that He spares the wicked, and from *P*9.13 it must follow that this is because of his justice.
de non bonis – Anselm makes a distinction between God making the good out of what is not good and out of the wicked. The latter deserve punishment and instead are shown mercy.
§9.15 Anselm's argument here is that it is not possible to deny God's attributes, and that therefore they must co-exist, although we cannot fully understand how or why this is the case. One could interpret Anselm's words as implying that a God who forgives *all* the wicked would be more merciful and more just than a God who forgives *some* of the wicked, since he does not employ a quantifier with the term '*malis*'. However, Anselm does not make this move, because he does not believe it to be consistent with Catholic belief.
§10.1 Anselm considers not just how different attributes can be reconciled, but also how different usages of the same attribute can avoid conflict or contradiction.
§10.2 If sparing the wicked is just, then the question for Anselm is how the apparently contradictory uses of 'just' here can be reconciled.
§10.3 Anselm finally begins to clarify what is going on with the linguistic usage here. It is just that the wicked are punished for their deeds and just that God forgives the wicked, because of His goodness.
§10.4 *secundum te & secundum nos* – God's attributes possess a different meaning when looked at from the perspective of God or from that of His creatures. In sparing the wicked, God acts justly, but they experience the effect of this just action as mercy. Furthermore, even when we experience God's justice we do so in our own way, for this is the action of Him, who is supremely good, doing as He ought to.[26]
§11.1 Anselm has to resolve an apparent contradiction between scriptural references to God's attributes of mercy and justice. If he cannot resolve this, then it is possible to think of something more merciful or more just than the God of Catholic belief, in which case He cannot be X. Again, although Anselm is influenced by Augustine here,[27] he takes a different direction. For Augustine, God is merciful and just because he delays justice and shows us mercy in the present time.
§11.2 If God is merciful only in relation to us and not to Himself, does this mean that this is true of his justice? Anselm's answer is, No. Not only that, but God is just in relation to Himself when he spares he wicked.
§11.3 By establishing this, Anselm is able to show that the apparently conflicting statements in *Psalms* 24:10 and 144:17 can be made consistent.
§11.4 If God wishes to punish or spare the wicked, this is just, because whatever God wills is just. Anselm does not state here whether he means that God's willing it is what makes it just, or that God only wills what is just. Given Anselm's

26 See Augustine, *Enarrationes in Psalmos*, CXLVII, 13.

27 See Augustine, *Sermo* XXII, 5, 5.

understanding of the identity of God's attributes, this juxtaposition of alternatives would be misleading; what God wills and His justice are identical, and neither is the cause of the other. God's goodness and justice are identical and therefore His mercy can be said to arise out of His justice.

§11.5 Whilst this helps us to understand how God can will good for the wicked, it is of limited use in showing us why God treats some of the wicked more mercifully than others, when they appear to possess the same lack of merit.

§11.6 Anselm has demonstrated the method establishing God's attributes by the principle that God is 'whatever it is better to be than not to be', and in the process has strengthened his case for the identity of God and X.

§12.1 Anselm argues from God's self-subsistence to the fact that all God's attributes are to be identified with Him.

§12.2 Unlike other beings, God exists through Himself (*per se*) and not through another (*per aliud*). God is the goodness by which He is good, etc. In *M*16, Anselm argues that for God to be just and to be justice are the same thing and similarly for other attributes.

§13.1 Anselm now seeks to address the question of how that which is attributed to others can be uniquely attributed to God, developing the theme that he had begun in *P*3 and *P*5. If God understood as X cannot be shown to be unique, then X cannot be identified with God.

§13.2 *maius te nichil est* – Anselm is talking here of God as X, i.e. nothing *can* be greater than God.

ubique et semper – This passage reflects the conclusion of *M*21 and the argument of *M*22 that the supreme nature or essence exists everywhere and always. God alone is unlimited and eternal, because He alone is not subject to the laws to which His creation is subject.

§13.3 The question arises of how then unlimitedness and eternity can be predicated of created spirits.

§13.4 *solus es eternus* – Anselm argues this point in *M*18.

§13.5 Only God can exist simultaneously everywhere. In this He differs from that which is corporeal which can only exist in one place at a time.

§13.6 Anselm argues there are spirits that can exist in more than one place at a time, citing the example of the way he understood the soul to inhabit the body.

§13.7 That which exists in different places, but not everywhere, is unlimited in one sense, but limited in another. However, only God is absolutely unlimited and eternal.

singulariter – Anselm has been able to show how the attributes, 'unlimited' and 'eternal', can be predicated of God 'uniquely': only God is unlimited and eternal in the fullest senses of the words. Although other spirits can be said to be unlimited and eternal, this is not meant in the same way when it is said of God. Only God is *absolutely* unlimited and eternal. The way in which the absolute unlimitedness and eternity of God is established marks an important step for the understanding of the argument of the *Proslogion*. Anything postulated of God or ascribed to Him is done so in a unique way, since His attributes are of an absolute nature, and in that differ from those of other things.

§14.1 Anselm turns his attention to the issue of how the unknowable God can be known. The approach he takes is different from, but not inconsistent with, that of *M*65, where he addresses the question of how dialectic can attain to the truth concerning the ineffable.

§14.2 Anselm summarises the outcomes of the previous chapters. He has established that nothing better than God can be thought, and thus that God as X cannot be thought of as not existing. And yet, he is not satisfied by the argument. His reaction is not to doubt the validity or soundness of the argument – he is certain that its conclusion is true – but to investigate what this might indicate about his (and our) relationship with God. The tension between God 'in relation to us' and 'in relation to Himself' is made more explicit.

summum omnium – This does not mean that God is the greatest conceivable being. As Anselm argues in the next chapter (*P*15), the '*summum omnium*' is greater than can be conceived.

§14.3 Anselm believes his argument shows that God as X exists in the understanding, otherwise he could not have made the progress he did. To exist in the understanding means that the concept of God is understood and therefore understandable. But how can this be possible, if God is beyond our understanding? Part of the problem lies in the 'gap' between the conclusions of dialectic, even if true and certain, and the experience of that which is true and certain. Dialectic is not a way of experience. Finding God via dialectic is only a limited kind of finding God.

§14.4 Anselm considers whether it is possible that it is not God whom he has found.

lucem & veritatem – *Psalm* 42:3. Dialectic achieves what it does by means of God's light and truth, and insofar as one grasps the truth of the argument one sees God's light. But it is not a direct vision or experience of God. It is rather an indirect experience of that which makes possible any 'vision' at all.

§14.5 *aliquatenus* – Even this indirect 'vision' is only vision to some extent, not simply because of its indirectness, as Anselm goes on to show.

sicuti es – *1 John* 3:2.

§14.6 *quae nullae sunt inte* – *1 John* 1:5. Anselm cannot see beyond what he has seen, not because of God's darkness, but because of a darkness that is in him.

§14.7 Anselm identifies the root of the problem as the difference between God's greatness and man's smallness.

§14.8 It is precisely that which enlightens which is not seen. Its immensity is overwhelming and explains why it cannot be seen and why the full significance of its attributes cannot be grasped in thought. Anselm's language is reminiscent of Augustine's doctrine of divine illumination.[28] Note also Anselm's use of the phrase '*lux rationis*' in *M*6. In *M*65, Anselm writes that when we speak of or see

[28] Augustine, *De Trinitate*, XII, 15, 24.

the ineffable God, we can only do so through another, '*per aliquam similitudinem aut imaginem*'. This similitude or image is the rational mind, where God is seen, if only indirectly (*M*67).

§15.1 Having made the point that there is more to God than the creature can understand, Anselm goes on to show in this chapter how this claim is entailed in his argument.

§15.2 *quo maius cogitari nequit* – Anselm omits both *aliquid* and *id* from his formula (a usage he repeats frequently in the *Responsio*). Given his use of *quiddam* and *aliquid* in the remainder of this chapter, I have chosen to understand him to imply 'something' here.

It is not possible to think of something greater than God, therefore God must be greater than can be thought. For whatever is greater than can be thought is greater than the greatest that can be thought. It is here that the strength and weakness of dialectic when addressing the question of God becomes clear. The Christian God cannot fall under the Aristotelian categories, and thus dialectic cannot in the end define or grasp Him. Anselm here does not follow the advice of Augustine in *De Doctrina Christiana*, I, 6, 6, that it is better to avoid disputation on the question of the speakability and unspeakability of 'God'. The fact that Anselm's argument can produce, through the use of the middle term 'X', the conclusion that it is greater than can be thought, is further evidence that this X is to be identified with God, and that his method of dialectical argument is justified. It is when we know something of God that we realise that He is unknowable.

§16.1 Anselm returns to the theme of the inaccessible light (see *P*1 and *P*9), relating it to the notion that God is greater than can be thought.

§16.2 *lux inaccessibilis* – *1 Timothy* 6:16. See also Boethius, in *De Consolatione Philosophiae*, V, Prosa 3. Anselm must show that the scriptural image of God's inaccessibility is consistent with an argument that appears to have 'discovered' Him. This 'discovery' is one where the discovered is known but not experienced.

16.3 *per lucem solis* – In *DIV*1, Anselm identifies those who argue against Catholic doctrine with bats and owls that cannot look directly at the light of the sun. Although, in Anselm's theory of vision it is possible to see the light of the sun directly, here he speaks of the weak eye that cannot do this. This is the state of mankind's 'intellectual' vision. Being weak it cannot look directly at the light, but it can only see at all, because what it sees is made visible by the light. It transpires that Anselm's striving to see God, the light, is the striving to see the light that enables us to see. This is entirely consistent with and supports the argument of *M*66–67, that the search for God should take place where the light is reflected, i.e. in the rational mind, which is the mirror and image of God. We find further evidence of this understanding of the relation between God, the sun and light in the *Dicta Anselmi*:[29] 'For just as we experience the sun through sunlight before we see it rise, so we experience God in the reflection of our mind, when we perceive something true in the light of truth.' Not that even the saints shall ever

---

29 See R.W. Southern and F.S. Schmitt, *Memorials of St Anselm*, Oxford 1969, p. 148.

see God fully, even though they shall see him as He is, because He would not be immeasurable, if anyone's understanding could grasp Him.[30]

§16.4 In spite of everything he knows about God, which the rational mind can uncover by means of dialectic, Anselm makes it clear that the understanding cannot attain or grasp God, who is great beyond understanding.

§16.5 *Ubique* – The relationship between God and His creatures is not symmetrical. God sees us, but we cannot see Him. He is distant from us, although we are close to Him. Although He is everywhere, and in Him 'we live and move and have our being' (*Acts* 17:28), we do not experience Him. How then can Anselm know God is within him and around him? In his intellectual striving after God, Anselm has found Him in the activity of intellectual striving itself, has pushed language to the point where the very use of language is revealed as possessing a necessary affirmation of God. The light, which Anselm seeks, is 'experienced' as the condition for the possibility of any experience at all.

§17.1 This chapter continues the theme of God's light, and expands the imagery to cover the other senses.

§17.2 It is not only to sight that God lies hidden, but to all the other senses as well, and thus God cannot be experienced in any corporeal way.

§17.3 Since God is 'greater than can be thought', He must be ineffable, and so all these scriptural attributes of God (i.e. harmony, etc.) – though they would at first sight appear to be accessible to the senses and to human understanding – are ineffable too, and consequently do not impair God's identity with X.

vetusto languore peccati – Because of sin, the soul's senses have lost their sensitivity. They cannot experience God, who possesses in His 'own ineffable way' qualities which make Him experienceable, and which He has given to His creatures 'in their own sensible way'. Man, made in the image of God, has no direct experience of God, because of his sinfulness. It should be noted that in *P*14 the lack of a direct experience of God was explained in quite different terms, i.e. as a result of man's limitedness. If one is to make sense of these two claims, one must understand Anselm as meaning that our limitedness excludes the possibility of experiencing God's fullness, and our sinfulness the possibility of any explicit experience of God at all. Our experience of God is that of the fallen, who have lost God's grace. Of our own accord we cannot experience God. Such an experience is a gift of grace, which Adam possessed and then lost for us (see *P*1). Even the limited understanding of God attained through this *argumentum* is a gift.

§18.1 In talking in our limited way of God's attributes, we make it sound as if God is made up of different parts. Anselm addresses this question here.

§18.2 In spite of all his success in arguing about God, Anselm remains dissatisfied. It follows from *P*16–17 that any experience of God must be indirect, and thus open to ambiguity and ambivalence. Hence, it cannot provide lasting satisfaction. The language here recalls Anselm's words concerning Adam's prelapsarian abundance

[30] Ibid., p. 149.

in *P*1. Reason and dialectic cannot give back what Adam lost, only God can do that.

§18.3 *Ante cecidi, quam – Psalm* 50:7. Anselm realises that his failure to experience God is not his alone. In fact, he had failed before he had started. He failed with Adam's sin.

§18.4 As a result of Adam's fall, every step of our striving for God goes wrong, thus even faith in seeking goes wrong, as does understanding in finding. What is worse, when we obtain what we sought, we find that it is not what we sought. The experience of God is not what we expect, for we cannot experience God as we are made to on account of sin.

§18.5 Anselm asks for God's aid to continue his search. This passage is made up almost entirely of quotations from scripture: *Psalms* 24:7, 26:8–9, 12:4 and *Song of Songs* 6:12.

§18.6 Our inability to 'see' God arises from two things: our limited understanding and our sinfulness. God overcame our limitedness by giving Adam the grace to 'see' Him, but Adam by his sin lost that grace for himself and all his progeny. Thus, the situation is worse than it would have been before Adam was given the grace to 'see' God, because we are no longer just limited by our understanding, but also by the distorting and darkening effects of sin. The attempt to 'see' God requires another act of God's grace, to remove the effects of sin and to help us see what is beyond our understanding.

§18.7 Having asked for God's help, Anselm returns to the difficult question of how apparently distinct attributes can be ascribed to God, who is not made up of parts.

§18.8 For Anselm God's unity is essential for the absolute identity of God and X. Here Anselm argues that if God is made up of parts He is not that than which a better cannot be thought. It is because of the limited nature of human understanding that God cannot be perceived in one glance, and therefore His attributes have to be posited by us as distinct.

§18.9 *tues ipsa unitas* – Anselm makes it clear that there is no sense in which God can be said to be made up of parts. He is utterly indivisible. This argument reflects that of *M*17, where Anselm is concerned to show that whatever attributes can be predicated of God's essence are identical with each other, for God is simple.

§18.10 Having argued in *P*13 that God is everywhere simultaneously, Anselm is now able to clarify this claim: since there cannot be parts in God, when we say God is everywhere simultaneously, we mean that He is present at every place and time in His entirety. Thus, although the inadequacy of human language concerning God follows inevitably from man's limited understanding and God's unlimitedness, Anselm shows that it is still possible to make some progress in understanding God through the application of the art of dialectic.

§19.1 Anselm turns to another apparent problem, that even if God is entirely everywhere simultaneously He still appears to be circumscribed by space-time. In *P*13, he showed that God's unlimitedness and eternity are of a unique kind, different from that of any creature. In this chapter, he attempts to show the nature of the uniqueness of God's eternity.

§19.2 If, because God is eternal, we have to say that He has existed, does exist and will exist, the problem arises how these different times can be simultaneous, since God must exist wholly at all times.

§19.3 Anselm initially offers the Boethian solution that God dwells in an eternal present,[31] but immediately qualifies it by suggesting that even talking of God as existing in the present is misleading, since God exists outside of time.

§19.4 *non es tamen inloco aut tempore* – See the argument of *M*21–22 that God can be said to exist in no place and no time and in every place and time. Notions such as past, present and future are not applicable to God since they are internal to time. One has to say God always is, but God exists outside all spatio-temporal limitations.

tu contines omnia – Time and space can be said to exist in God, rather than God in them. Anselm reinforces the idea of God's transcendence, yet closeness. We are reminded of his words in *P*16.5: 'How distant You are from my sight, whilst I am so present to Your sight.' The relationship of God and man is from the divine perspective one of immanence, and from the human perspective one of transcendence. It is this immanence of God, which in man takes on a special significance, since he is created in the divine image, which makes possible the knowledge of God's transcendence.

§20.1 Anselm now seeks to explain in more detail the difference between God's eternity and that of creatures.

§20.2 *Psalm* 89:2. Following scripture Anselm uses the present tense in a context in which common usage would normally use the past, i.e. in referring to God's existence prior to that of the universe. He attempts to explain how it is possible to use the term 'before' in a context in which there is no time. God can be said to exist before creation, because He exists before it is made. He does not succeed in justifying this usage, because there can be nothing 'before', precisely because there is no time without creation. God exists out of time apart from creation, and does so whether creation exists or not.

§20.3 Anselm's discussion of how God can be said to be beyond other things addresses this issue more successfully. God is beyond other things, because He is not lessened by their non-existence, whereas they cannot exist without Him.

§20.4 The question remains as to how that which is really eternal can be said to have something that is beyond it. Anselm finds the answer in God's undeniability. Only the Creator cannot be thought not to exist. Even those created things that possess eternal existence can be thought not to exist, since creation can be thought of as not having taken place. In this sense they can be said to have an end, whereas God cannot, and is consequently beyond them.

§20.5 Following Boethius, Anselm also distinguishes between the eternity of God and that of creatures. According to Boethius, God's eternity is 'the total,

---

[31] See *De Consolatione Philosophiae*, V, Prosa 6.

simultaneous and perfect possession of unending life',[32] whereas the 'eternity' of the world does not involve such a complete possession, since it does not yet possess the future and no longer possesses the past. Although Anselm's discussion here bears a close resemblance to that of Boethius, it is worth noting that his vocabulary is different.

§20.6 At last, we can understand properly how God can be said to be beyond all things, even the 'eternal'. Since He is present at every time and place, He is present at those times and places that creatures have not yet arrived at. In this chapter Anselm has offered three complementary answers to the question: how can God be beyond all things? God is beyond these things, because (i) they cannot exist without Him, but He can exist without them, (ii) they can be thought to have an end, but He cannot, and (iii) He is 'always present in that place at which they have not yet arrived, or rather since it is always present to [Him]'. God's eternity is wholly present to Him, whilst their eternity is an endless movement, an endless discovery of new moments. God's unlimitedness is absolute, that of creation is relative and asymptotic. God is already and always 'there', creation is forever approaching 'there'. The implication of this view of God is that man can never finally understand Him, for there will always be new moments of discovery, God will always be beyond man, and consequently will always be 'greater than can be thought'.

§21.1 Anselm seeks to resolve the problem of how without contradiction God's eternity can be spoken of in scripture in both the singular and the plural.

§21.2 *saeculum saeculi* – This phrase occurs twenty-eight times in the *Psalms*, but only twice elsewhere (in *Isaiah* 45:17 and *Hebrews* 1:8).

saecula saeculorum – This phrase occurs thirteen times in the *Apocalypse*, and twelve times elsewhere in scripture.

Anselm here shows how dialectic can be used in scriptural exegesis. Through his analysis of the notion of God's eternity and that of creation in the previous chapters, he seeks to show that the singular usage (the age of the age) refers to God's eternity, whilst the plural usage (the ages of the ages) refers to God's containing of creation's perpetuity. God's eternity is singular because of its unity (the age) and plural because of its greatness (the ages).

§21.3 Anselm briefly alludes to the fact that, in the same way that God's eternity is not circumscribed by time, His greatness is not circumscribed by space. It is not possible to talk of God properly in spatial terms, just as it is not possible to talk of God properly in terms of the temporal.

§22.1 Anselm seeks to confirm God's uniqueness and unity, because if He is not unique and is made up of parts, then something greater than Him can be thought and He is not X.

§22.2 *tues qui es* – *Exodus* 3:14.

aliquid est mutabile – In *M*25, Anselm argues that God is not the subject of any accidents since accidents are properly speaking characterised by mutability. Here

32 Ibid.

he adds that this characteristic of mutability applies to that which is not fully what it is.

§22.3 *proprie & absolute* – All those attributes that do not apply to God, which Anselm has discussed in the previous chapters, e.g. coming into being, being able to be thought not to be, etc., are to be identified with that which does not exist properly and absolutely. Anselm here recalls the argument of *M*28: God's immutability means that He alone can be said to exist simply, absolutely and perfectly, and, in some sense, alone can be said to exist.

§22.4 It is because God is always wholly what He is and cannot be thought of in any other way, as Anselm has already shown, that He is said to exist truly, simply and properly.

tantum praesens esse – See Augustine, *Enarrationes in Psalmos*, 89, 3. Anselm follows Augustine in believing that God is substantially immutable, and that therefore He cannot be subject to the past, present and future of time. Although Anselm says here that God only has present existence, he makes it clear that this is not a presence in time.

§22.5 The God, X, who has been the subject of Anselm's argument is revealed more and more to be consistent with the God of Catholic belief, so that this statement of what this God is is also a statement of its identity with the God of Catholic belief.

summum bonum ... ut bene sint – Anselm 'repeats' the phrase from *P*0.2. He has accomplished the second of the tasks he set himself.

Not only God's unlimitedness and eternity, but also His existence is of an absolute kind, qualitatively different from that of other beings, which do not exist in a 'proper and absolute' sense, since they come from nothingness and will return there unless they are held in being by another. But God is always what He is, which follows from His absolute unity, maintained by Anselm in the previous chapter. God exists absolutely, for He is completely self-sufficient, whilst all other beings need Him.

§23.1 The third goal Anselm set for his argument in the Preface was to prove 'whatever else we believe about the divine substance'. In this chapter, he seeks to prove that the God of his argument is consistent with what Catholics believe about the Trinity, as he must do, if his argument is to be seen to work. However, Anselm does not attempt to repeat, except in the briefest form, what he had said about the Trinity in *M*29–63.

§23.2 *simplex* – The doctrine of God as Trinity appears to create a problem for Anselm's argument, because God as X must be simple. Anselm identifies God the Father with the *summum bonum* (see *P*22.5) that brings all things into existence. This Father begets a Word, His Son, who is identical with Him and is also the *summum bonum*.

§23.3 The *summum bonum* is also to be identified with the Holy Spirit, which is the love of Father and Son for each other. Anselm's argument here contains a statement of Catholic belief about the procession of the Holy Spirit, i.e. the

Holy Spirit proceeds 'from both' ('*abutroque*') the Father and the Son. (See *DPSS*, *passim*; also *M*57.)

§23.4 Anselm seeks to show the identity of the Persons of the Trinity with each other as the one God. If the Persons are different or distinct, then they cannot be identical and God cannot be the highest simplicity. This means that the Trinity itself is identical with each of the Persons, and is therefore simple and one.

§23.5 *unum est necessarium – Luke* 10:42. It is only in this chapter that Anselm explicitly introduces the notion of necessity, and that in relation to the unity of the Trinity. In *DIV*11, Anselm points out that the same set of properties cannot be applicable to diverse persons. The implication for Anselm's *argumentum* is that God and X are one, because the same set of properties is applicable to both.

§24.1 Having established the existence of X and its identity with the God of Catholic faith, Anselm considers the implications of the reality of this God, and what it means for the creature.

§24.2 *excita* – Anselm here recalls the *excitatio mentis* of *P*1, seeking to reflect on how great the *summum bonum* is.

§24.3 In language reminiscent of but not derived from Boethius, Anselm speaks of how the good is both the source of, and yet distinct from, other goods.

§24.4 In a series of rhetorical questions, Anselm stresses the qualitative difference between God (the *summum bonum*) and all other things: that that which creates, saves, is the source of wisdom, and which makes delightful things delightful, is even better, more delightful and more worthy of love.

§25.1 Anselm seeks to understand what the goodness of God means for his creatures, once they share His life in heaven. This chapter is full of scriptural allusions, as Anselm moves from expounding scripture through dialectic to expounding on the results of his dialectical argument by means of scripture.

§25.2 *quicquid volet erit* – Whatever man wills in heaven will come about, because his will is united with that of God.

nec cor hominis cogitavit – I Corinthians, 2:9.

§25.3 *homuncio* – As in the previous chapter, Anselm makes an allusion to the *excitatio mentis* of *P*1 through his reference to himself as 'little man'.

The one good, the unique good, is the only real good. For Anselm we can now understand and not simply believe how God is the only good who alone satisfies our desires. The *unum argumentum* has led to the *unum necessarium*, which is the *unum bonum*.

§25.4 Man's end is with God in heaven, and whatever he loves or desires is to be found there with God. There follows a scriptural reflection, in which Anselm considers what this statement means for those who possess God, whose being and attributes his argument has confirmed. Anselm lists the different physical and spiritual goods that men seek and shows how in God they find their real and transformed fulfilment.

§25.5 *Matthew* 13:43.

§25.6 *Matthew* 22:30 and *I Corinthians* 15:44.

§25.7 *Wisdom* 5:16 and *Psalm* 36:39.

§25.8 *Psalm* 16:15.
§25.9 *Psalm* 35:9a.
§25.10 Here Anselm departs from the series of scriptural quotations and makes reference to the Preface for Pentecost in the *Roman Missal*: '*angelicae potestates hymnum gloriae tuae concinunt sine fine.*'
§25.11 *Psalm* 35:9b.
§25.12 Although there is no direct citing of a particular text here, this sentence is clearly influenced by the first chapter of *Ecclesiasticus*, especially verses 6–7.
§25.13 Here Anselm mentions the term '*amicitia*', which occurs more than 200 times in the works of Cicero, and which in *James* 4:4 is identified with opposition to God: '*amicitia huius mundi inimica est Dei*'. This earthly love will be transformed in heaven into that love to which Jesus calls men in *Mark* 12:29–31 and *Matthew* 22:37–39.
§25.14 In *Ecclesiasticus* 25:2, concord is identified as one of the things that pleases God's spirit. It is because in heaven man's will is united with God's that Anselm was able to say in *P*25.2 that whatever he shall will shall be.
§25.15 Even the desire for power will be transformed by the uniting of man's will with God, in which he will share God's omnipotence. Since whatever God wills must come to pass, and whatever He does not will cannot happen
§25.16 *Matthew* 25:21, 23, *Psalm* 81:6, *Matthew* 5:9, *John* 14:3 and *Romans* 8:17. The pursuit of worldly wealth and honour is transformed into the spiritual inheritance of Christ.
dii – Peter Damian saw the use of the plural of *deus* as an invention of the serpent (whom he equates with the *artifex doctor*, i.e. the teacher of the liberal arts) in *Genesis* 3:5.[33] Anselm may obliquely be criticising this view here.
§25.17 Man will experience true security in heaven, since it will not be possible for him to lose the good. *Romans* 8:38–39.
§25.18 Anselm returns to himself from the *excitatio* and considers the great joy that awaits those who currently suffer and are afflicted.
§25.19 The greater the number of those who themselves share in the blessedness and joy of heaven, the greater will be the joy of each one of them.
§25.20 Anselm asks how it will be possible for the human heart to contain all this joy. For not only will he experience the joy of all men, but will share in God's joy which is even greater.
§25.21 *Matthew* 22:37. In loving God as completely as humanly possible, the return (the joy) itself will be more than the human can encompass. We shall never experience God's love completely, but the experience we have of this love draws us on eternally towards Him. As we shall see in the final chapter of the *Proslogion*, Anselm has to address the scriptural statement that 'your joy will be full'. Although God's joy may fill us, we cannot contain it. God is not simply the greatest that we can experience, but is also greater than we can experience.

---

[33] *De Sancta Simplicitate*, 1.

§26.1 Anselm asks whether the fullness of joy he has just described is what God has promised. In *CDH*II:1, Anselm states that rational nature was created so that rejoicing in God it might be blessedly happy.
This chapter of the *Proslogion* has to be approached with more care and attention than is usually paid to it. It is not simply a prayer appended to the book, but contains a statement about the result of the 'search' that the book describes, a statement most fittingly in the form of a prayer, given that result.
§26.2 *John* 16:24. This discussion of joy brings us back to the beginning of the *Proslogion*, where Anselm alluded to *Isaiah* 7:9 '*Nisi credideritis, non intelligetis*'. In an important passage in Augustine entitled, 'The incomprehensible God is always to be sought',[34] we find a discussion of whether joy comes from seeking or finding. Augustine quotes *Ecclesiasticus* 24:29 that those who eat and drink God will still hunger and thirst. In searching for the incomprehensible God, we find that we can make progress, that what we search for is not nothing, but that of course we can never comprehend it. The task is to understand what we can in an unending search after God. In fact, according to Augustine the purpose of understanding is to seek God. In *P*14, Anselm asked how it was that he had both seen and not seen, found and not found God. The answer lies in the incomprehensible nature of God and in the fullness of joy that those who find Him experience, which completely overwhelms them. It more than fills them, and they cannot contain it.
§26.3 Thus, the fullness of joy cannot enter into man, but man can enter into the fullness of joy.
§26.4 *Matthew* 25:21, 23.
Again, Anselm seeks to determine what scripture says about this joy.
§26.5 *I Corinthians* 2:9.
For Anselm the reality of the divine life is beyond the capacity of any human word or concept to convey meaning. In the final analysis, even language which employs phrases such as '*supra modum*', since it is the language of approximation concerning the absolute, must fail to uncover the reality that it is striving to reach. In spite of all he has written and all he has experienced, Anselm states that what he has understood still remains unknown to him. It is the inadequacy of the human capacity for experiencing the divine (through its sinfulness and limitedness), which explains why the argument does not satisfy Anselm. It must necessarily be unsatisfactory, if it is an argument about the real God.
§26.6 Anselm repeats the allusion to *I Corinthians* 2:9. What is said there concerning joy is also true of love and knowledge of God. We in this life cannot imagine how great that will be in heaven.
§26.7 For Anselm the purpose of knowing and loving God is to experience the fullness of joy in heaven. We cannot have this experience in this life, except in the form of intimations. We can come closer to it, but not attain it. Thus, his argument can bring us closer to knowledge of God, but cannot attain for us that knowledge,

[34] *De Trinitate*, XV, 2, 2.

because even logically sound arguments do not possess the capacity to deliver to us in His fullness the God who is our final end.

§26.8 See Augustine, *Sermo* XXI, 1. The point is not to be discouraged, but to seek to make progress in knowing and loving God, in hopeful anticipation of the fullness of joy to be experienced in heaven. In this section Anselm appears to contradict what he has said about man's relationship with God in earlier chapters. He suggests that in heaven our knowledge of God will be 'full', appearing to deny the asymptotic character of man's relationship with God. The contradiction is only apparent, for he does not know what this fullness could mean. It is a fullness that goes beyond our understanding of fullness, a fullness that overflows.

§26.9 *John* 16:23f. Anselm fulfils the injunction of Jesus that he should ask so that he may receive. It is only in his asking and in God's giving that Anselm will understand the significance of his argument.

§26.10 *desideret* – Anselm's conclusion is reminiscent of the words of Augustine in *De Libero Arbitrio*, II, 2, 6: 'All these things are to be desired and loved now.' We are to believe and love the things that others understand more fully than us, so that we may experience them in the next life.

The limited success of his argument does not discourage Anselm. His realisation is that if it is sound, then its success must be limited.

Matthew 25:21, 23 and *Romans* 1:25.

§26.11 Anselm believes he has established the existence of God and the nature of His attributes. Although God as X is a legitimate subject of dialectical investigation, He is greater than any dialectician can grasp. It took Anselm most of the *Proslogion* to establish the identity of God and X. It is only towards the end of his investigation, with his realisation of its limits, that Anselm can claim to have achieved what he set out to do.

Chapter 5
Anselm's Defence and the *Unum Argumentum*

Introduction

In this chapter, I shall look at Anselm's defence in the *Responsio* of his argument against the objections presented in the *Pro Insipiente*, a work traditionally ascribed to a monk named Gaunilo. My purpose here is not to reiterate the text of the debate, but to shed light on what Anselm was doing in the *Proslogion*. The *Responsio* shows that:

(i) the *Proslogion* was intended as a 'philosophical' argument, the understanding of which was accessible to anyone who possessed the power of understanding;
(ii) the identity of God and X is central to the argument of the *Proslogion*;
(iii) God as X is a special case, which creates a problem for objections employing a similar logical form;
(iv) terms which are perfectly legitimate in themselves when applied to God, e.g. 'greater than everything' and 'necessarily existent', cannot be substituted for the terms that Anselm uses, such as X and 'that which cannot be thought not to exist'; and
(v) the argument of the *Proslogion* is concerned with the act of thinking about God and not merely with an analysis of the concept of God.

Anselm's defence of his argument in the *Responsio* is not a restatement or development of the *Proslogion*, but nevertheless does help to clarify what Anselm meant by the term '*unum argumentum*'. In the final section of this chapter, I attempt to provide an account of the form and structure of Anselm's argument, insofar as it is possible to reconstruct it.

The *Pro Insipiente* and its Author

Neither Anselm nor his biographer, Eadmer, refer to the author of the *Pro Insipiente* by name. Anselm appears to be unaware of the identity of the author, given the manner in which he addresses him at the beginning of his *Responsio*: 'Indeed you say – whoever you are …'. Eadmer refers to Anselm's opponent simply as 'someone'.[1]

[1] Eadmer, *Life*, p. 31.

However, this may be a literary conceit, and it is not impossible that Anselm knew who the author was, or even that the *Pro Insipiente* was the product of Anselm's own 'school' (as perhaps is the second half of the *Responsio*, *R*5–10). Whatever is the case, it is certain that the author was not an unbeliever, since, in spite of his claim to be speaking on behalf of the fool, in *Pro Insipiente*, 7.8 (=*G*7.8) he states: 'I understand indubitably that that which is supreme, namely God, truly both exists and cannot not exist.'

Of the extant early manuscripts, only one mentions Gaunilo as the author of the *Pro Insipiente*, a late eleventh century/early twelfth century manuscript from Jumièges, now in Rouen – Ms 539 (A 366). This is presumably one of the two manuscripts referred to in Migne: '*In mss. Gemmeticensi et Sancti Michaelis notatur hujus libri auctor fuisse Gaunilo monachus Majoris-Monasterii, vulgo, Mair-Moutier*'.[2] This, then, would appear to be the basis of the tradition of Gaunilo's authorship, but as there is no separate manuscript tradition for the *Pro Insipiente* to that originating with Anselm at Bec (not even at Marmoutiers), it is possible that this ascription is the result of a scribal fancy.

The preservation of the text of the *Pro Insipiente* is due to Anselm's own action. Eadmer relates how Anselm requested that anyone who wanted to make a copy of the *Proslogion* should append to it copies of the *Pro Insipiente* and Anselm's *Responsio*.[3] Southern points out that since all the earliest copies of the *Proslogion* also contain the *Pro Insipiente*, the latter must have been produced very shortly after the *Proslogion*.[4] This is perhaps evidence that it had its origins at Bec. The *Pro Insipiente* is a response to *P*2–4, the *Sumptum*. In B, the scribe indicates this by placing it after the *Sumptum*, with the inscription: 'How someone might reply to these [words] on behalf of the fool.' The author of the *Pro Insipiente* also makes it clear that he is only responding to part of the *Proslogion*, saying in *G*8.1: 'The remainder of this little book is argued so truthfully and so clearly and magnificently.'

Anselm's *Responsio*

When we compare Anselm's *Responsio* with the *Proslogion*, we see a marked difference in the style of the two works and, even more significantly, variations in the arguments employed. Given that there exists little development in Anselm's writings generally (they are all the products of his mature thought), and the shortness of the period between the composition of the two works, the differences between them must be explained, not by any change of view on Anselm's part, but on other grounds. The form of the *Responsio* is dictated by the content of the *Pro Insipiente*, whose major objections Anselm is concerned to answer. However, in one extremely important respect, his *Responsio* diverges from addressing the

2 *PL*158 coll. 241/242 n. 930.

3 Eadmer, *Life*, p. 31.

4 Southern, *Saint Anselm*, p. 65.

avowed intention of the *Pro Insipiente*. Anselm is concerned to argue, not against the fool, but against the Catholic who argues on the fool's behalf: 'may it suffice for me to reply to the Catholic' (*G*1.1). This is not because Anselm has missed the point of the *Pro Insipiente*, but rather because the latter is not really arguing on behalf of the fool at all. Its purpose is clearly to argue from the perspective of the Catholic who does not accept that Anselm provides an indubitable proof of God's existence.

Anselm states explicitly at the beginning of his *Responsio* that the *Proslogion* was directed against the fool, i.e. the unbeliever: 'the fool, against whom I spoke in my little work.' The traditional view that the *Responsio* is the more philosophical work must be turned on its head. It will become clear when we look at the details of Anselm's defence that the argument takes place in the context of a shared faith. Thus, Anselm's main thrust in the *Responsio* is to show those persuaded by the argument of the *Pro Insipiente* that what must be said of X must also be said of God, and that consequently the objections put forward against Anselm's argument are not consistent with Catholic belief. The argument of the *Proslogion*, on the other hand, is intended to meet any doubt or denial concerning the existence and nature of God. It is not a debate with the fool in the sense that it looks at his arguments for saying there is no God and attempts to refute them. Anselm rather seeks to take *anyone* through a process at the end of which the denial of God is seen to make no sense. For Anselm the soundness of his argument is recognisable whether one is a believer or not.

Anselm's Defence

The main objections that Anselm addresses in the *Responsio* are found in *G*4, *G*5.1–3, *G*6 and *G*7. Anselm replies to them in this order: to *G*4 and *G*5.1–3 in *R*l and *R*2, to *G*6 in *R*3 and to *G*7 in *R*4. Anselm deals at greatest length with the objections in *G*4 and *G*5.1–3, which concern the sense in which X is 'in the understanding' and what follows from this. The reason for this approach is clear. The main thrust of the *Pro Insipiente* is that God and X are not to be identified (an objection more easily made since it ignores those parts of the *Proslogion* where this identification is established). Anselm's primary purpose in the *Responsio* is to show that such an identification is unavoidable. For Anselm two possibilities follow from his opponent's objections: either we can have an idea of God, but He is not supreme, or He is supreme, but we can have no idea of Him. These options are ones which a Catholic must regard as opposed to his faith and conscience (*R*1.4).

Before turning to the argument of *R*1 and *R*2 in which Anselm meets the objections of *G*4 and *G*5.1–3, I shall present first a synopsis of the arguments of the *Pro Insipiente* in these sections:[5]

[5] I shall abbreviate as Y the phrase '*maius omnibus*' and its variants, which are used by the author of the *Pro Insipiente* as an alternative to X.

(1) Y can no more be thought of or possessed in the understanding 'in the manner of something known to me under the categories of species or genus' than can God, who, therefore, can be thought not to exist (*G*4.1).

(2) For this thing is not known, nor can an idea of it be gained by comparison with other things (*G*4.2),

(3) since, as Anselm maintains, 'there cannot be anything similar to it' (*G*4.2).

(4) Neither God nor Y exists in thought or in the understanding 'in terms of something true and known to me', but as 'the sound of letters or syllables' (*G*4.5).

(5) But thinking of any true thing is thinking about the meaning of the word (*G*4.5).

(6) Y is not thought of 'in the way that someone who knows what is customarily signified by the word thinks of something, who at least thinks of it in terms of something true in thought alone' (*G*4.5).

(7) 'Rather, it is thought of in the way of someone who does not know that thing and only thinks of it in terms of an activity in his soul' (*G*4.5).

Having dealt with Y in the understanding, the author of the *Pro Insipiente* moves on to treat of Y in reality:

(8) Anselm claims to have proved that Y 'necessarily exists in reality' from the fact that otherwise really existent things would be greater than it, and thus it would not be that greater than everything which had already been proved to exist in the understanding (*G*5.1).

(9) However, if something exists in the understanding in the sense of point (7), I do not deny that it is in the understanding (*G*5.2).

(10) But, since to be in the understanding in this way cannot lead to a conclusion about existence in reality (*G*5.3).

(11) I will not concede that it exists, unless this is proven by an 'indubitable argument' (*G*5.3).

The aim of the author of the *Pro Insipiente* in *G*4 is to maintain that there is no significant sense in which Y can be thought of or be in the understanding. It follows that Anselm cannot provide a proof concerning the actual existence of Y (G5). In spite of these objections, Anselm insists that, 'if [X] can be thought at all, it is necessary that it exists' (*R*1.12). (Anselm reserves the task of explaining that X is not the same as Y for the section of the book which deals with obvious weaknesses in the *Pro Insipiente*.) It is interesting to note that Anselm had not used the word 'necessary' in this way in the *Proslogion*. The author of the *Pro Insipiente* had introduced the idea of necessary existence: 'it is then also proved to me that this necessarily exists in reality' (*G*5.1). Anselm does not dispute this use of 'necessary'. In *R*1, he states three times that X necessarily exists, but always in conjunction with the conditional, 'if it can be thought'. Anselm argues that if X can be thought of as existing, it exists necessarily (*R*1.7). For X cannot be thought of as having a beginning, and what can be thought of as existing, but does not exist can be thought of as having a beginning (*R*1.8–9). However, someone may refuse to accept that X can be thought of as existing, so he goes on to argue, that if X can simply be thought of, it necessarily exists (*R*1.12). If X were to exist, it could not not exist either actually or intellectually, otherwise it would not be X (*R*1.13–14). 'But whatever can be thought and does not exist, if it were to exist, would be able not to exist either in actuality or in the understanding' (*R*1.15). Therefore, if X can be thought, it cannot not exist (*R*1.16). Even if we attempt to postulate the non-existence of X, we are led to conclude that it is not X whose non-existence we have actually postulated. For, if something's non-existence is postulated, it is not X, for something greater than it can be thought, i.e. something whose non-existence cannot be postulated (*R*1.17–19). Anselm's argument proceeds from the possibility of thinking of X as existing to its necessary existence, because X cannot be thought of as having a beginning, i.e. as not existing.

How are we to evaluate these arguments for the necessary existence of X? We should note that Anselm's argument here concerns X and not God. It is clear from the beginning of the *Responsio*, that he wishes to prove the identity of X and God. He has already tried to show the author of the *Pro Insipiente* that to deny this identity goes against his faith. Now he is trying to show that there must be a sense in which X says something about God. If X cannot be thought of as having a beginning (a characteristic clearly shared with God), it exists necessarily. The reason for this conclusion lies in the apparent identification of 'necessary existence' with 'cannot be thought of as not existing'. Although Anselm had avoided talking of 'that which cannot be thought not to exist' as 'necessarily existent' in the *Proslogion*, he makes this identification here. In this context, 'necessarily existent' refers to that whose existence has no beginning, which is a peculiar characteristic of 'that which cannot be thought not to exist' as opposed to other 'necessarily existent' things, which are dependent on 'that which cannot be thought not to exist' for their existence.

In *R*1, Anselm does not attempt to justify the claim that X can be thought. The meaningfulness of X cannot be a problem for the Catholic, so it should not be necessary to show that X can be thought, except when dealing with the unbeliever. It is only in *R*8 that Anselm provides an explanation of how X can be thought in some significant sense.

The remainder of *R*1 concerns the idea that there are no spatial or temporal parts in X, but that X exists as a whole at every time and in every place. Whilst God is the subject of such discussions in the *Proslogion*, in the *Responsio* they concern X. If we remember the words of *G*8.1: 'The remainder of this little book is argued so truthfully … that in no way should it be condemned on account of those assertions at the beginning', and that the author of the *Pro Insipiente* already accepts in *G*7.8 that God cannot be understood not to exist, then we can see precisely what Anselm is doing in *R*1. He is demonstrating that what is said of God in *P*18–20, which the author of the *Pro Insipiente* accepts, must also be said of X. It cannot be objected that the same language does not make sense when applied to X, but does make sense when applied to God. Since the author of the *Pro Insipiente* understands that God necessarily exists, he must also understand that X necessarily exists, and that consequently his objections are unsuccessful.

At the end of *R*l, Anselm asks his opponent whether he now considers that X 'can in some way be thought or understood'. He continues: 'For if it cannot, then these things concerning it cannot be understood', things which his opponent has already accepted can be understood of God. However, if he still (inconsistently) says that X cannot be understood because they cannot be fully understood, 'you might as well say that he who cannot look at the pure light of the sun does not see daylight, which is nothing other than the light of the sun' (*R*1.37). The opponent is misled by the fact that the terms, 'God' and 'X', are apparently different. As words, they are. However, their meaning is the same (as is the meaning of 'sunlight' and 'daylight') and it is this that gives the force to Anselm's argument in the *Proslogion* and to his response to the *Pro Insipiente*.[6]

In *R*2, Anselm continues his treatment of *G*4 and *G*5.1–3, making closer reference to the actual arguments put forward there. He begins by suggesting that the understanding of X is not a problem even for the fool unless he is incapable of understanding anything. However, Anselm goes on to answer the objection of *G*4.5 that X (which for the sake of argument he continues to equate with Y) only exists in the understanding as something unknown, and therefore as not understood. The inconsistency of Anselm's opponent is once more revealed, since to understand and to be in the understanding have the same meaning (*R*2.7). He must accept that X is understood, since he accepts that it is in the understanding.

Anselm then suggests in reply to *G*5.3 that the step he took in *P*2, from the existence of X in the understanding to its existence in reality is perfectly coherent. He presents a similar argument to that at the beginning of *P*3. If X exists only in the understanding it is not X. But for any understanding, not-X is not X. It follows that if X exists in any understanding, it does not exist only in the understanding, for then it would be not-X. This is not a restatement of the *unum argumentum*, but rather a clarification of elements of the argument disputed by Anselm's opponent. Once the latter has accepted that X can be in the understanding meaningfully, then he cannot coherently avoid concluding that it cannot be even thought not to exist. And, since this can only be said of God, and he understands that God cannot not exist, he must agree that X is to be identified with God and 'does not exist in the understanding alone' (*R*2.16).

*R*3 contains Anselm's refutation of the lost island argument (*G*6). This objection, similar in form to Anselm's argument, was employed to show the impossibility of providing a proof from the mere idea of something. The author of the *Pro Insipiente* envisages a lost island, whose wealth excels that of all other lands. He can easily understand what is meant by such a concept. However, if someone were to conclude that it existed 'somewhere in reality', because otherwise any other land that exists in reality would be greater than it, he would not be able to take him seriously. He must first be convinced that it actually exists, and does not exist in the understanding as 'something false or uncertain', before he can be convinced that it is more excellent than other lands.

---

6 See *DG*4: it is the meaning rather than the words that give force to a syllogism.

Anselm's answer to his opponent is to stress that his argument cannot apply to anything other than X. The similarity of form has misled his opponent. In a reference back to his earlier arguments in *R*1, Anselm states: 'Moreover, it has already clearly been seen that something than which a greater cannot be thought, which exists by such certain logic and truth, cannot be thought not to exist. For otherwise it would in no way exist' (*R*3.3–4). The meaning of this last phrase becomes clearer if we look at his conclusion: 'Therefore, he who thinks [X], thinks something which cannot be thought not to exist. Clearly, he who thinks this, does not think that this very thing does not exist. Otherwise he is thinking what cannot be thought' (*R*3.10–12). The first statement (*R*3.3–4) refers to the object of thought, and the second to the one who thinks (*R*3.10–12). Anselm is putting forward the principle that if one is forced to conclude that one has to say or think that God exists, then one has to say or think, 'God exists'. X cannot be thought not to exist. To think it cannot exist is to think the unthinkable. Anselm is insistent on this assertion both in the *Proslogion* and in the *Responsio*. X cannot be thought not to exist, because the condition governing the possibility of thinking the concept, X, is that X is understood and understood to exist. This explains further Anselm's use of the verb 'to think' in the second statement above. If one tries to think that X does not exist, then a contradiction arises between what is thought and the active process of thinking it; what Coreth called 'a contradiction in performance'.[7] It is obvious that there is a sense in which X can be thought not to exist, but thinking in this way is of no significance. It is simply employing the concept without content, or, if one uses the concept with content, it is knowingly to postulate a contradiction. Anselm has made explicit this 'contradiction in performance' by means of an analysis of the act of thinking about God, and not simply by an analysis of the concept of God.

Central to Anselm's response to the lost island parody and to the other objections of the *Pro Insipiente* is the idea that X is a special case. This is not an arbitrary assertion, but follows from the results of his dialectical procedure. It is only in the case of X that certain things follow; it is only the existence of the supremely existent that can be established by this argument. Islands and all those things that exist and do not exist in their entirety in all places and times, that have a beginning or are dependent on something else for their existence, cannot be made the subject of the *ratio Anselmi*.

In *R*4, Anselm treats of the objection in *G*7 to the use of the verb 'to think' rather than 'to understand', in the statement, the 'supreme reality cannot be thought not to exist'. The author of the *Pro Insipiente* equates understanding with understanding that something exists in reality (*G*2.2), a view Anselm does not hold, since false things can be understood. Anselm sees clearly that given this meaning of 'to understand', if he were to say that X cannot be understood not to exist, then his opponent would object 'that nothing that exists can be understood

---

7 E. Coreth, 'Dialectic of performance and concept', in F.E. Crowe, *Spirit as Inquiry: Studies in Honor of Bernard Lonergan*, Minnesota 1964, pp. 147–54, p. 153.

not to exist'. The implication of this would be that 'not to be able to be thought not to exist' would not be uniquely applicable to God, but would apply equally to any existing thing that was understood. On the other hand, if it were possible to understand the non-existence of anything which certainly existed, then God could be understood not to exist. Anselm writes, 'this objection cannot be raised against thought, if it is considered properly' (*R*4.6). For everything that has a beginning or an end, is made up of parts, or does not exist wholly everywhere and always, can be thought not to exist. Only in the case of the supreme being which is not such a thing can this not be thought. Thus, his opponent must accept that God cannot be thought not to exist, and, since this description also fits X, then neither can X be thought not to exist. Once again Anselm has tried to establish that what his opponent must say of God, if he draws the correct inferences from his argument, he must also say of X.

Anselm expresses surprise at his opponent's suggestion in *G*7.9 that he does not know if he can think of himself as not existing. In fact, 'we can think that something does not exist, while we know that it does exist', since knowing and thinking are not the same operation (*R*4.12). However, we cannot simultaneously think of something as existing and not existing. It is only God as X that cannot be thought not to exist, when the distinction between knowing and thinking is made, since the possession of the concept of X in thought in any meaningful sense already presupposes that it is understood to exist. In this sense, it is a distinguishing characteristic of God that He cannot be thought not to exist (*R*4.15). God can be thought not to exist only in the sense indicated in *P*4.

Anselm originally ended the *Responsio* at *R*4.16, adding the later sections as a reply to those elements of the *Pro Insipiente* that he had considered unworthy of a response. From *R*5 onwards the style changes and the sentences become less polished and longer. The difference between the two sections is sufficiently great to suggest that Anselm was not the sole author of the *Responsio*, and that parts of it may have been a product of the schoolroom. Note how in *R*7.1 Anselm says: 'Those who have attained even a little knowledge of disputation and argument might reply on my behalf' – a reference perhaps to those who are students of dialectic at Bec. The lesser objections do not require someone who is wise to answer them (*R*5.1). Given that the *Pro Insipiente* and the *Responsio* were produced very soon after the *Proslogion* (all the early manuscripts contain them) and the controversy and opposition within Bec (the likeliest explanation of the fate of the early wax tablet drafts of the argument), it is quite possible that these later chapters were a product of debate amongst Anselm's students (guided by Anselm), seeking to answer the outstanding objections of the *Pro Insipiente*, objections which they themselves may also have generated. The 'certain readers', who had wanted him to elaborate on his response to the objections, may also have included his students.

In *R*5, Anselm finally points out that X and Y are not equivalent for the purposes of his proof. The two terms do not function in the same way. Consequently, any conclusions arrived at in relation to Y constitute *non sequiturs* when applied to X. Y cannot be incorporated into an argument of the logical form used in the

Proslogion to prove X without adding further steps to the argument. It might be possible, even if 'the greater than everything' existed, that something greater than it could be thought, even if the latter did not exist. However, since X is understood and is in the understanding, and therefore its existence in reality is affirmed, the conclusion that 'the greater than everything' exists in reality is true. In other words, the proof of the latter (Y) is dependent on that of the former (X), whereas there is no reciprocal dependence of X on Y.

Holopainen has suggested that in *R*5, Anselm equates the *unum argumentum* with X.[8] However, as we saw in Chapter 2, Anselm's use of the term '*argumentum*' is not clearly differentiated from that of '*argumentatio*'. In fact, the evidence points to the *unum argumentum* being the proof of God based on the proof of X (see below). In *R*5.16 Anselm does not equate X with the *unum argumentum*, but with the category of argument that the *unum argumentum* falls under.

In *R*6, Anselm explains that the objection that X is in the understanding in the same way as unreal or doubtfully real things is irrelevant. For, even if one attempts to postulate X as in the understanding in this sense, one discovers that, if one has understood it correctly, it is already understood as existing. He also points out the inconsistency in the notion of 'to understand' in the *Pro Insipiente*. The author has said he can understand unreal things and also that to understand something is to know with certainty that it exists.

Anselm then indicates in *R*7 why he employed X in his proof, rather than God. It is possible to have no idea of what the word God means, whereas the meaning of X is directly accessible to the hearer, if only partially understood or understandable.

According to Anselm (*R*8), the objection that X is not like the unexecuted picture in the painter's mind serves no good purpose. Anselm had used this image, not as a direct analogy in relation to X, but rather to show that something can be both in the understanding and understood not to exist. The remainder of *R*8 concerns the meaningfulness of X in reply to the objection in *G*4.1–2. We can conjecture much about X by comparison with those things than which a greater can be thought, 'ascending' from the less good to the more good. Thus, according to Anselm, if something that has a beginning and an end is good, then that which is without beginning is better, and that which is without beginning or end is even better, even if its eternity is sequential. And 'that which is in no way lacking nor is thought to change or to be in motion is very much better than [that]'. In this way, the concept of X can be formed 'from those things than which something greater can be thought'. If the fool says that to form such a concept is impossible, he 'can easily be refuted'. Whereas, the Catholic should remember the words of *Romans* 1:20, that God is understood through his creation. If the author of the *Pro Insipiente* can form a concept of God, then he must also be able to form a concept of X.

---

8 T. Holopainen, 'Anselm's *Argumentum* and the Early Medieval Theory of Argument', in *Vivarium*, 45 (2007) 1–29, 24.

In *R*9, Anselm makes an important distinction between the object of which X is the concept and the concept itself. Although the former can never be grasped by thought, just as the object that is qualified as ineffable or unthinkable can never be grasped by thought, it is still possible to think and understand it in the same way that we think and understand the concepts, 'ineffable' or 'unthinkable'. In the same way, 'X' can be thought, although its object is beyond thought. Anyone who says X does not exist, 'understands and thinks of the denial that he makes'. He must understand and think of X, in order to deny it. But, when someone thinks of X as able not to exist, it is not X he is thinking of, since 'not to be able not to exist' is greater than 'to be able not to exist'. The same thing cannot be thought and not thought simultaneously. When one thinks of X one thinks of something that cannot not exist. 'Therefore, it is necessary that what he thinks exists, because whatever is able not to exist, is not what he thinks' (*R*9.14). This explains how it is that X is undeniable.

Anselm began his argument in the *Proslogion* with a discussion of the possibility of the non-existence of X, and established in *P*3 that it cannot be thought not to exist. Here, he concludes that X exists necessarily from the fact of the inconceivability of its non-existence. In fact, as we have already seen, the two phrases 'necessarily existent' and 'not able to be thought not to exist' are treated here by Anselm as having the same meaning, the former phrase being drawn from the *Pro Insipiente* and its meaning subsumed under the latter. Central to Anselm's argument is the claim that there is no conceivable state of affairs in which the existence of X can be denied meaningfully. This is not so much an ontological assertion as a statement concerning the conditions governing an ontological assertion.

Anselm begins the final section (*R*10) by stating that the argument of the *Proslogion* was successful and remains unrefuted. In his *Responsio*, Anselm has been concerned to clarify the nature of the argument in the *Proslogion* in the light of certain misunderstandings of it, and not to reformulate the *unum argumentum*. If Anselm had needed to reformulate it, then this would be to admit some weakness in it, something he is not prepared to do.

The *unum argumentum* aims to establish that X 'which is of necessity understood and thought of by itself' (*R*10.2) is proved to exist in reality and to be whatever ought to be believed about the divine substance. The force of the argument is not found in the analysis of the concept, X, but is revealed in the analysis of the act of understanding or thinking which grasps the concept. Anselm ends his *Responsio* with a reiteration of the identity of X and the 'divine essence', which was the basis of his answer to the objections of the Catholic.

Our detailed consideration of Anselm's response to the objections of the *Pro Insipiente* makes two further points clear. Firstly, Anselm is concerned primarily with arguing the case for the Christian acceptance of the possibility of a rational proof of God's existence. Anselm shows that the objections fail from a Catholic perspective, because they are objections to any thought about God. Thus, the *Responsio* does not constitute a restatement or development of the *Proslogion*. It has a different purpose and is the secondary of the two works. Secondly, the notion of 'necessary existence', introduced into the debate in the *Pro Insipiente*, is employed by Anselm precisely because it is part of the argument of his opponent. The argument of the *Proslogion* did not require such terminology. For Anselm, terms like 'existing necessarily' and 'greater than everything' may be legitimately applied to God. However, they have no place within the framework of the *unum argumentum*, because, when applied to God, they derive their real meaning from the notions of 'that which cannot be thought not to exist' and 'that than which a greater cannot be thought', but fail to convey the full significance of these notions.

The *unum argumentum*

The *Responsio* can help us to clarify what Anselm meant when he spoke of the *unum argumentum*. I have already mentioned Anselm's use of the term *argumentum* in *R*5 and the suggestion that it is to be equated with X. Other suggestions are that it is to be equated with the proof(s) of *P*2–3. But neither of these positions is justified, since Anselm's argument was intended as a proof that *God* exists. Of course, Anselm introduces *P*2 by saying that we believe that God is X, but he says in *P*0.2 that he is going to prove what we believe about the divine substance, including that God exists, so clearly neither this statement of *belief*, nor the proof concerning *X*, even when combined can deliver what Anselm sets out to achieve.

In the *Responsio*, the issue of the identity of God and X is revealed to be one of the key elements of Anselm's argument, and this has important implications for what constitutes the *unum argumentum*. Leaving aside the possibility (a) that the *unum argumentum* is simply to be identified with the *Proslogion*, since Anselm says that he is going to talk about other things (*P*Preface) and in fact does so (see, for example, *P*1, *P*25, *P*26) and (b) that Anselm is confused about the term '*unum argumentum*' (for this view can only follow an attempt to understand what the *unum argumentum* is), it seems that there are four options for what constitutes the *unum argumentum*.

[A] A categorical syllogism of the form:
  1. God is X (minor premise)
  2. X is F (major premise)
  3. Therefore, God is F (conclusion)

(F stands for 'existent *in re*' or any attribute of God.)

[B] A *reductio* argument of the form:
  1. If X is not F, it is not X,
  2. X cannot be X and not X
  3. Therefore, X is F

  (Proof of [A]2, i.e. of the major premise of [A].)

[C] The middle term itself:

  X

[D] A categorical syllogism of the form:

1. God is G (assumption)
2. X is G (by definition)
3. There is only one thing that is G (established in *P*5, 13, 22, 23; see also *M*15 and *R*5, 10)
4. Therefore, God is X

(G stands for 'whatever it is better to be than not to be'.)

(Proof of [A]1, i.e. of the minor premise of [A].)

In *P*Preface, Anselm says that his argument must meet two criteria: it must (α) suffice on its own to (β) establish that God exists etc. It would seem that only [A] could fit the criterion (β), but [A] is dependent on [B] (to establish the major premise) and [D] (to establish the minor premise), so can it fit the criterion (α)? X is the middle term of [A] and [B], but is not the middle term of [D], which is G. It seems unlikely therefore that the middle term 'X' is the *unum argumentum*, in spite of its central role, since [C] does not fulfil criterion (β), if it is not the middle term of [D]. [D] itself cannot be the *unum argumentum*, because it does not meet criterion (β).

It appears that all of the above options fail to meet the criteria of the *unum argumentum*. This suggests that there is no straightforward, easily recognisable account of it that anyone with a good knowledge of the *Proslogion* and its background would automatically accept. Nevertheless, a case can be made that [A] is the *unum argumentum*, since it alone can meet the major criterion (β). The fact that it does not appear to meet criterion (α), therefore needs explanation.

The premises [A]1 and [A]2 employ the middle term X, the use of which from Anselm's perspective is unchallengeable. The *reductio* argument [B] establishes [A]1 and the categorical syllogism [D] establishes [A]2 (if one accepts [D]3). Thus, it would seem that the *unum argumentum* involves a chain of three arguments and that it is also dependent on the claim that there is only one thing that is G (which for Anselm one understands to be true, if one understands the argument). Is the *unum argumentum* then a hypothetical version of [A]: if God is X, then God is F, since X is F? But here we come to *R*10, where as we saw above, Anselm addresses the identity of God and X, having stated in *R*5 that it is certain that nothing similar to X can exist. Anselm believes that his argument establishes [D]4, since it shows that X and God have identical attributes (they are both G, and their being G entails that they have certain attributes). Thus, from Anselm's perspective there is no requirement for the hypothetical version of [A]. The categorical version of [A] is the *unum argumentum*, and the minor premise, [A]1, is established simply by understanding what X means (as [D] shows). Anselm appears to be employing a version of an identity of indiscernibles argument: I am looking for an object Z, which is recognised by attributes H, J, K (at least one of which is exclusive to object Z). I have found an object with attributes H, J, K. Therefore I have found object Z.

Although we may no longer have a chain of three argument, do we not now have a chain of two arguments, [A] and [B]? Clearly [B] can be understood as a separate argument, but for Anselm it is not, since it is simply the means by which the major premise, [A]2, establishes itself. The establishing of the premises [A]1 and [A]2 is internal to the *unum argumentum*, and follows on from understanding what we believe about God and understanding X. Thus there is no chain of arguments, and Anselm's argument proves from itself alone that God exists, etc.

If, as Boethius stated, the *argumentum* is to be identified with the finding of the middle term,[9] then this would explain what such a finding would be. To 'find' the middle term is not simply to come across it but to show that it is employed with justification in the major and minor premises of the syllogism. Finding the middle term is, then, the argument that the middle term is justifiably the predicate of the minor premise and the subject of the major premise. Once the middle term has been justified in this way, Anselm's proof is achieved, since the formally valid nature of the argumentation itself does not require further justification. Anselm's *argumentum* can be seen to fit his description of it as self-sufficient, since the justification of the middle term is internal to it.

That may be as close as it is possible to get to understanding what Anselm means by the term '*unum argumentum*'. However, it shows that we can still understand that there is an *unum argumentum*, and this should make us wary of accounts which in practice ignore Anselm's claim that he is proving by means of a single argument.

It is often stated that the later objections of Aquinas, Kant and others were anticipated in the *Pro Insipiente*. If that is the case, then we might hope to find in the *Responsio* an indication of how Anselm would have replied to such objections. In fact, we do find such an indication in the idea that the case of God is unique. Arguments and objections concerning those things than which a greater can be thought (not-X) cannot be deployed against that than which a greater cannot be thought (X). As the history of the reception of Anselm's argument will confirm, objections that employ similar logical forms or similar premises or terms do not operate successfully against Anselm's argument. To be successful an objection must show that there is something wrong with the particular and distinctive logical form, premises and terms Anselm uses. We shall see in the following chapters that this constitutes an eminently difficult task.

---

9 See Stump, *In Ciceronis*, p. 32.

Chapter 6
The Medieval Reception

After the initial interest expressed by the author of the *Pro Insipiente*, little attention appears to have been paid to the *Proslogion*. Even within the writings of Anselm's immediate circle, there is a surprising lack of interest. Although Gilbert Crispin uses a variant of the formula 'X',[1] he does not do so in the context of a discussion of Anselm's argument. Even a follower such as Rodolfus Monachus, who, like Anselm, is concerned to address the unbeliever, fails to advert to the argument of the *Proslogion*, presenting instead an argument for the existence of God as first cause in his *Libellus de Nesciente et Sciente*.[2]

Twelfth Century

There are a few references to Anselm in the writings of his younger contemporary, Peter Abelard. He is aware of the text of the *Proslogion*,[3] but does not address Anselm's argument. In fact, the twelfth century is notable for its lack of consideration of Anselm's argument, even though there are sufficient extant manuscripts to suggest that the work was not unknown. Perhaps, then, it was not ignorance but fashion that determined the response of Anselm's immediate successors to his work. The growth of the schools in Northern France, and the development of a scholastic culture, with an emphasis on expounding the scriptures and comparing authorities may partly explain the lack of interest. That Anselm's work did not possess, or at least was not presented in, the systematic form required by twelfth century teachers and students meant that it was less likely to find an audience at that time.[4] It is also possible that philosophers and theologians felt unequipped to

---

1 Gilbert Crispin, *De Angelo Perdito*, [23]: '*Deus enim est quo nichil melius excogitari potest*'; A. Sapir Abulafia and G.R. Evans (eds), *The Works of Gilbert Crispin Archbishop of Westminster*, London 1986, p. 106.

2 The work (contained in Bodleian Ms Laud misc. 363) is anonymous. For the attribution to Rodolfus, see R.W. Southern, 'St. Anselm and his English pupils'. in *Medieval and Renaissance Studies*, I (1941–3) 3–34, but see also Southern, *Portrait*, p. 373, esp. n. 6.

3 See M. Perkams, '*Rationes necessariae – rationes verisimiles et honestissimae*: Methoden philosophischer Theologie bei Anselm und Abaelard', in Gasper and Kohlenberger, pp. 143–54, p. 148.

4 J. de Ghellinck, *Le Mouvement Théologique du XII*^{e} *siècle*, 2nd edn, Bruges, Brussels, Paris 1948, pp. 82ff.

deal with the argument of the *Proslogion* or viewed it as too rationalistic and too independent of authorities to earn a place in the schools.

William of Conches (fl. 1120–1154) provides an example of the lack of influence of the *Proslogion* in the period following Anselm's death. He writes that to know God perfectly is to know him according to the categories, but He transcends the categories, and therefore we cannot know Him perfectly. Although he says that nevertheless we know that God exists, he does not attempt to demonstrate this in the manner of the *Proslogion* argument.[5] Others, who look to Anselm as an authority, also take the view that God is beyond comprehension, and as a result appear to conflict with Anselm's apparent claim in *P*2 that God can be understood. Thus, Walter of Saint Victor in his *Contra Quatuor Labyrinthos Franciae* uses Anselm as an authority in his attack on Abelard, Gilbert de la Porrée, Peter Lombard and Peter of Poitiers. But, in language that could be directed at Anselm's discussion of the fool in *P*2, he states that there is nothing more stupid than wishing to grasp that which is beyond our understanding.[6]

Allusions to the argument of the *Proslogion* are occasionally to be found, for example in the *De Trinitate* of Richard of Saint Victor (d. 1173). Richard states that nothing greater or better that God can be conceived by even God Himself. The more that human thought approaches that which is better and more perfect, the closer it comes to God, but without ever reaching Him.[7] Herbert of Boseham (c. 1120–c. 1194) shows an awareness of Anselm's *Proslogion* argument in developing his own argument in the *Liber Melorum* (written 1186/87). He asks whether there is something so powerful that there can be nothing more powerful,[8] but omits the verb, *cogitare*, from his formula. The twelfth century attempt to produce a theological compendium based on sentences from Anselm's work (the *Bamberger Kompendium*) does not contain any texts derived from the *Proslogion*. It is worth noting, then, what Nicholas of Amiens says about knowledge of God in his *Ars Fidei Catholicae* (written c. 1190). God cannot be grasped by human understanding, nor signified correctly by a word. He is understood by faith alone (*sola fide*) and not by knowledge.[9] Here without explicitly saying so or referring to the formula 'X', he appears to be undermining the argument of *P*2, that X can be understood, and interpreting *P*15, that X is greater than can be thought, to support his view. The structure and arguments of Book 1 of the *Ars Fidei Catholicae* are clearly influenced by the *Proslogion*, and yet the argument for God is one based

---

5 William of Conches, *De Philosophia Mundi*, Liber I, c. 4. See G. Maurach (ed.), *Philosophia Mundi: Ausgabe des 1. Buchs von Wilhelm von Conches' 'Philosophia'*, Pretoria 1974, pp. 10f.

6 *PL*199 col. 1145A.

7 Liber 1, cc. 18f.

8 *PL* 190 col. 1359B: '*quaero ab insipiente an aliquid ist adeo potens quo sit nihil potentius*'.

9 M. Dreyer, *Nikolaus von Amiens: Ars Fidei Catholicae – Ein Beispielwerk axiomatischer Methode*, Münster 1993, pp. 82 l.27– 83 l. 25.

on causation. By his reference to '*sola fide*', Nicholas appears to be setting himself up against Anselm's '*sola ratione*' method. Perhaps here we have a reason for the silence concerning the *Proslogion*. It may have appeared as abrogating the requirement for faith concerning Catholic belief, in spite of what Anselm says about 'faith seeking understanding'.

Thirteenth Century

Alexander Nequam (1157–1217) has been identified as first important reviver of Anselm's works, including the *Proslogion* argument.[10] Alexander wrote the *Speculum Speculationum* at the beginning of the thirteenth century, citing the *Proslogion* extensively, and providing a brief account of Anselm's argument in a chapter entitled, 'That the Godhead cannot be defined'. Alexander introduces Anselm's argument in the form that God is that than which nothing better can be understood.[11] Whoever understands 'God' correctly, understands that God exists. For it is greater for a thing to be understood and to exist than to be understood and not to exist. In the same way, it is greater for God to exist *in re* and *in intellectu* and not to be able to be understood not to exist than to exist *in re* and *in intellectu* and to be able to be understood not to exist. Therefore God is that which exists *in re* and *in intellectu* and cannot be understood not to exist.

In the *Summa Aurea* of William of Auxerre (d. 1231), written between 1215 and 1229, Anselm's argument is one of four disparate proofs for God.[12] William first notes John Damascene's claim in *De Fide Orthodoxa*, I, 1, that knowledge of God's existence is inserted in us, and then states that the darkness of sin causes such madness, that the fool says in his heart, There is no God. Thus it is necessary to show that God exists. He presents the argument of '*magister Anselmus Cantuariensis*', employing a variant of X not found in the *Proslogion*, '*aliquid quo maius excogitari non potest*', which is closer to the formula of *P*3 than of *P*2, and which becomes standard in William's successors. Stressing the intelligibility of X, he follows a compressed version of Anselm's argument, but with a significant difference of emphasis. When someone hears the words that make up 'X', he understands their meaning. Thus, it is clear that X is intelligible. If someone understands X, what he understands either exists or does not exist. If it is said that X does not exist, then what he understand exists *in intellectu* but does not exist *in re*. But it is greater to exist *in intellectu* and *in re* than *in intellectu* alone, which is clearly intelligible. Therefore something intelligible is greater than the thing he thinks. Therefore he does not understand X. But this contradicts what has already

---

10 R.M. Thomson (ed.), *Alexander Nequam: Speculum Speculationum*, Oxford 1988, p. xv.

11 I, 18, 4.

12 Liber I, t.1. See J. Ribaillier (ed.), *Magistri Guillelmi Altissiodorensis Summa Aurea [: Liber Primus]*, Paris 1980, pp. 21–4.

been established, therefore it remains the case that that which he understands exists. Therefore X exists and is the *summum bonum* or God. William's variant of X and the context in which he presents Anselm's argument – John Damascene's view of the innateness of the knowledge of God's existence, and the fool's denial – is to have a significant influence on later scholastic interpreters of Anselm (including Aquinas), representing 'a widely received *status quaestionis*'.[13]

Robert Grosseteste (c. 1168–1253) does not discuss Anselm's argument as a proof of God's existence, exhibiting little interest in such proofs. However, he shows his awareness of the text of the *Proslogion* in his *De Decem Mandatis*, written between 1220 and 1235. Anselm's formula 'X' and his assertion that God is greater than can be thought (*P*15.2) are used with approval by Grosseteste in his comments on the first and second commandments, in which he discusses how we should think of God. If we are to avoid taking God's name in vain, he declares: 'We should understand Him to be that than which nothing is superior, nothing is better; He is not only the best that can be thought [*excogitari*], but is also better than can be thought [*excogitari*].'[14] And, in his 'sermon' on confession, '*Deus est*', Grosseteste begins (and ends) with a variant of Anselm's formula, God is 'that than which nothing greater can be thought [*excogitari*]', self-sufficient and sufficient for everything else.[15]

A significant number of thirteenth century discussions of Anselm's argument appear in commentaries on Peter Lombard's *Sentences*. Although he discussed briefly four proofs of God's existence in *I Sententiae*, d. 3, c. 1, Lombard did not mention Anselm's argument. It is not from him that the commentators on his *Sentences* obtain their interest in Anselm, but given the similarities of these treatments to that contained in the *Summa Aurea*, it appears likely that it is William of Auxerre who reawakened this interest, and influenced the form it took.

Alexander of Hales (c. 1185–1245), the first Franciscan to hold a university chair (at Paris), was the teacher of Bonaventure and Richard Rufus. He treats of Anselm's argument in his commentary on the *Sentences* and in his *Summa Theologica*. In the former work, he presents an accurate precis of Anselm's argument in *P*2–4.[16] In the latter work, Alexander presents Anselm's *Proslogion* argument in two quotations taken from *P*2.3–2.5 and *P*2.9–2.12 with no comment, other than to say that Anselm demonstrated (*declarat*) the necessity of his

---

13 J. McEvoy, *Robert Grosseteste*, Oxford 2000, p. 167.

14 See R. Grosseteste, *De Decem Mandatis*, edited by R. Dales and E. King, Oxford 1987, p. 24 ll. 17–19. See J. McEvoy, 'Robert Grosseteste's use of the argument of Saint Anselm', in J. McEvoy (ed.), *Robert Grosseteste: new perspectives on his thought and scholarship* (*Instrumenta Patristica*, vol. XXVII), Turnhout 1995, pp. 257–75.

15 S. Wenzel, 'Robert Grosseteste's Treatise on Confession, "Deus est" ', in *Franciscan Studies*, 30 (1970) 218–93, pp. 239 and 293. Anselm's formula also appears in Sermon 14, in Ms Bodley 830 (SC2713) fol. 184rb ll. 22f.

16 *Glossa in Quatuor Libros Sententiarum Petri Lombardi*, I, d. 3, a. 12, 1. He refers to the *Proslogion* as '*De personislogion, id est divinis personis*'.

reasoning in many ways (*multipliciter*) in his *Responsio* to the *Pro Insipiente*.[17] It is clear from this and from what follows that Alexander had read *P*2–4 (the *Sumptum*) and the *Responsio*. In a chapter entitled 'That it cannot be thought that God does not exist',[18] he addresses two questions: (i) whether it is necessary that the divine essence is known to exist in such a way that it cannot be thought not to exist (article 1); and (ii) whether it is a property of God's essence not to be able to be thought not to exist (article 2). In article 1, Alexander extracts *P*3.3–3.6 (with some minor textual variants) to support the view that God cannot be thought not to be, and follows it by a reference to John Damascene's claim that the knowledge of God's existence is innate in us. He then presents objections to these views, citing the fool of the *Psalms* to argue that God's existence can be denied. In his response to this objection he quotes from Anselm. This time the extract comes from *P*4.2–4.5: God's existence can be denied in the sense that one can use words without understanding their meaning, but it is not possible to deny His existence if one understands what the word God means. In article 2, Alexander asks whether not being able to be thought not to be is proper to God's 'essentiality'. His treatment of this question is made up completely of extracts from Anselm's debate with the author of the *Pro Insipiente*.

Alexander of Hales' reception of Anselm's argument marks a significant step forward in two ways: firstly, the argument is presented in some detail by someone who is clearly well acquainted with it; and, secondly, it sets the direction in which future discussions will go with its concentration on the *Sumptum*. It also reinforces the identification of X's inconceivable non-existence with the notion that knowledge of God's existence is implanted, impressed or innate in us. This latter position is not contained in Anselm's argument, but will come to play an important role in its medieval reception.

The Dominican, Richard Fishacre (d. 1248), the first Oxford commentator on the *Sentences*, addressed Anselm's argument in his *Quaestiones Super I–IV Sententiarum*, I, d. 3 (written between 1241 and 1245).[19] He writes that God's existence can be shown in many ways, presenting ten arguments, including a very abbreviated version of the argument of *P*2. Fishacre explains the fool's ability to deny God by suggesting that he is not speaking of God, but of something less than God. The fool denies that which, according to John Damascene, is implanted in him by God (knowledge of His existence), because of the malice (*malitia*) of corrupted human nature. Like William of Auxerre and Alexander of Hales, Fishacre makes a connection between God's undeniability and John Damascene's view that knowledge of God's existence is innate.

---

[17] *Summa Theologica*, I, p. 1, i. 1, t. 1, q. 1 – 'On the essentiality of the divine substance'.

[18] *Summa Theologica*, I, p. 1, i. 1, t. 1, q. 1, c. 2.

[19] R. Long and M. O'Carroll, *The Life and Works of Richard Fischacre OP: Prolegomena to the Edition of his Commentary on the Sentences*, Munich 1999, pp. 26 and 41.

In spite of his importance in the history of medieval philosophy, Albert the Great (c. 1200–1280) offered no new insights into Anselm's argument. He addresses it briefly in his *Summa Theologiae*,[20] which he wrote towards the end of his life, but does not include it in his proofs of God's existence. He asks whether God's existence is *per se notum*,[21] and introduces the psalmist's fool to suggest that it is not. Against this view he puts forward the argument that the fool is someone who does not know even himself,[22] but that if he did know himself properly, he would not say that God does not exist, nor could he think it, 'as Anselm says'. Thus, Albert equates Anselm's position on the undeniability of God with the view that God's existence is *per se notum*. There is no evidence that Albert accepts the argument of the *Proslogion*, even though he does not explicitly reject it. When Albert 'quotes' from the *Proslogion*, the text appears to be a simplified version of the arguments Anselm employs in *R*1 and *R*4.[23]

A particularly influential interpreter of Anselm was Bonaventure (1221–1274).[24] He first addresses the argument of the *Proslogion* in his *Commentaria in IV libros Sententiarum* (1250–1252), in a question concerning whether the divine being exists so truly that it cannot be thought not to exist.[25] Bonaventure presents an abbreviated form of Anselm's argument with a Boethian influence. Anselm argues, says Bonaventure, that God is X 'according to a common conception of the mind' ['*secundum communem animi conceptionem*'].[26] This is an important adjustment by Bonaventure, since such a 'common conception' would be *evidens in se* or *per se notum*, and Anselm does not employ this Boethian usage. Bonaventure continues that not to be able to be thought not to exist is greater than to be able to be thought not to exist, therefore, since nothing greater than God can be thought, divine being is such that it cannot be thought not to exist. He follows this by what has become the standard association with John Damascene (knowledge of God's existence is naturally impressed in us), and explains the sense in which God can be thought not to be without reference to the *Proslogion*.

At the beginning of the *Quaestiones Disputatae de Mysterio Trinitatis* (1253–1254) Bonaventure takes up the Anselmian argument in more detail. In question 1,

---

20 Albert the Great, *Summa Theologiae, sive De Mirabili Scientia Dei*, edited by D. Siedler et al., Aschendorff 1978. Albert's commentary on the *Sentences*, unlike those of Fishacre and Alexander of Hales does not contain a reference to Anselm's argument.

21 *Summa*, I, t. 3, q. 17.

22 Citing Aristotle, *Nichomachean Ethics*, 1.4 c.9 [1125 a 27–28]; *Aristoteles Latinus*, XXVI, 1–3, p. 216 l. 20: '*Chauni autem insipientes et se ipsos ignorantes.*'

23 *Summa*, I, t. 4, q. 19, c. 4.

24 On this see J. Chatillon, 'De Guillaume d'Auxerre à saint Thomas d'Aquin: l'argument de Saint Anselme chez les premiers Scolastiques du XIIIe siècle', in *Spicilegium Beccense. Congrés International du IX Centenaire de l'arrivée d'Anselme au Bec (vol. I)*, Paris 1959, pp. 209–31.

25 Bonaventure, *Commentaria in IV libros Sententiarum*, I, d. 8, p. 1, a. 1, q. 2.

26 Boethius, *De Consolatione Philosophiae*, III, 10. See Chapter 4 §2.5.

article 1, which asks whether the existence of God is indubitably true, he identifies three ways of answering this question:

(1) Every truth impressed on every mind is an indubitable truth.
(2) Every truth that every creature proclaims is an indubitable truth.
(3) Every truth most certain and most evident in itself is an indubitable truth.

Not surprisingly amongst the ten arguments Bonaventure puts forward to support the first way is that of John Damascene that knowledge of God's existence is implanted (*inserta*) in us. There follow another ten arguments intended to support the second way. These show that no matter under what categories existence is conceived, God's existence is to be inferred necessarily. However, it is only with reference to the third way that Bonaventure makes use of Anselm's argument to support the view that the existence of God is so certain that He cannot be thought not to exist. The first four of the remaining nine arguments are derived from Anselm. The first (i.e. no. 21 of 29) consists of a direct quotation (with a minor variation) of *P*4.6. The second argument (no. 22) is an abbreviated form of Anselm's argument derived from *P*2.3 and *P*3.3-3.5, and similar to that presented in his commentary on the *Sentences*. In the third argument (no. 23), Bonaventure again presents a version of *P*3.3: if X exists only in thought it is not X, therefore if it exists in thought, it must also exist in reality, and cannot be thought not to exist. X possesses 'such a nature (*natura*) that it cannot be thought unless it exists *in re*'. This claim reflects Anselm's summary of his argument so far in *P*4.5, where he says X 'exists in such a way that not even in thought can it not exist', and accords with Alexander of Hales' reading of the text. The fourth argument (no. 24) takes the claim of *P*5.1/*P*5.7, that God is whatever it is better to be than not to be, to establish that God exists indubitably, since indubitable existence is better than dubitable existence. According to Bonaventure, doubt can only arise as a result of a lack of understanding of what the word 'God' means. The evil man and the fool of the *Psalms* are able to deny God because of a defect of reasoning in their understanding. Furthermore, since the understanding is capable of comprehending and judging correctly in this matter, their error arises from an act of the will rather than because they are obliged to think this way. For Bonaventure, the point of proving God's existence is not to gain knowledge of what we do not yet know, but to remove doubt or ignorance that result from a defect in our reasoning.

In some ways, Bonaventure is at his most Anselmian in the *Itinerarium Mentis in Deum*, presenting there a variant of Anselm's argument (c. 6, n. 2). His use of the imagery of sight and light in c. 5 is in many ways reminiscent of Anselm, as is his approach to God in c. 3 through the trinitarian image of memory, understanding and will in the mind, to which nothing but God is superior. The similarity arises as a result of a shared Augustinianism. However, Bonaventure possessed 'a richer Augustinianism' than Anselm,[27] and his call to contemplate pure and absolute

---

27 A. Pegis, 'Four medieval ways to God', in *The Monist*, 54 (1970) 317–58, 321.

being (c. 5) represents a step beyond Anselm, as does his identification of the light of the intellect with the divine light.

The effect of Bonaventure's discussion of the inconceivability of God's non-existence on the history of the reception is wide ranging, because of the issues he raised in association with Anselm's argument, but which are not derived from it. Thus, in his response to the seventh objection in his *Quaestiones Disputatae de Mysterio Trinitatis*, he argues that God's existence 'is evident in itself and certain to the knower'. Combined with the view that knowledge of God's existence is innate in us, this position helps to set the scene for the next important phase in the development of the reception of Anselm's argument. Aquinas will criticise Anselm in the mistaken belief that his argument is to be identified with these Bonaventurean accretions. In fact as, Weisheipl suggests, Thomas considered Anselm to be arguing that God's existence is self-evident and not in need of proof.[28]

It should be noted that not all Franciscans accepted Anselm's argument, as the case of Richard Rufus of Cornwall confirms. Rufus wrote his *Lectura Oxoniensis super libros i–iii Sententiarum*[29] in 1250 before he went to Paris. In this work, he develops an original interpretation of Anselm, which may have influenced both Bonaventure and Aquinas. Rufus says of Anselm's arguments in *P*2 and *P*3 that, although subtle, they appear to be sophistical.[30] He puts forward an objection to Anselm's argument, that the fool can deny that X has a referent.[31] Although he *cannot* think that than which a greater cannot be thought can be thought not to exist, he *can* think that there is nothing than which a greater cannot be thought.[32] Anselm is correct in his view that it is impossible to think that something X can be thought not to exist, since the predicate contradicts the subject.[33] However, it does not follow that the same argument applies to a second 'hypothesis': it can be thought that there exists no such being [*nullum entium*], X. If someone thinks that there exists no such being, X, he cannot be thinking of something, X. Therefore, he does not think that something, X, does not exist. It does not follow, then, that every object, X, exists. For concerning no X does the fool think it exists and does not exist (which would involve the contradiction noted above), but concerning every being he thinks that it is not X. Thus, God's existence cannot be proved in this way. The fact that 'something X' is contradicted by the predicate 'able to be thought not to be' does not mean that 'God' is contradicted by the same predicate. In the case of the word 'God', which designates an absolute divine nature, 'being able to be

---

28 J. Weisheipl, *Friar Thomas D'Aquino: His Life, Thought, and Works*, Oxford 1975, p. 226.

29 See R. Raedts, *Richard Rufus of Cornwall and the Tradition of Oxford Theology*, Oxford 1987, pp. 20–39. Text contained in Balliol College, Oxford, Ms 62.

30 G. Gál, 'Viae ad exsistentiam Dei probandum in doctrina Richardi Rufi OFM', in *Franziskanische Studien*, 38 (1956) 177–202, 191 l. 36.

31 Ibid., 191 ll. 40f.

32 Ibid., 193 ll. 20–28.

33 Ibid., 193 ll. 24f.

thought not to be' is an accidental quality, and a contradiction cannot arise between these terms as it does between something, X, and 'being able to be thought not to be'. God and something, X, do not function in the same way in relation to what is predicated of them. Presumably, to make the case that they could so function, one would need to show the absolute identity of something, X, and God. But this, as we saw, is a key part of Anselm's argument. Anselm does not simply to leave off the argument (mere assertion of such an identity) at the point where Rufus appears to think he does (*P*2/*P*3). There are certain similarities between the objections Rufus puts forward prior to his presence in Paris and some of the subsequent positions taken by Aquinas. As they were contemporaries at Paris this is not at all surprising, and suggests that Aquinas' response to Anselm's argument may have been influenced by Rufus.

According to Thomas of York (d. c. 1260) in his *Sapientiale*, to say that God does not exist is to say that God is not God, and thus to acknowledge that God exists. This argument may have influenced or have been influenced by Bonaventure's claim that if God is God, then God exists. (The two were contemporaries for a time in Paris.) Thomas identifies the origins of Anselm's formula 'X' in Cicero's *De Natura Deorum* (see Chapter 4 §2.3). He defends Anselm's argument against the claim that the fool can deny that X has a referent, by employing Anselm's distinction in *P*4.3 between thinking a word signifying something and understanding the thing itself. Like Anselm, he argues that, in the latter sense, God cannot be thought not to exist.[34]

The Dominican, Peter of Tarentaise (c. 1225–1276), presents Anselm's *P*2 argument in favour of the view that God's existence can be proven and is thereby not *per se notum*, and Anselm's *P*3 argument (substituting *melius* for *maius* in the formula 'X' – *P*14.2) to put the case against the existence of God (since there is nothing than which a better cannot be thought). He distinguishes between God's being *per se notum* in Himself and *per se notum* in relation to us, and uses Anselm to argue that one can understand that God is thought not to exist in two ways: firstly, when the words signifying this are used, and, secondly, when the thing signified is thought. He then adds another distinction to this second one: what is thought is either specifically God or generally truth, goodness, etc. God can be thought not to exist in the specific sense, but not in the general sense, because we cannot think that truth does not exist, since for this to be true, truth must exist.[35] Peter holds, then, that Anselm's argument shows that God is *per se notum* to us in the general sense (as truth, etc.), but not in the specific sense and consequently does not succeed in showing the undeniability of the God of Catholic faith.

Although Anselm is a frequently cited source in the writings of Thomas Aquinas (c. 1225–1274),[36] references to the *Proslogion* are relatively rare, and he

---

34 See S. Matthews, *Reason, Community and Religious Tradition: Anselm's Argument and the Friars*, Aldershot 2001, pp. 110f., nn. 128 and 129.

35 *Sententiarum*, I, d. 3, q. 1, a. 2.

36 For example, in Aquinas' *De Veritate*, Anselm is cited in 43 articles.

may not have been directly acquainted with the text of this work.[37] In fact, it is well attested that in his treatment of Anselm's argument Aquinas was responding to the use of the argument by thirteenth century scholastics, in particular Bonaventure.[38] According to Gilson, Aquinas was opposing an Augustinian idea of a direct knowledge or awareness of God, against which he put forward the thesis that our knowledge derives from material objects by way of the senses.[39]

Aquinas addresses Anselm's argument in the following works:[40]

In Primum Librum Sententiarum, dist. 3, question 1, article 2 (1252–1256)
Quaestiones Disputatae De Veritate, question 10, article 12 (1256–1259)
In Boethii De Trinitate, pars 1, question 1, article 3 (1258–1259)
Summa contra Gentiles, I, 10f. (1259–1264)
Quaestiones Disputatae De Potestate, 7, 2 (1265–1266)
Summa Theologiae, Ia, question 2, article 1 (1266–1273)
Super Psalmos, 13 and 52 (1272–1273)

It is possible to identify seven recurring objections to Anselm's argument in these works, which can be summarised as follows: [41]

(AQ1) Not to be able to be thought not to exist is to be equated with being *per se notum*. Being *per se notum* excludes the possibility of being established by a demonstration, but God's existence is established by demonstration, therefore it is not *per se notum*. From this it follows that it is not the case that God cannot be thought not to exist.
(AQ2) The fool was able to think that God does not exist, therefore God can be thought not to exist.
(AQ3) Anselm's argument only works if one presupposes the existence of X, but that is the question at issue.
(AQ4) God is *per se notum* in Himself and not to us. The proposition, 'God exists', differs from a principle such as 'the whole is greater than the part', which is *per se notum* through an immediate perception and does not have to be demonstrated.
(AQ5) Philosophers have regarded God differently to Anselm, either as not X or X as something different to the God of Catholic belief.

---

37 See B. Davies, *The Thought of Thomas Aquinas*, Oxford 1992, p. 24 n. 17.

38 See, for example, Chatillon, 'De Guillaume d'Auxerre', esp. p. 228. See also B. Bonansea, 'The ontological argument: proponents and opponents', in *Studies in Philosophy and the History of Philosophy*, 6 (1973) 135–92, p. 149 and n.35.

39 E. Gilson, *The Philosophy of Thomas Aquinas*, Cambridge 1929, p. 62.

40 Dates of authorship based on Weisheipl, *Friar Thomas D'Aquino*, pp. 355–405, and G. Emery, 'Brief Catalogue of the Works of Saint Thomas Aquinas', in J.-P. Torrell, *Saint Thomas Aquinas*, vol. 1: *The Person and His Work*, Revised edition, Washington D.C. 2005, pp. 330–61.

41 I number Aquinas's objections AQ1, AQ2, etc.

(AQ6) We can think God does not exist, because of the weakness of our intellect.
(AQ7) God is known through His effects, not through Himself.

Aquinas first treats of Anselm's argument in his commentary on the first book of Peter Lombard's *Sentences* in an article entitled: 'Whether God's existence is known through itself [*per se notum*]'. In this article Aquinas sets out the problem he thinks exists with the argument: the conclusion that God cannot be thought not to exist is to be taken to mean that God is *per se notum* (AQ1). Aquinas goes on in the *Contra* to argue (i) that the example of the fool in the Psalms shows that God's existence can be denied, not merely in words, but also 'in the heart' (AQ2), and (ii) that whatever is concluded by means of a demonstration is not *per se notum* (AQ1). According to Aquinas we only arrive at God through argument. In his reply to the fourth objection, Aquinas suggests that Anselm supposes that X exists, even though it is possible to think that no such thing exists (AQ3).[42]

In his *De Veritate*, Aquinas's response to Anselm's argument undergoes some development. In a change of position from the commentary on the *Sentences*, he refers to Anselm's use of the Psalmist's fool to support the position that knowledge of God's existence is not innate.[43] He continues to hold that Anselm's argument is intended to show that God cannot be thought not to exist and that therefore His existence is *per se notum* (AQ1), but says that it contains some truth, since God's existence is *per se notum* in itself (a point made by Bonaventure, rather than Anselm), though not to us. If we could understand God in Himself (His essence), He would be undeniable in thought, but since our understanding is inadequate, He is not undeniable in our thought.

In his *In Boethii De Trinitate*, Aquinas identifies not being able to be thought not to be with the first objects of knowledge that are known naturally and are innate (*inserta*) in us. He repeats the argument of *De Veritate* that God's existence is *per se notum* in itself, because His essence is identical with His existence, but that it is not *per se notum* to us because we do not see His essence (AQ4).[44] Aquinas ascribes the view he is opposing here to Anselm, although in *De Veritate*, he associates it with Boethius.[45] Aquinas accepts that we possess innate principles, but these do not include knowledge of God's existence. Rather, they provide us with the means to determine that God exists.

In the *Summa contra Gentiles* Aquinas does not mention Anselm by name but uses the wording employed by Anselm in *P*3: '*aliquid quo maius cogitari non potest*' (*P*3.4) and '*aliquid quod non possit cogitari non esse*' (*P*3.3).[46] He

---

42 *In Primum Librum Sententiarum*, d. 3 q. 1 a. 2 ad 4.

43 In the first of the 'Answers to Contrary Difficulties'.

44 *In Boethii De Trinitate*, p. 1 q. 1 a. 3 ad 6.

45 *De Veritate*, q. 10, art. 12, responsio.

46 Thus, Hartshorne was mistaken in claiming that in rejecting Anselm's argument in *ScG* and *ST*, Aquinas only refers to *P*2. See C. Hartshorne, *Anselm's Discovery: A Re-examination of the Ontological Proof for God's Existence*, LaSalle, Illinois 1965, p. 155.

again equates Anselm's position with the claim that God's existence cannot be demonstrated since it is *per se notum* (AQ1), and explains why he takes this view of the argument. That is *per se notum* which is known immediately its terms are known. Aquinas repeats here objections AQ4 and AQ3, and also produces some new objections:-

Many ancient philosophers identified God with the world and therefore, did not consider God to be X in the sense Anselm intended. Thus, it is possible to have X in the understanding, and still not identify it as God in Anselm's sense (AQ5).

It does not follow that something greater than God can be thought, if He can be thought not to be, since this arises from a weakness in our understanding and not from any weakness erroneously imputed to God (AQ6).

God is known indirectly through His effects, not through Himself, and in particular through the likenesses to Him in His effects (AQ7).

In the *De Potestate*, Aquinas again discusses without explicit reference to Anselm the issue of whether God's existence is *per se notum*. For something to be *per se notum* in relation to us, we must understand the terms of the proposition, but in the case of the proposition, 'God exists', we cannot, since we cannot know what God is (AQ4).

In Aquinas' much cited 'reply' to Anselm's argument in *ST*, Ia, 2, 1, there is once again no explicit mention of Anselm. He amends Anselm's formula to 'that than which a greater cannot be signified [*significari*]'. Once one understands what the word 'God' signifies, God's existence in reality is recognised, since God exists in the understanding and it is greater to exist in reality as well. 'Therefore that God exists is *per se notum*.' However, it is possible to think that God does not exist, as the fool of the Psalms shows, and therefore that God's existence is not *per se notum* (AQ2). Aquinas resolves this contradiction, as he had done previously, by arguing that there are two senses in which something is *per se notum*. But here the distinction is more accurately expressed. Something can be *per se notum* (i) in relation to itself and not to us or (ii) in relation to itself and to us. The proposition, 'God exists', is *per se notum* in relation to itself since God's existence and essence are identical, but not to us, since we do not know what God is (AQ4), but must rather establish this by demonstration from his effects (AQ7). Aquinas also repeats objections (AQ5) and (AQ3).

In his final, incomplete work, *Super Psalmos*, Aquinas addresses the question of what the fool of the Psalms is doing in denying God's existence (exposition of *Psalms* 13 and 52), reiterating objections AQ2, AQ4 and AQ7.

It is clear that Aquinas's aim was not to present an accurate exposition of the *Proslogion*. He had a particular interest in the argument of *P*3 that God cannot be thought not to be, and identified this proposition with the view that 'God exists' is *per se notum*, which for him involved the unacceptable claim that we have direct knowledge of God apart from sense experience. The question is whether any of his objections successfully address the argument of the *Proslogion*. I shall consider each of them in turn to see whether this is the case.

(Ad AQ1) Although Aquinas asserts that 'not to be able to be thought not to exist' and to be *per se notum* are to be identified, nowhere does he explicitly show this to be the case. Rather, it seems to be a position held by his opponents, and for his purposes that is sufficient. Aquinas would have to justify this position in the following way: a proposition is *per se notum*, in which the predicate is contained in the subject, so that once we understand the terms of the proposition, we understand that it is true. For something to be unable to be thought not to be, the predicate 'existence' must be contained in it, so that as soon as one understands the meaning of the something and the predicate 'existence', one understands that it is true. For this reason, it cannot be thought not to exist. The difficulty with such a justification is that, whilst there may be a sub-set of *per se notum* propositions that involve inconceivable non-existence, it does not necessarily follow that this sub-set contains the set of all propositions involving inconceivable non-existence. In fact, as we can see from Anselm's discussion of seeing and not seeing in *P*14, he does not adhere to the view that God is immediately intuited in such a way that His existence is known as undeniable. The term 'God' in the proposition 'God exists' is in a sense beyond understanding (*P*16.4). If it can be understood at all, it is only a partial understanding (*P*14.5). If Anselm had thought that the undeniability of God's existence arose from the fact that it was *per se notum*, he would presumably have finished the argument of the *Proslogion* at *P*3. In fact, he has to show that he has not understood God, who is greater than can be thought (*P*15),[47] for just as the creature cannot judge the Creator (*P*3.6), which is what he does when he denies His existence, so it cannot claim that knowledge or understanding which is only available in the fullness of heaven (*P*26). In this life, God is only seen indirectly (*P*16.3). If one were to understand the term 'God', it would not be God that one understood.

(Ad AQ2) The use of the fool of the Psalms by Aquinas is surprising, since it is precisely this 'person' Anselm uses as a foil in his argument in *P*2. For Aquinas, the fact that the fool can say God does not exist in his heart shows that he can think that God does not exist. Anselm does not deny this, but distinguishes two types of thinking, that in which the words are thought, and that in which what is signified by the words is understood. The fool can say in his heart that God does not exist in the first sense, but not in the second. The fool says in his heart in the first sense what cannot be thought in the second sense, i.e. what he says lacks understanding. For Anselm, the fool is foolish, not because he fails to possess a full understanding of God, but because not fully understanding God, he judges Him, and fails to possess the limited understanding available to him. The fact the fool can behave in this way shows that God's existence is not *per se notum* in relation to us, but must be arrived at through a process of ratiocination.

(Ad AQ3) According to Aquinas, Anselm is to be understood as arguing that when we understand God it is not possible to understand that God should exist and

[47] In this he would agree with Aquinas, who states in *ScG*, I, 5, that we only know God truly insofar as we believe that He is above whatever we can conceive of Him.

should be able to be thought not to exist. However, it is a *non sequitur* to draw the conclusion that someone could not think that God does not exist, since it is possible to think that there is no such thing as X. Anselm presupposes that something X exists. His argument claims too much, either because to be unable to be thought not to exist is to be *per se notum*, which 'X exists' clearly is not, or because the undeniability of X's existence has not been demonstrated, since to be undeniable it would have to be *per se notum* and therefore indemonstrable. In either instance, Aquinas' objection to Anselm's argument is based on his view that being *per se notum* is to be identified with being unable to be thought not to exist, a connection not made by Anselm, nor one that his argument requires.

(Ad AQ4) Anselm would agree with Aquinas that God is not *per se notum* in relation to us, since if He were there would be no need to undertake the dialectical task of supplying a proof for a matter in doubt. He thinks that we cannot understand God in Himself: 'not only are You that than which a greater cannot be thought, but You are also something greater than can be thought' (*P*15.2). That we cannot know God's essence does not mean for Anselm as it does for Aquinas that His non-existence can be thought. To know that God is, it is necessary to know what God is, but only to the extent that we know the manner of His existence as undeniable in thought, which follows from His being identified with X. Again, Anselm would agree that God is known through His effects, one of which is the *imago dei* in the *ratio* of man.

(Ad AQ5) Anselm's use of Seneca's formula 'X', which the latter applied to a god he identified with the world, suggests that he was aware of the different meanings God and X could have ascribed to them. That people misunderstand the terms, God or X, is an important reason for producing the *Proslogion*, for it is this misunderstanding (not to be confused with a failure to understand fully) that allows them to deny the God of Catholic belief. Anselm uses X precisely because people have tried to signify something other than the Christian God by it.

(Ad AQ6) Anselm is in complete agreement that our intellect is weak, likening it to the weak eye that cannot see the sun (*P*16.3). The weakness of our intellect prevents us from seeing or understanding God directly or fully. However, Anselm's argument is intended to show that we can know that God exists, even if our vision and understanding are limited. On one hand, the 'ability' to deny God's existence is a result of the weakness of our intellect, since we are prone to misunderstanding. On the other hand, our intellects are not so weak that we cannot know that God exists, if we understand what we are doing when we talk or think of God.

(AD AQ7) This objection is based on the assumption that Anselm views our knowledge of God as derived directly from God (*per se notum*), whereas, for Thomas, all knowledge of God can only be derived from the world of experience, i.e. through His effects. However, Anselm's argument does not require that knowledge of God is derived directly from God. In fact, the aetiology of our knowledge of God is irrelevant for Anselm. What matters is that we can have a notion of what God is as X. The argument of the early part of the *Monologion* shows how such a notion might be constructed from our experience of God's effects.

That Aquinas did not deal a decisive blow against Anselm is unsurprising, since it was not Anselm's argument that he was addressing. Aquinas' intention was to protect the Aristotelian principle that all knowledge is derived through (though not limited to) the senses[48] against the extra-sensory origins of knowledge of God proposed by Bonaventure and his supporters. However there is no doubting the influence of Aquinas' position, even amongst some Franciscans, such as Richard of Middleton (c. 1249–c. 1305).[49]

Henry of Ghent (c. 1217–1293) treats of Anselm's argument in his *Summa* (*Quaestiones Ordinariae*), which postdates the writings of Bonaventure and Aquinas. In a. 21, q. 1,[50] Henry makes use of Anselm's argument as the counter position to the objection that God is X and therefore cannot exist, because it is always possible to think of something greater. In his response to this objection, Henry defends Anselm's use of the formula 'X' arguing that something greater can only be thought of a finite being. Henry follows the traditional references to John Damascene concerning the malice of human nature, the role of the fool, and that knowledge of God is inserted in us. However, he also cites the *Magna Glosatura* on *Romans* 1, to put forward the idea that we come to knowledge of God through creatures. In a. 22, q. 2,[51] Henry seeks to show that Anselm's argument does not prove that God's existence is *per se notum*. Like Peter of Tarentaise he distinguishes between a general and a specific sense in which God's existence can be understood. The former refers to a 'confused' implanted knowledge of God (as being, one, good) and the latter to a particular knowledge of God as the referent of the term 'God'. In this latter sense, it is possible to deny God's existence. To be *per se notum* for Henry it must be the case not only that the subject of a proposition contains the predicate, but that the truth of the proposition must also be obvious or spontaneously known to, and assented by, us. For those who think that it is the purpose of Anselm's argument to show that God's existence is *per se notum*, this might appear to be proof that the argument fails. However, for those who do not think that this is its purpose, it is evidence that Anselm's argument is safe from objections against the *per se notum* character of God's existence.

William of Ware, another Oxford Franciscan (fl. 1290–1305), is part of a growing trend to 'mine' the *Sumptum* to put forward arguments that have little or no bearing on Anselm's argument. Thus, he employs the formula 'X' in his *Questiones super libros Sententiarium*, q. 14, to put an argument against the existence of God. By William's time, it is the commonly held view that Anselm's argument is a statement of the *per se notum* character of God's existence. In q.

---

48 ST I, 84, 6.

49 Richard of Middleton, *Super Quattor Libros Sententiarum*, Brixiae 1591, I, d. 3, a. 1, q. 3. That Richard did not take an entirely negative view of Anselm's argument can be seen from his appeal to Anselm in *Sententiarum*, I, d. 43, a. 1, q. 1, *contra*.

50 J. Decorte and R.J. Teske, *Henry of Ghent's* Summa: *The Questions on God's Existence and Essence (Articles 21–24)*, Louvain 2005, pp. 40–47.

51 Ibid., pp. 108–23.

21, William employs Anselm's argument to support this view.[52] According to William, Anselm states in *P*2 and *P*3 that God's existence is *per se notum*, and in his *Responsio* that God's existence is most known or evident (*notissimum*), because it is not possible to conceive correctly its opposite. However, Anselm's texts support neither of these claims.

Giles of Rome (c. 1243–1316) too identifies Anselm's argument in *P*3 that God cannot be thought not to exist with the view that His existence is *per se notum* (*Sententiarium*, I, d. 3, q. 1, a. 2), offering no argument for this identification.[53] Anselm's explanation of the fool's denial in *P*3.8 is taken by Giles as evidence that God's existence is *per se notum* only to the wise. Only they possess this 'common conception of the soul', since only they can know what it is that is meant by the word 'God'. Thus, it is only in the case of the wise that God's non-existence cannot be thought.[54] According to Giles, demonstrating the existence of God as X is not inconsistent with the notion that it is *per se notum* to the wise, precisely because it is not evident to everyone.[55]

In his *Quaestiones de deo cognoscendo*,[56] Peter Olivi (1248–1298), does not see any contradiction between God's existence being *per se notum*, demonstrable by reason and believed on faith. Anselm is again cited alongside John Damascene as arguing that God's existence is *per se notum*, since what is indubitable is '*per se notissimum*'.[57] Against this Olivi cites the psalmist's fool. He then uses Anselm's argument against the view that God's existence is demonstrable '*per rationes necessariae*'.[58] This is not because it shows God's existence is *per se notum*, but because the argument seems to fail. If X exists in the understanding alone, it is not the highest, but if one allows that it exists, then one can think of something which is the highest, without having to postulate its actual existence. Anselm's argument shows that if such a thing exists in act [*actu*], it exists necessarily in reality [*in re*].[59] However, Olivi does not leave the matter there, but later seeks to rehabilitate Anselm's argument.[60] A hypothetical existence of God is not what Anselm's argument involves. In fact, according to Olivi, if X does not exist, then X refers to the supreme impossibility and the supreme contradiction. However, this cannot be true for X, since it is clearly the case that when we are talking of X

[52] See A. Daniels, *Quellenbeiträge und Untersuchungen zur Geschichte der Gottesbeweise im Dreizehnten Jahrundert, mit besonderer Beruchsichtigung des Arguments im Proslogion des Hl. Anselm*, Münster 1909, pp. 98–104.

[53] Ibid., p. 72.

[54] Ibid., p. 75.

[55] Ibid., pp. 76f.

[56] *Fr. Iohannis Petrus Olivi O.F.M., Quaestiones in secundum librum Sententiarum quas primum ad fidem codd. mss.*, vol. III, edited by B. Jansen, Florence 1926, pp. 453–554.

[57] *Quaestiones*, p. 517.

[58] Ibid., p. 518.

[59] Ibid., pp. 523f.

[60] Ibid., p. 527.

we are referring to that which is above all perfection, and lacks all imperfection and limitation, which is after all what we mean by the word 'God'. And therefore, according to Olivi, Anselm correctly regards this method of investigating God's existence as superior to all others, since the notion of God or X can be formed by anyone from the sum of things lacking imperfection (such as being, the good, the true, the one).[61] Original and interesting as Olivi's approach to Anselm was, it was not influential.

The influence of Duns Scotus (1265/6–1308), on the other hand, was significant. Scotus argued that the proposition 'X exists' is not *per se notum*.[62] In his *Lectura* (I, d. 2, p. 1, q. 2) and *Ordinatio*, (I, d. 2, p. 1, q. 2), Scotus first puts forward Anselm's argument (referring to *P*2 in the *Lectura* and *P*5 in the *Ordinatio*) in support of the view that God's existence is *per se notum* alongside that of John Damascene that knowledge of God's existence is inserted in us, but then takes the words of the fool to indicate that God's existence cannot be *per se notum*, since if it were no mind would be able to deny it. He then makes it clear that it was not Anselm's intention to assert that God's existence is *per se notum*, but to show that the proposition, 'God exists', is true.[63] The problem with Anselm's argument is that Anselm says that the fool understands X, but he does not show that X is understandable as something that can exist, that does not contain any inherent contradictions. Thus, Scotus adds the phrase 'without contradiction' to the Anselmian argument: when thought without contradiction, God is that than which a greater cannot be thought without contradiction.[64] This 'colouration' of Anselm's argument, in which the invisible structure of the argument is supposedly made visible by additional content, marks a significant contribution to the history of interpretation, since it helps us to identify the limitations of the argument of the *Proslogion*, the validity of which needs to be established within the context of a wider set of questions than addressed by Anselm in the *Proslogion*. This is not to say that Anselm's argument requires Scotus' colouration, since in the *Monologion* Anselm had provided for the kind of objection that Scotus' colourations were designed to meet.[65] However, it suggests that Anselm's argument does not possess the self-sufficient character he claimed, unless we consider the fool's acceptance of X as in his understanding as sufficient for Anselm's purposes. For, in a dialectical disputation a conceded premise would not after all require justification.

In his Parisian proof for God's existence, Scotus makes it clear how he understands Anselm's argument: as a proof that there exists an infinite being,

---

[61] Ibid., p. 528.

[62] *Ordinatio*, I, d. 2, p. 1, q. 2, n. 26.

[63] *Lectura*, I, d. 2, p. 1, q. 2, n. 35. See also *Ordinatio*, I, d. 2, p. 1, q. 2, n. 35.

[64] A. Wolter, *John Duns Scotus: A Treatise on God as First Principle* [De Primo Principio], Chicago 1966, §4.65, p. 123. In the *Ordinatio*, I, d. 2, p. 1, q. 2, Scotus uses 'cognito' rather 'cogitato'.

[65] See B. Bonansea, 'Duns Scotus and St. Anselm's ontological argument', in *Studies in Philosophy and the History of Philosophy*, 4 (1967) 128–41, 138.

which exists of itself. He does not limit Anselm's proof to the *Sumptum*, but sees the argument of *P*5.3, that X exists through itself alone, as an indispensable part of the argument. Anselm's proof works, according to Scotus, if one can show that there is no contradiction in the concept of X, for only then is it thinkable.[66] Without his colouration, Scotus would not accept Anselm's argument, but with it he is prepared to give Anselm a supporting role in his proof of God's existence.

Fourteenth Century

William of Ockham (c. 1285–1347) reads Anselm through Scotus' colouration. In *Quodlibeta Septem*,[67] I. q. 1, Ockham considers whether it can be proved by natural reason that there is only one God. He identifies two 'descriptions' of God: (i) that God is something that is more noble and better than everything else besides Himself and (ii) that God is that than which nothing is better and more perfect. Insofar as a proof is based on an article of faith rather than a *per se notum* principle or one that is known from experience, it cannot succeed as a demonstrative proof. Thus, the former description can only be used to prove that if God were to exist, there could only be one God, but not that God exists (argument 1). However, according to Ockham, it is possible to prove that God or a God exists using the second description, since we would be involved in an infinite regression if there were not something to which nothing is prior and than which nothing is more perfect (argument 2). This demonstration does not establish that there is only one such thing. The problem with Ockham's account is that neither of the formulae employed by Ockham are identical with that of Anselm. From an Anselmian perspective, X provides the basis of a single argument for both the unity and uniqueness (argument 1) and the existence (argument 2) of God.

In *Quodlibeta Septem*, VII, q. 15, Ockham states that in *P*2, Anselm argues that 'that than which a greater cannot be thought without contradiction (=X^*) is infinite'. God is X^*. Therefore God is infinite. In other words, he incorrectly ascribes the Scotist 'colouration' to Anselm. In his account of this Scotist proof, Ockham almost immediately slips into Scotist talk of the 'greatest thinkable being' ['*summum cogitabile*'], which from our reading of *P*15 we know cannot be equated with X, since X is greater than can be thought (*P*15.2). Ockham responds to this proof. He states that the minor premise (i.e. God is X^*) is to be denied according to the philosophers. Ockham asks what Anselm's proof in *P*2 has achieved. He states that there are two senses in which something is X: (a) that nothing can be thought that is *de facto* greater than it; (b) that if this something were to exist, then nothing greater than it could be thought. Only if one understands Anselm's argument as employing sense (a), does it work (assuming that there is no infinite regress of

---

[66] *Reportatio 1A*; Wolter, 'Parisian Proof', in Frank and Wolter, *Duns Scotus*, p. 64.

[67] William of Ockham, *Opera Theologica*, vol. 9, edited by J. Wey, Bonaventure NY 1980.

greater beings). In other words, Anselm's argument can establish the real existence of a being than which no other is greater, but not that of a being than which it is not logically possible that there is a greater.[68] Ockham then goes on to outline the argument of *P*3.3–4 that God cannot be thought not to exist, but when he comes to provide a reply, we find that the page is blank.

Robert Holcot (c. 1290–1349)[69] again deals with Anselm's argument alongside that of John Damascene that knowledge of God is inserted in us. Holcot presents Anselm's *P*2 argument, Anselm's conclusion to *P*4 (*P*4.6), the lost island objection, and Anselm's response in *R*3.[70] Holcot believes Anselm's argument is obviously fallacious and goes into some detail to show that it fails,[71] because one cannot grasp the meaning of X, any more than one can grasp the magnitude of what is infinite. By parity of reasoning, one could prove that something better than God can exist, on the basis that you can understand the terms involved when you hear 'something better than God', and therefore something better than God is in your understanding. And it cannot only be in your understanding but must exist *in re* otherwise a better than God is not a better than God, since it is better to exist *in re* and *in intellectu* than *in intellectu* alone. The weakness of Holcot's interesting objection is that it fails to deal with Anselm's premise that God is whatever it is better to be than not to be. If something is better than God then it is better for God to be it. But since God, who is the best there can be cannot be it, this means that there can be no such thing as a better than God. For Holcot, the existence of God is to be believed on faith and not demonstrated.[72] With nominalist thinkers such as Holcot we experience the loss of confidence in '*sola ratione*', and a move in the direction of '*sola fide*'.[73]

This is not to say that Holcot's contemporaries necessarily share his views. Thomas of Buckingham (c. 1290–1351), in his *Questiones in quattuor libros Sententiarum* (1335–1343), q. 5, provides a detailed account of Anselm's argument in *P*2–4 as well as Anselm's *Responsio*, in particular the discussion of the lost island. In what is clearly a response to Holcot's rejection of Anselm's argument, Thomas argues that it is sufficient to prove that God is the highest good, omnipotent, and similar such things.[74] He also believes Anselm's discovery of the argument to have been divinely inspired, and that those such as Holcot, who regard Anselm as 'sophistically deceived' in his arguments, simply do not understand him.[75]

---

68 See M.M. Adams, *William Ockham*, vol. 2, Notre Dame 1987, p. 972.

69 *Quaestiones super quatuor libros sententiarum*, Lyons 1497.

70 I, q.4 fo. D.vi^{rb} l. 52 – D.vi^{va} l. 24.

71 I, q.4 fo. D.vii^{rb} l. 12 – vii^{va} l. 4.

72 I, q.4 fo. D.v^{va} ll. 4f.

73 I, q.4 fo. D.v^{rb} ll. 43f.: 'sola fide tenetur'.

74 See Thomas of Buckingham, *Questiones in quattuor libros Sententiarum*, Paris 1507, i.viii^{vb} ll. 6–9.

75 Ibid., i.viii^{vb} ll. 34–9.

In his *De Ente*, I, t. 2, c. 2,[76] John Wyclif (c. 1320-1384) suggests that in the *Proslogion* Anselm sought to determine whether 'that than which there is no better' exists *in intellectu* alone or *in intellectu* and *in re*. Although he clearly accepts Anselm's argument, he does not put it forward on its own terms, but in the context of showing that the highest good is identical with the highest being [*ens*]. In *De Ente*, II, t. 1, c. 1, Wyclif seeks to prove that God has knowledge of all intelligible things. To understand is the most perfect act possible or is concomitant with such an act, and therefore since whatever it is better to be than not to be is to be attributed to God, to be in possession of understanding must be attributable to God.[77] Wyclif makes reference to Anselm's principle in *P*5.7, that God is whatever it is better to be than not to be, to support his argument that every 'probable' attribute of God can be proved in this way.

Other fourteenth century writers are also aware of the text of the *Proslogion*. One example is Jean de Ripa, who alludes to Anselm's discussion of eternity in *P*21–22,[78] and the discussion of the inaccessible light in *P*16,[79] as well as providing a brief account of the *ratio Anselmi*, in which God is proved to exist on the basis that it is better to exist than not to exist, and to be a being rather than nothing.[80]

Fifteenth Century

Anselm continues to interest philosophers in the fifteenth century, but they no longer wish to repeat his argument, even if they are sympathetic to it. See for example, Nicholas of Cusa (1401–1464), who does not explicitly defend or oppose Anselm's argument, but makes use of Anselm's formula 'X' and the notion that God is greater than can be thought, pushing beyond Anselm's position on God's unknowability to an almost apophatic view of God's inconceivability. His own argument for the necessary existence of God from possibility in *De Apice Theoriae*, 13, follows Anselmian lines, but is quite distinctive.[81]

---

76 S. Harrison Thompson (ed.), *Johannis Wyclif Summa de ente: libri primi tractatus primus et secundus*, Oxford 1930, p. 79.

77 M. Dziewicki (ed.), *Johannis Wyclif De ente liborum duorum excerpta: Libri I, Tractatus tertius et quartus: Liber II, Tractatus primus et tertius, et fragmentum De annihilatione*, London 1909, p. 50 ll. 12–20.

78 P. Vignaux, 'La preuve ontologique chez Jean de Ripa', in *AA*, IV/1, pp. 173–94.

79 See Paul of Venice's abbreviation of Jean de Ripa's *Super Primum Sententiarum*, q. III, art. 2 in F. Ruello (ed.), *Paul Venetus: Super primum Sententiarum Johannis de Ripa lecturae abbreviatio. Prologus*, Florence 1980, p. 199.

80 Vignaux, 'Jean de Ripa', p. 179 n. 24.

81 Nicholas de Cusa, *Opera Omnia*, vol. 12, edited by R. Klibansky and J.G. Senger, Hamburg 1982, p. 126. See J. Hopkins, 'Nicholas of Cusa's intellectual relationship to Anselm of Canterbury', in P. Casarella (ed.), *Cusanus: The Legacy of Learned Ignorance*, Washington D.C. 2006, pp. 54–73, esp. pp. 57–60.

Gabriel Biel (d. 1495), shares the Ockhamist/nominalist distrust of reason as a way to knowledge of God. In his *Collectorium circa quattuor libros sententiarum*, he asserts that God is not the object known, but rather the principal and efficient cause of our knowledge (of Him).[82] In the question concerning whether God's existence is *per se notum*, he argues that the fool's doubt shows that knowledge of God is not *per se nota*.[83] Any demonstration can only be based on probabilities and will lack the force that Anselm claims for his argument.[84]

For the nominalist tradition, Anselm's argument must fail as a logically rigorous demonstration of God's existence, since all such arguments must fail in a world where man's reason is corrupted by sin and can only attain to God as a result of faith. These thinkers clearly saw that Anselm was not one of them. Thus, at the end of the medieval period, with the apparent victory of the *via moderna*, it is unsurprising that interest in Anselm's project wanes. That said, it is important to note that the continued interest at the beginning of the modern period, owed more to Aquinas than to any other interpreter. His rejection of Anselm's argument was decisive for those who rejected the argument and the starting point for justifying the argument to those who sought to defend it. Thus, although the interpretations of Bonaventure, Scotus and others might have been more interesting, that of Aquinas was more influential.

---

82 *I Sententiarum*, d. 3, q. 1, a. 2. See Gabrielis Biel, *Collectorium circa quattor libros Sententiarum: Prologus et Liber primus*, edited by W. Werbeck and U. Hofman, Tubingen 1973.

83 *I Sententiarum*, d. 3, q. 4, a. 2, concl. 1.

84 *I Sententiarum*, d. 2, q. 10, a. 2 concl. 3.

Chapter 7
The Modern Reception

Sixteenth Century

Interest in Anselm's argument had waned by the end of the fifteenth century, whilst the great debates of the sixteenth century were concerned with the nature of Christian faith and the means of salvation, rather than the existence of God. The weight placed upon the principles of '*sola scriptura*', '*sola fide*' and '*solus Christus*' by the 'reformers' meant that it became difficult, if not impossible, to accept the Anselmian principles of *sola ratione* and *remoto Christo*. Luther himself possessed a copy of Anselm's works, which he glossed in his own hand (1513–1516).[1] However, he appears to have had no interest in the *Proslogion*, and it does not merit a single comment. Nevertheless, the ongoing scholastic tradition continued to address Aquinas's objection to the argument that God's existence is *per se notum*, and, however mistakenly, to address Anselm's argument from this perspective. Thus, the commentator on Aquinas and opponent of Luther, Thomas de Vio Cajetan (1449–1534), expands on Aquinas's objections, making the important point that for something to be *per se* means that it excludes another, middle term,[2] but like Aquinas fails to see that therefore Anselm's demonstration of God's existence can in no way be classified as a proof of God's self-evidence. As we saw in Chapter 5, X functions as a middle term in the proof of God. The minor premise, God is X, is demonstrated by establishing the identity of the attributes of God and X in the main body of the *Proslogion*. The proof of the proposition, 'X exists' (the major premise), is achieved by a *reductio* demonstration (in two stages, that X exists, that the existence of X is undeniable). At no point is there a claim that God or X is *per se notum*.

Francisco Suarez (1548–1617), Jesuit priest and theologian, refers to the *Proslogion* in his *Disputationes Metaphysicae*, 29 section 2. Taking his lead from Aquinas, *ST* Ia, 2, 1, Suarez states that Anselm in *P*2, *P*3 and the *Responsio* appears to have held the view that God's existence cannot be demonstrated, because it is self-evident.[3] Later he says that Anselm's formula 'X' is taken from Augustine's *De Doctrina Christiana*, but that it is not clear whether X signifies something true

---

1 *D. Martin Luthers Werke: Kritische Gesamtausgabe*, vol. 9, Weimar 1893, pp. 104–14.

2 *Sancti Thomae Aquinatis Opera Omnia, vol. 4: Pars Prima Summa Theologiae (ad q. 49) cum commentariis Thomae de Vio Caietani*, Rome 1888, p. 28.

3 Francisco Suarez, *The metaphysical demonstration of the existence of God: metaphysical disputations 28–29*, translated and edited by J. Doyle, South Bend, Ind. 2004, pp. 83f.

or imagined.[4] In other words, the claims for self-evidence involving X do not hold water. No serious attempt is made by Suarez to engage with Anselm who is merely one amongst many competing and possibly dated (pre-Aquinas) authorities.

Seventeenth Century

Rene Descartes (1596–1650) famously presents different versions of an argument for the existence of God that is traditionally classed together with that of Anselm as 'ontological', although, as in the case of Anselm, he had not himself applied this epithet to his argument(s). In terms of the reception of Anselm's argument, Descartes's work marks a significant step, not because Descartes was an interpreter of Anselm, but precisely because he was not that. In fact, Descartes does not explicitly discuss the thought of Anselm at all. It is not until he has already published the *Discourse on Method* (1637) and completed the manuscript of the *Meditations on First Philosophy* (published in 1641) that for the first and only time he refers to Anselm in a letter to Mersenne (December 1640): 'I shall look at Saint Anselm at the first opportunity.'[5] The inference to be drawn is that he was unacquainted with Anselm's argument.

The 'classic' presentation of Descartes's argument is to be found in the fifth meditation:[6]

> [I]t is quite evident that existence can no more be separated from the essence of God than the fact that its three angles equal two right angles can be separated from the essence of a triangle, or than the idea of a mountain can be separated from the idea of a valley. Hence it is just as much of a contradiction to think of God (that is, a supremely perfect being) lacking existence (that is, lacking a perfection) as it is to think of a mountain without a valley.

Whether this argument was derived from earlier scholastic sources or was an independent discovery, its influence on the tradition of reception of Anselm's argument arises from the attempt of others to classify the two arguments together and to read Anselm's argument as that of Descartes and through the lens of discussions of the latter's argument.

It was Johannes Caterus (1590–1655), in the first set of his objections to the *Meditations*, who identified Descartes's argument in the fifth meditation with the version of Anselm's argument rejected by Aquinas in *ST* Ia, 2, 1, equating Thomas's version of X, '*id quo maius* significari *non potest*', with Descartes's 'supremely

---

4 Ibid., p. 144.

5 C. Adam and P. Tannery, *Oeuvres de Descartes*, vol. III, Paris 1899, p. 261.

6 J. Cottingham, R. Stoothoff and D. Murdoch (eds), *The Philosophical Writings of Descartes* (=*CSM*), vol. II, Cambridge 1984, p. 46.

perfect being', since nothing greater than the latter can be thought.[7] Caterus called this a definition of God. In his reply, Descartes seeks to distinguish his argument from that to which Thomas objected. The conclusion to be drawn from the argument as conveyed by Thomas concerns the meaning of the word 'God', which we understand to involve existence in reality as well as in understanding. 'Yet,' Descartes writes, 'because a word conveys something, that thing is not therefore shown to be true'.[8] Descartes regards his argument as quite different:[9]

> That which we clearly and distinctly understand to belong to the true and immutable nature, or essence, or form of something, can be truly asserted of that thing. But once we have made a sufficiently careful investigation of what God is, we clearly and distinctly understand that existence belongs to his true and immutable nature. Hence we can now truly assert of God that he does exist.

This follows because (1) 'whatever we clearly and distinctly understand is true' and (2) the idea of God contains necessary existence. Descartes's introduction of the concept of clear and distinct ideas does not mean that the object of thought is fully understood. Thus, in the case of the 'infinite', having a clear and distinct understanding that no limitations can be found in it is to understand it, although the infinite is not thereby grasped. It is sufficient then for Descartes as for Anselm that there is some understanding of God,[10] although Descartes is much more explicit about what this means. For Descartes shows that it is not necessary to have a vision of God in order to understand something of his essence, and it is not necessary to fully understand God's essence in order to be able to say something about it. The clear and distinct idea of God is sufficient to provide us with the basis for an *a priori* proof of God's existence. On the other hand, Descartes's response can be seen as important for the reception of Anselm's argument, because it shows that, even without a grasp of God's essence, God's essence can be sufficiently understood ('insofar as the feebleness of our nature allows',[11] 'so far as the eye of my darkened intellect can bear it'[12]) for the purposes of his *a priori* proof. For

---

7 *CSM*, II, p. 71.

8 *CSM*, II, p. 83

9 Ibid.

10 It should be noted that this is not an understanding of a part of God, but a real understanding, the full implications of which are not grasped. See Descartes's analogy of the novice in geometry, who understands a triangle, since he understands that it is a 'figure bounded by three lines'. More experienced geometers know of other properties of the triangle of which the novice is not aware. (*CSM*, II, p. 254.)

11 *Principles of Philosophy*, I, 22; *CSM*, I, p. 200.

12 *Third Meditation*; *CSM*, II, p. 36.

Descartes as for Anselm a fully comprehended God could not be proven to exist. The proof must be the proof of what is beyond the grasp of thought.[13]

Descartes's suggestion that the idea of God is innate in us reinforces the scholastic tradition of interpretation,[14] and the subsequent Thomist reaction to Descartes tells us something about the Thomist understanding of Anselm. In the *Dream of Descartes*, Maritain writes of the ontological argument as a 'substitute' for the immediate intuition of God.[15] The two notions are inextricably linked and the former is a kind of statement of the fact of the latter. But we do not have such an immediate intuition *in via*, and therefore there can be no successful argument of the kind put forward by Descartes and, by implication, Anselm. There is a supposition here that Anselm's argument assumes that God is in some sense directly perceivable, manifesting Himself directly to the human mind without any mediating realities, that X constitutes a definition of God and thereby a kind of grasping of God's essence. But Anselm makes no such assumptions, and his argument does not require them. Anselm assumes rather that the God of Catholic faith, whose reality he seeks to establish by reason, is beyond man in his sin and ignorance (*P*1). It follows from this assumption that there can be no immediate vision of God, no definition of God, no grasping of God's essence. Rather, God dwells in inaccessible light. Anselm's argument helps to explain how this is the case, by showing that it follows from the fact that He is X. That which is X is greater than can be thought (*P*15) and is therefore knowable in one sense, but unknowable in another.

Caterus was not the only philosopher to provide a noteworthy objection to Descartes which is relevant to our considerations. Pierre Gassendi (1592–1655) anticipates Kant's objection that existence is not a predicate, saying that existence is not a perfection in God just as it is not a perfection in a triangle (or, at least, if it is a perfection, it operates no differently in God than in a triangle). By making existence a perfection in a distinctive sense, Descartes is begging the question, since he has introduced what is to be proved into the idea of God.[16] Descartes's reply is that the 'necessary existence' of God is different from the 'possible existence' of the triangle, and it is this that justifies his treatment of God's existence. The actual existence of that which necessarily exists follows from the fact that it is necessarily existent, whilst the actual existence of the triangle that possibly exists has to be established by further investigation. In that sense, existence in God is equivalent to the necessary properties of the triangle (e.g. that the sum of its angles

---

[13] See J.-M. Beyssade, 'The idea of God and the proofs of his existence', in J. Cottingham (ed.), *The Cambridge Companion to Descartes*, Cambridge 1992, pp. 174–99, p. 185.

[14] See *Principles of Philosophy*, I, 22; *CSM*, I, p. 200:'For when we reflect on the idea of God which we were born with'.

[15] J. Maritain, *The Dream of Descartes*, London 1946, p. 107.

[16] *CSM*, II, p. 225.

equals 180 degrees), rather than to the possible existence of the triangle itself.[17] Descartes's reply to Gassendi has been influential in the later interpretation of Anselm's argument, since it suggests that a successful 'ontological' argument would have to address the necessary existence of God. This is then read back into Anselm's argument in the *Proslogion*, where Anselm is supposed to have put forward an argument concerning God's existence in *P*2 and another argument concerning his necessary existence in *P*3.[18] However, as we saw in Chapter 5, Anselm does not engage in a discussion of necessary existence in the *Proslogion*, but with that which cannot be thought not to exist.

Gottfried Leibniz (1646–1716) identifies Descartes's *a priori* argument for God with that of Anselm, believing that Descartes borrowed it from Anselm.[19] The account he gives of Anselm's argument reflects this fact. According to Leibniz 'the Scholastics' were wrong to regard this argument as fallacious. However, although it is not fallacious, it is incomplete. It assumes that the idea of God is possible and without contradiction. Thus it established no more and no less than that 'if God is possible, He exists'.[20]

Leibniz's older contemporary, Baruch Spinoza (1632–1677), appears to raise, if only indirectly, a particular difficulty for Anselm's argument, since he identifies God with the natural universe.[21] How, then, are we to know that X is to be identified with the God of Catholic belief rather than Spinoza's God? As we have already seen, Anselm may well have employed the formula 'X' because of its non-Christian history, and Seneca's identification of it with the world. If that is the case, then he would not have been unaware of the possibility raised by Spinoza. It would also explain why most of the *Proslogion* is taken up with establishing the identity of X and the God of Catholic belief. Spinoza's own argument for God's necessary existence indicates a sympathy with the Cartesian project that overrides any interest he may have had in the specifics of an Anselmian argument.[22] In fact, there is no evidence that Spinoza was acquainted with Anselm's work.

---

17 *CSM*, II, p. 263.

18 The classic presentation of this viewpoint it to be found in N. Malcolm, 'Anselm's ontological arguments', in *The Philosophical Review*, 69 (1960) 41–62. Copyright, 1960, Sage School of Philosophy at Cornell University. All rights reserved. Used by permission of the present publisher, Duke University Press.

19 Leibniz, *New Essays on Human Understanding*, Open Court, LaSalle Ill. 1949. Book IV, 10, §7.

20 Leibniz's position shares elements of that of Peter Olivi and Duns Scotus.

21 See Spinoza, *Ethica, pars* I, *propositio* XIV: '*Praeter Deum nulla dari, neque concipi potest substantia.*'

22 See *Ethica*, propositio XI: '*Deus, sive substantia constans infinitis attributis, quorum unumquodque aeternam, & infinitam essentiam exprimit, necessario existit.*'

Eighteenth Century

Christian Wolff (1679–1754) stated that Anselm affirmed that the existence of God is to be inferred from the notion of the most perfect being, linking the argument of Descartes with that of Anselm.[23] He understood Aquinas' criticism to be that God's existence can only be proved from the notion of a most perfect being, if it can be shown that this notion accords (*convenire*) with some being, and took the view that it was a similar criticism to that of Leibniz, that existence cannot be established from such a notion until one has shown that the most perfect being is possible. Wolff appears uninterested in the question of whether and in what sense one could have knowledge of God, and therefore is able to disregard the basis of Aquinas' criticism that God's existence is not *per se notum*. Although aware of a medieval dispute concerning Anselm's argument, there is no evidence in his discussion that Wolff was acquainted at first hand with any of the texts.

Of particular interest for the development of the reception of Anselm's argument is Wolff's use of the term 'ontology', which he defined as 'the science of being in general insofar as it is being',[24] for it was Immanuel Kant's reaction to 'ontology' as a science that was to determine so much of what came later in the reading of Anselm.

Immanuel Kant (1724–1804) is determined to put aside a proud ontology 'that presumptuously claims to supply, in systematic doctrinal form, synthetic *a priori* knowledge of things in general' for a modest 'analytic of pure understanding'.[25] What Wolff and others[26] treated as a set of principles which demonstrate with mathematical rigour claims about the real world, Kant attempts to show are 'merely rules for the exposition of appearances'. But, whether his critique addresses the nature of Anselm's proof is a question Kant does not pose, because he appears to have had no direct, and virtually no indirect, knowledge of Anselm's argument. There are, for example, no references to Anselm in Kant's writings prior to the publication of the *CPR* (1781; revised 1787). However, it seems likely that Kant would have noted the reference to Anselm in Wolff's *Theologia Naturalis*, II, §13, in which Wolff identifies Anselm as a participant in a scholastic dispute concerning a 'Cartesian' proof of God's existence. In *Reflexionen* 6214 (dating from the early 1780s) we find a reference to Anselm's Ontotheology.[27] There is also a reference

[23] C. Wolff, *Theologia Naturalis – Pars II*, Editio Novissima Emendiator, Verona 1779, Sectio I, Caput 1, §13, '*Ens perfectissimum possibile est*'.

[24] C. Wolff, *Philosophia prima sive ontologia methodo scientifica pertractata qua omnes cognitionis humanae principia continentur*, Frankfurt 1730, §1: '*scientia entis in genere, quatenus ens est*'.

[25] I. Kant, *Immanuel Kant's Critique of Pure Reason (=CPR)*, translated by N. Kemp Smith, 2nd impression with corrections, Macmillan, London 1933, A247; B303. All quotations from *CPR* are reproduced with permission of Palgrave Macmillan.

[26] E.g. Alexander Baumgarten (1714–1762) in his *Metaphysica*, Halle 1739.

[27] *Kants Gesammelte Schriften (=GS)*, hrsg. von der Königlich Preussischen Akademie der Wissenschaften, Berlin 1900– , vol. XVIII, p. 500.

to Anselm in the *Lectures on the philosophical doctrine of religion*.[28] And in 1791 Kant writes of Leibniz as adding to or supplementing Anselm's argument.[29] Particularly revealing is the reference dating from 1794, in which Kant calls Anselm a Parisian scholastic, who first put forward the argument developed by Descartes and Leibniz.[30] Without any knowledge of Anselm's argument, Kant has placed it under the category of 'ontological arguments'.

Kant claims that in the end all arguments for God boil down to the ontological argument as he has refuted it in the 'Transcendental Dialectic'. This ensures that ontological arguments in the weak sense (any arguments that make real claims about existence, i.e. all arguments for the existence of God) are swept up with ontological arguments in the strong sense (arguments which follow the particular approach of seventeenth and eighteenth century rationalism). Kant's claim cannot have apodictic force, since it would be dependent on considering all the arguments for God's existence (including that of Anselm) to see whether they did indeed fall under the category of ontological arguments in the strong sense.[31] Of course, one might take as axiomatic Kant's uncritical empiricist assumption that all knowledge of objects is to be limited *to* as well as *by* sense experience,[32] i.e. that defines out of existence objects not given to us in experience. But, even abstract and *a priori* arguments for God are not to be dismissed by a vague appeal to an empiricist epistemology of the kind we encounter in the 'Postulates of Empirical Thought'.[33]

Kant's specific objections to ontological arguments can be summarised as follows: **(K1)** that if both the predicate and the subject of a judgement are rejected, then no contradiction can result,[34] **(K2)** that ontological arguments assume what has been called into question,[35] erroneously treating God as a special case, and **(K3)** that existence is not a predicate.[36] Let us deal with these in turn.

(Ad K1) The question is not whether there is a general principle that subject and predicate can both be rejected without contradiction, but whether any such principle is applicable in the case of God. The example Kant provides of a similar case is that of the triangle: 'To posit a triangle, and yet to reject its three angles, is self-contradictory, but there is no contradiction in rejecting the triangle together

---

[28] *GS*, XXVIII, p. 1003.

[29] *GS*, XX, p. 349.

[30] *GS*, XVIII, p. 782.

[31] In the *CPR*, Kant ignores his own version of the ontological argument. For the significance of this, see I. Logan, 'Whatever happened to Kant's ontological argument?', in *Philosophy and Phenomenological Research*, 74 (2007) 346–63.

[32] See *CPR*, B75: 'Our nature is so constituted that our intuition can never be other than sensible'.

[33] A.W. Wood, *Kant's Rational Theology*, Ithaca/London 1978, p. 96.

[34] *CPR*, A594; B622.

[35] *CPR*, A595; B623.

[36] *CPR*, A598; B626.

with its three angles.' Whilst in this instance there may be no self-contradiction, it does not follow that there is no contradiction at all. If I say there is no such thing as a triangle in the sense that there is no actual triangle instantiated in the universe, there may turn out to be a contradiction between my concepts of the triangle and of the universe, since it may be the case that the universe cannot exist without there being triangles (i.e. the existence of triangles is a necessary condition for the existence of the universe).

Let us assume that the existence of triangles is not a necessary condition for the existence of the universe. In this case, there would be no contradiction involved in denying the existence of triangles. But in making this assumption we have made an assumption that could not be made in the case of God without contradiction, for it is 'definitional' of Anselm's God that He is a necessary condition for the existence of the universe, since He is its Creator. Thus, the example of the triangle does not stand on all fours with the case of God. 'That than which a greater cannot be thought' is not like 'that than which a greater can be thought', precisely because it is the condition governing the possibility of the latter.

(Ad K2) This leads directly to the second objection Kant produces:[37]

> The only way of evading this conclusion [i.e. K1] is to argue that there are subjects that cannot be removed, and must always remain. That, however, would only be another way of saying that there are absolutely necessary subjects; and that is the very assumption which I have called in question, and the possibility of which the above argument professes to establish.

Anselm it seems is wrong to argue that God is a special case that cannot be removed without contradiction, since that is the point to be established. The key move here for Anselm comes in the early stages of his argument, when he says in *P*2.5 that the fool, on hearing 'something than which nothing greater can be thought', 'understands what he hears, and what he understands is in his understanding, even if he should not understand that it exists', i.e. he has already committed himself to accepting the existence of God, even if he does not understand this yet. In the same way, he has already committed to understanding that God is a special case. For God is X, and X is distinct from not-X, and the term 'X' operates in a different way to all other terms that concern not-X. God is 'by definition' a special case. The issue is how this works out in our thinking about Him. Anselm's argument seeks to show that one way in which God is a special case is that His existence cannot be denied, because unlike all other things, whether real or chimerical, a contradiction arises when one tries to deny His existence. This is not an internal contradiction, but a contradiction between the contents of the assertion, 'God does not exist' and my saying it, a contradiction in performance. Kant's **K1** objection has missed an important implication of the *reductio* nature of Anselm's argument, that there are other types of contradiction

---

[37] *CPR*, A595; B623. The Cartesian argument he is responding to in K1 likens the property of existence in God to that of angles in the triangle

in addition to internal contradictions. As I type these words, I can type, 'I am not typing and will not have typed these words'. There is no internal contradiction in these words, and they could very well be true. There is a contradiction, however, between my actual typing of these words and their content. And it would seem that this is just as significant a contradiction as an internal contradiction. When Kant says, 'in the absence of contradiction I have, through *a priori* concepts alone, no criterion of impossibility',[38] he is referring to internal contradiction and not to the type of contradiction identified by Anselm in the *Proslogion*.

But Kant does not accept that God constitutes a special case, because this does not fit in with his presuppositions concerning the exhaustive nature of the analytic/synthetic distinction as understood by him. The proposition 'God exists' would be 'a miserable tautology', if it is analytic, and the predicate would merely repeat what was contained in the subject. If the proposition is synthetic, 'as every reasonable person' will admit of all existential propositions, then the predicate can be rejected without contradiction, since it is only in the case of analytic propositions that the predicate cannot be rejected without contradiction.[39] But we have already seen that for Anselm, God as X constitutes a special case in such a way that if one does not allow this special case, then one is not talking about God in the sense of X. In other words, one cannot say that God as X is not a special case.

(Ad K3) We now come to the infamous slogan, 'Existence is not a predicate'. Kant argues that *Sein* (existence/being) is not a real predicate, i.e. 'it is not a concept of something which could be added to the concept of a thing'.[40] The little word 'is' does not add anything to the concept of God when one says, 'God is'. Thus, a 'hundred real thalers do not contain the least coin more than a hundred possible thalers', for the real contains no more than the merely possible.[41] There appears to be something counter intuitive about this claim, given that a hundred real thalers contains a hundred more real thalers than a hundred non-real thalers. And a hundred possible thalers if they are not real thalers are in fact non-real thalers. Kant attempts to pre-empt such an objection by admitting that real thalers have a significance in financial affairs not possessed by possible thalers, arguing that this is precisely because their existence is not contained in the concept (i.e. is not analytic), but is added to the concept synthetically. The concept of a hundred thalers is a concept of the possible and it is only when existence is added that it is a concept of something real. The addition of existence is not something that happens in the concept, but is something that happens in the real world. There is an obvious weakness with this argument for in this foregoing discussion we encountered the concepts of a hundred thalers, a real hundred thalers, a non-real hundred thalers and a possible hundred thalers. These concepts are not identical, but they must be if Kant is correct. Although Kant's claim that existence is not a predicate appears

---

38 *CPR*, A596; B624.

39 *CPR*, A598; B626.

40 Ibid.

41 *CPR*, A599; B627.

unconvincing, I do not intend to pursue the matter here, because the question is not whether existence is a predicate in the case of not-X, but whether it is a predicate in the case of X. Anselm does not claim that the argument he employs to prove that God exists can be applied to what is not God. In fact, he says that it cannot. It is not so much that existence adds anything to the concept of God, but that existence subtracted from the concept of God (X) leaves one with a concept of something else (not-X). This might be taken to mean that the only concept of God we can have is of a non-existent God. However, this non-existent God would not be X, and Anselm has shown that God must be X or one is not talking about God. This is why for Anselm it is not possible to say with understanding that there is no God. For understanding the concept of God (as X) involves understanding that God exists, regardless of whether or not existence is a predicate in the case of not-X.[42]

Kant's failure to recognise the special nature of the case of God had been anticipated by David Hume (1711–1776). As an historian, Hume was well aware of the role Anselm had played in the affairs of England, but there is no mention of Anselm in his philosophical works. Hume addresses *a priori* arguments for God in his *Dialogues concerning Natural Religion*.[43] Here he has Cleanthes argue that if we can think of something existing, we can also think of it as not existing, and thus there can never be a contradiction involved in denying the existence of something. Such an objection applies to any *a priori* argument making existential claims. But Anselm has made it clear that God as X is a special case, and that some conclusions (at least) concerning not-X may well not be applicable to X. The problem here is that Cleanthes is begging the question. He says that whatever can be thought of as existing can also be thought of as not existing. However, he needs to establish this 'fact'. But how can he establish it, other than by looking at attempts at such instances and showing that they cannot work? A particular problem arises when he seeks to apply the outcome of such an investigation to the question of God. God is not one of a series of facts in the world. He is distinct from everything given with the world. Thus, a conclusion *drawn from* facts in the world, which is a conclusion *about* facts in the world (the realm of not-X), is not a conclusion about God (X). To defeat Anselm's argument it is necessary to establish that Anselm's reasoning does not lead to his conclusion. One cannot do this by appealing to principles relevant to another sphere of investigation.

Nineteenth Century

In *Zur Geschichte der neueren Philosophie*, Schelling (1775–1854) identifies Anselm as advancing 'a similar argument' to that of Descartes.[44] He does not

---

42 See Hartshorne, *Anselm's Discovery*, p. 247.

43 D. Hume, *Dialogues concerning Natural Religion*, 2nd edn, London 1779, Part IX.

44 English translation by A. Bowie: F.W.J. von Schelling, *On the History of Modern Philosophy*, Cambridge 1994, p. 50.

address Anselm's argument directly, but that of Descartes. Schelling holds that Kant and others have missed the point in their refutations of the Cartesian ontological argument, since Descartes does not argue that existence is a perfection, but that 'it would contradict the nature of the perfect being to exist just contingently (...), therefore the most perfect being can only exist necessarily'.[45] Descartes has shown that if God exists, He exists necessarily. However, he believes mistakenly that he has shown that God necessarily exists, which is not the same. There is more in the conclusion than there was in the premises. Schelling argues, then, that Descartes (and, by association, Anselm) has established the manner of God's existence but not the fact of it. What is more, this proof concerning the necessity of God's existence cannot give us God as we understand him (i.e. the God Anselm wants to prove), but a necessary being (that which cannot not be), which is bound by its necessity, lacking the freedom to be called for instance a creator: 'the so-called proof of Anselm comes down to *this*.'[46] According to Schelling, this explains what he incorrectly believed was the universal rejection of Anselm's argument by the scholastics.

Later in the *History*, Schelling provides further evidence of what is going on here. He employs the Latin phrase '*Deus est id, quod non* ***cogitari*** *potest nisi existens*', which is translated by Bowie as 'God is that which cannot be thought unless it exists',[47] that is, if God does not exist, He cannot be the object of thought. However, Schelling's meaning appears to be better conveyed by translating this statement as 'God is that which cannot be thought except as existing', that is, whether or not God exists, He cannot be thought as not existing. This distinction tells us something about the difference between Anselm and Schelling, and about the nature of Anselm's argument. Anselm's position is closer to the meaning of Bowie's translation: if God does not exist, He cannot be the object of thought, even of a thought which seeks to deny His existence. Possession of the concept of God is for Anselm evidence of God's existence, and to talk of the possibility of God's non-existence (even in the case of a hypothetical syllogism which is intended to demonstrate God's existence) is to have failed to address God. In this sense, the denial of God constitutes a starting-point for the demonstration of God's existence, since the denial is revealed as resulting from the failure to understand the concept of God, which concept can only be had because God actually exists.

G.W.F. Hegel (1770–1831) treats of Anselm's argument in several of his works. He claims that Anselm is the originator of the ontological argument,[48] and identifies him as the first to make the transition from the concept of God to being,

---

45 Ibid. This appears to be closer to the argument of Spinoza than that of Descartes.

46 Ibid., p. 54.

47 Ibid., p. 88.

48 Hegel, *Enzyklopädie der philosophischen Wissenschaften im Grundrisse (1830)* (=*EPW*) §193; *HW*, vol. 8, p. 348. References are to G.W.F. Hegel, *Werke*, 3rd edn, Frankfurt 1993–96 (=*HW*).

something that neither Greek philosophy, nor earlier Christian thought achieved.[49] He also states that Anselm can be regarded as the 'founder of scholastic theology'[50] with its attempt to construct the doctrinal faith of the Church on metaphysical foundations.[51] In the section on Anselm in the *Lectures on the History of Philosophy*, Hegel's knowledge of Anselm appears to be derived exclusively from the excerpts contained in the eighth volume of Tennemann's *Geschichte der Philosophie*.[52]

Hegel's exegesis of Anselm's argument is not based on a close reading of the text. It reflects rather the transitional role ascribed to it (and more generally to medieval scholasticism) by Hegel within his account of the history of philosophy. As such, for Hegel, it cannot succeed as a proof of God, even though for him its fundamental insight is correct. Anselm's argument shares with scholastic thought a formal logical character that is empty (**H1**). It is based on a presupposition (the unity of concept and being), which, although correct, is not shown to be so by Anselm (**H2**). Anselm remains with the concept, the subjective, and does not attain to being, the objective, although he understands the need to do this (**H3**). If God is merely a subjective idea, then He is not perfect (**H4**). Thus, Kant's objection to ontological arguments works against Anselm's subjective argument (**H5**). However, Kant fails to recognise the uniqueness of the concept of God. In the end, the success of the ontological argument is determined by its starting-point (**H6**), the identity of thought and being in the infinite, but this has to be demonstrated by Hegel's account of the self-manifestation of the absolute Idea in human history.

I shall expand on these points in turn, in order to assess the significance of Hegel's 'reading' of Anselm, bearing in mind his very limited knowledge of the text of the *Proslogion*.

(**H1**) Hegel regards scholasticism as possessing a fundamental weakness in its purely formal nature. It is 'a quite barbaric philosophy of the understanding … which gads around in groundless connections of categories and determinations of the understanding'.[53] Anselm's argument falls victim to this weakness, insofar as it too is constructed in a formal logical manner.[54] It remains within the confines of scholastic dialectic (the form); it remains within the realm of thought and concept.

---

49 Hegel, *Vorlesungen über die Philosophie der Religion* (=*VPR*); *HW*, vol. 17, p. 523.

50 Hegel, *Vorlesungen über die Geschichte der Philosophie* (=*VGP*); *HW*, vol. 19, p. 555.

51 *VGP*; *HW*, vol. 19, p. 553.

52 See W.G. Tennemann, *Geschichte der Philosophie*, vols 1–11, Leipzig 1798–1819. Tennemann provides fairly extensive quotations from the *Monologion* and *De Veritate*, but cites only *P*2.5–2.12 and *P*3.2–3.4 and nothing from the *Responsio*. He provides in fact far more detail of the argument of the *Pro Insipiente*, citing from *G*2 (twice), *G*3, *G*5 and *G*7.

53 *VGP*; *HW*, vol. 19, p. 587.

54 *VGP*; *HW*, vol. 19, p. 557.

The unity of thought and being in the infinite is lacking in Anselm,[55] which is unsurprising, given the stage he represents for Hegel in the history of philosophy.
(H2) Anselm presupposes that there is a unity of concept and being, but he fails to show that this is the case. This explains why his proof is unsatisfactory, for it is precisely what he presupposes that is in question.[56] Although the content of Anselm's idea is 'true' and 'necessary' according to Hegel, its form is defective, since the unity of concept and being is presupposed.[57]
(H3) The implication of the problem posed by what Hegel regards as Anselm's presupposition is that the Kantian criticism appears to be justified in relation to Anselm's argument, since it is caught up in the subjective nature of thought, making an unjustified assumption that the object of the concept is an object in reality. It is because Anselm attempts to prove God's existence, rather than recognising God's self-manifestation in thought that this problem arises. The point is not to attempt to bridge the gap between concept and reality, but to recognise their unity in the infinite God. That constitutes the proof. It is only in the case of that which is not God (of concepts which are finite and in a sense untrue) that this unity is lacking and existence is not contained in the concept.[58] Anselm's aim is too narrow. It is not *unum argumentum* but the totality of thought that is required to attain to the ontological proof. Hegel sees Anselm as a kind of forerunner, who seeks to explain God in terms of philosophy, but who remains in the realms of religion, for whom philosophy is the 'handmaid of theology'.[59]
(H4) In the *Lectures on the Philosophy of Religion*, Hegel gives an account of Anselm's argument which reveals the implications of the subjective nature of Anselm's argument for the concept of God.[60] If God is conceived in such a way that he remains a subjective idea, then He is not the most perfect, something more perfect can be conceived, which is an objective idea, possessing existence. That idea of the most perfect is the idea of God, and thus to limit God to the subjective idea is at best to misunderstand what God is.[61] This argument is reminiscent of Anselm's *argumentum*, so it is not surprising to read in the *Encyclopedia*:[62] 'Anselm has … correctly declared as perfect that which exists not merely in a subjective manner, but at the same time in an objective manner.' Nevertheless for Hegel, Anselm fails to achieve his proof, because he has not demonstrated the unity of thought and being.

---

[55] See J. Biard, 'The Middle Ages in Hegel's History of Philosophy', in *The Philosophical Forum*, 31 (2000) 248–60, 255.

[56] *VPR*; *HW*, vol. 17, p. 211.

[57] *VPR*; *HW*, vol. 17, p. 527.

[58] *EPW* §24; *HW*, vol. 8, p. 86.

[59] See esp. *Lectures on the Philosophy of History*; *HW*, vol. 12, pp. 476f.

[60] *VPR*; *HW*, vol. 17, pp. 209ff.

[61] See also *Lectures on the Proof of God's Existence* (*VPR*); *HW*, vol. 17. pp. 523f. and 529f.

[62] *EPW* §193; *HW*, vol. 8, p. 349.

(**H5**) For Hegel, Kant's objection to ontological arguments works only if thought and being are differentiated. Hegel's criticism of Kant's objection is not that the concept of a hundred thalers cannot be differentiated from its existence, but that Kant equates God with the hundred thalers. It is precisely the differentiation of concept and being that is definitional of finite things, whereas any 'definition' of God requires that His concept and His being are '*unseparated* and *inseparable*'.[63] Whilst it is the case that in a sense concept and being are distinct from each other, it is even more true that God is different from the hundred thalers and from other finite things.[64] Anselm, in accepting in the form of his argument that this differentiation applies to God, opens himself up to Kant's objection. However, Kant fails to show that his objection applies to God properly conceived. The weakness of Kant's critique of the ontological proof is that it addresses the finite, i.e. that which is distinct from God,[65] rather than the God who is supposed to be the object of the proof. Hegel recognises that it is the uniqueness of God that protects the concept of God against the criticisms of Kant and others.

(**H6**) According to Hegel, Anselm's *presupposition* of the unity of concept and being provides him with a defective starting-point for his argument. On the basis of this presupposition Anselm starts from the concept and treats being as a predicate of God.[66] In setting out to establish that being belongs to the concept of God, Anselm has already set concept and being over against each other, which cannot be the case for God (unlike the finite[67]). Having broken the egg we cannot put it back together again. The point is not to break the egg, not to posit the concept in such a way that it is separated from being. Hegel's philosophy can be characterised as the attempt to establish the ontological proof in a way that avoids this 'error'. To do this, Hegel has to develop an entire philosophy, in which the identity of being and thought turns out to be the starting-point. Kant's objection does not work against Anselm if we understand that God is not the concept (thought) without reality (being), that there is an identity of being and thought in the infinite. This alone is the starting-point.[68] The form of Anselm's argument is incorrect, since it commences with the concept and attempts the transition to being. From his starting-point in scholastic philosophy Anselm could get no further than he does. For philosophy is with him at the stage in which thought and being are seen as opposed, even though Anselm makes a valiant attempt to construct a 'connection' between the two. The form of the ontological proof has to be radically different if it is to present the content correctly, and clearly for Hegel this means it must be in the form of Hegelian logic.

---

63 Hegel, *Die Wissenschaft der Logik* (=*WL*); *HW*, vol. 5, p. 92.

64 Ibid.

65 *VPR*; *HW*, vol. 17, p. 532.

66 J. Rohls, *Theologie und Metaphysik: der ontologische Gottesbeweis und seine Kritiker*, Gütersloh 1987, p. 395.

67 *VPR*; *HW*, vol. 17, p. 530.

68 *VGP*; *HW*, vol. 19, p. 559.

For Hegel, what is required is a more exhaustive ontological proof, in which the possibility of '*thinking* the finite' arises from the '*being* of the infinite'.[69] This proof is achieved by a process of understanding the movement of spirit in human history, which is the self-manifestation of the infinite in the finite. Hegel's absolute philosophy constitutes the proof, whilst Anselm's argument like that of Descartes exhibits 'the erroneous form of the formal syllogism'.[70]

It was clear from the outset that Hegel's reading of Anselm was inadequate. Thus, when he refers to Anselm's key concept as 'the thought of a highest',[71] he is unaware that for Anselm the '*summum omnium*' (*P*14.2) is not simply the highest thinkable, but is even greater than that which can be thought. The thought of the highest thinkable becomes the thought of the unthinkable, in the sense that it cannot be grasped by thought in its totality. If it could be grasped in this way, it would not be the highest thinkable, since it would then be possible to think of something higher (*P*15.2). His lack of awareness of the direction of Anselmian dialectic, may explain why Hegel sees in Anselm's argument the weakness of empty formal syllogisms,[72] which cannot escape the world of sense, representation and understanding (*Verstand*) nor attain to the world of concept and reason (*Vernunft*). Anselm did not know of the Kantian criticism and thus Hegel is able to argue that he is open to that criticism, since he nowhere refutes the argument that existence is not a predicate. However, a more detailed reading of Anselm reveals that it is entirely consistent with his position that existence has to be seen as a predicate in the particular case of God (reflecting the distinction between X and not-X), if by this proposition is meant that one cannot possess the concept without affirming the existence of its referent, even if it should be the case that Kant has shown that existence is not a predicate in the case of what is not God, a point which itself is debatable.

Arthur Schopenhauer (1788–1860) famously quipped that the ontological argument (by which he meant Descartes's argument) 'is a charming joke'.[73] He regarded Descartes as its inventor, seeing it in Anselm 'only indicated in a general manner'. In his 'Criticism of the Kantian philosophy', Schopenhauer writes that one can hear Anselm's voice in the section on the Transcendental Ideal.[74] Schopenhauer's view was that Aristotle had already provided a refutation of the ontological argument in *Posterior Analytics*, II, 7: 'But being [*existentia*] is not the substance [*essentia*] of anything.'[75]

---

69 See Q. Lauer, *Hegel's Concept of God*, Albany 1982, p. 228.

70 *WL*; *HW*, vol. 6, p. 402.

71 *VGP*; *HW*, vol. 19, p. 557.

72 What Hegel calls elsewhere 'the cobwebs and hazy forms of abstract understanding'. (*EPW* §38; *HW*, vol. 8, p. 109.)

73 A. Schopenhauer, *On The Fourfold Root of the Principle of Sufficient Reason and On the Will in Nature*, translated by Mme. K. Hillebrand, Revised edition, London 1903, p. 11.

74 A. Schopenhauer, *The World as Will and Idea*, vol. II, translated by R. Haldane and J. Kemp, 3rd edn, Boston 1887, p. 125

75 Ibid. p. 130. *Posterior Analytics*, 92^{b}13f.; Barnes, *Aristotle*, vol. I, p. 152

Schopenhauer's words indicate that he has no direct knowledge of the content of Anselm's argument, since no reader of Anselm would seriously suggest that Anselm's voice is to be found in the text of 'The Transcendental Ideal'. In spite of this, he raises implicitly an interesting question: if Anselm had been aware of the *Posterior Analytics*, would he have been able to put forward his argument as a proof of God's existence? In fact, Anselm would not have found Aristotle's text disconcerting, since it is clearly addressing that which is not God, i.e. that which falls under the Categories. It may well be true that here existence does not pertain to essence. Aristotle concludes that nothing is demonstrated by a definition, but, as we have seen, for Anselm as a Christian dialectician God cannot be defined, since He is not the differentiated species of a genus and does not fall under the Categories. Once again we are reminded of the distinction between X and not-X and Anselm's insistence that the two are not subject to the same rules of argument.

Another reading of Anselm can be found in the work of L. Feuerbach (1804–1872). Although his knowledge of Anselm is perhaps greater than that of Hegel,[76] in his *Essence of Christianity* (1841) he follows in outline Hegel's account of the ontological argument,[77] which he believes to be 'in essence' that of Anselm.[78] Feuerbach's particular view of the ontological argument is based on the notion of X as a 'limit concept', i.e. the highest point that human thought can attain. This is then taken to be God, since there is nothing higher for man. What is internal to man, his highest thought, is then made external to him. Feuerbach follows Hegel's notion that the key concept in Anselm's argument is that of the highest thought. In doing this he equates Anselm's *summum omnium* (understood as X) with the *maius omnibus* of the *Pro Insipiente*. He sees in Anselm's argument a presentation of the highest that can be grasped by man, which is put forward as the concept of God. But Anselm explicitly rejects the *maius omnibus* formulation (*R*5) precisely because of its limited nature, and its consequent failure to deliver what can be delivered by X in his argument. It is entailed necessarily in the notion of X that it is *maius omnibus*, but it does not follow necessarily from the notion of *maius omnibus* that it is X. That which is greater than everything that exists is not necessarily the greatest thing that can exist. X is greater than can be thought (*P*15.2), i.e. it is greater than any limit concept, and as such is not a projection of the limits of man's abstractive power, but transcends that abstractive power. For Feuerbach, any talk of God's real rather than ideal existence is illegitimate. It therefore *follows* that Anselm has made his move illegitimately. But Anselm's argument is a philosophical argument, and even if it were the case that he had

---

[76] He quotes at length from *P*17 and *P*25 in *Wider den Dualismus von Leib und Seele, Fleisch und Geist*. See *Ludwig Feuerbach's Sämmtliche Werke*, edited by W. Bolin and F. Jodl, vols 1–10, Stuttgart 1903–1910 (=*FW*), vol. 2, pp. 352f.; from *M*66 and *P*22 in the Appendix to *Das Wesen des Christenthums* (=*WC*); *FW*, vol. 6, pp. 338 and 357.

[77] *WC*, c. 21; *FW*, vol. 6, pp. 239f.

[78] *Geschichte der Neueren Philosophie*; *FW*, vol. 3, p. 214.

objectified a subjective notion of God, it would not follow *from this* that his argument is invalid or unsound.

One nineteenth century commentator on Anselm, Robert Flint (1838–1910) was strongly convinced of Anselm's rationale for the special case nature of God. He writes:[79] 'The Creator Himself – the absolutely perfect God – The Highest God – is, as Plato and Anselm so profoundly taught, the only best possible Being. In Him alone the actual is coincident and identical with the possible, the real with the ideal.' Although Anselm had his precursors he was 'the first to endeavour to show that from the very idea of God as the highest Being his necessary reality may be strictly deduced'.[80] In his account of Anselm's argument, Flint only considers the text of *P*2, substituting the term 'highest Being' for Anselm's formula 'X'. Yet, in spite of this carelessness in interpretation, Flint makes an insightful observation about the objection that 'the ideal can never logically yield the real'. This is 'merely an assertion that the argument is fallacious'. But such an assertion 'cannot fairly be made until the argument has been exposed and refuted'. Concerning the objection that existence is not a predicate, he writes:[81]

> 'That the exclusion of existence – which here means real and necessary existence – from the idea of God does not leave us with an incomplete idea of God, is not a position, I think, which can be maintained. Take away existence from among the elements in the idea of a perfect being, and the idea becomes either the idea of a nonentity or the idea of an idea, and not the idea of a perfect being at all.'

Again we come across the idea that to subtract existence from God conceptually is not to think of God. Flint concludes that all the objectors show is that 'if our thought of God be imperfect, a being who merely realised that thought would be an imperfect being'.[82]

Twentieth Century

As we enter the twentieth century, there appear other thinkers who attempt to read Anselm apart from the traditions of Thomas, Kant, Hegel, etc., although not necessarily by a return to the detail of Anselm's text. R.G. Collingwood (1889–1943) represents a case in point. He suggests that we should refer to 'Anselm's proof', saying of Kant's description of the 'ontological proof' that it was invented by someone who did not understand Anselm's argument and possesses no authority.[83]

---

79 R. Flint, *Theism: The Baird Lecture for 1876*, 9th edition, Edinburgh 1895, p. 240.

80 Ibid., pp. 277f.

81 Ibid., p. 280.

82 Ibid.

83 R.G. Collingwood, *An Essay on Metaphysics*, Oxford 1940, p. 189 n. 1. However, see his earlier view in *An Essay on Philosophical Method*, Oxford 1933, p. 126.

According to Collingwood Anselm is not trying to prove that God exists, but that we are committed to this belief in the existence of God.[84] For Anselm, he argues, the fool is foolish because he does not realise that he presupposes this belief.[85]

Collingwood makes the important observation that the reason the objections of such as Kant do not work against Anselm's argument is that it applies to thought about a unique object, X, and not to thought in general.[86] Collingwood's view was that since Hegel's ontological proof, there had been no serious criticism of the argument.[87] This view, somewhat surprising in the light of subsequent developments, arises because of the place the proof has in Collingwood's own philosophical system, and the fact that, historically, following Hegel there had been no new objections to Anselm – all the old objections having been shown to be flawed. When we get into the detail of Collingwood's reading of Anselm, we see that he is not really interested in *Anselm's* argument. He claims, for instance, that it does not prove the existence of what people think of as God.[88] However, for Anselm it is central to his argument that it does indeed prove what Catholics happen to believe about God. Nevertheless, Collingwood has two important insights for those who wish to read Anselm: that God is a special case; and that Anselm's argument concerns the presupposition that God exists (i.e. that to possess the idea of God is already to think of Him as existing).

Mention should be made at this point of a particular strand of twentieth century interpretation, in which it is considered unnecessary to treat Anselm's text at all seriously, with the result that his argument is simply caricatured. Thus, Hans Reichenbach (1891–1953) presents Anselm's argument thus: beginning with a definition of God as an infinitely perfect being, which possesses the property of existence, since it possesses every essential property, it proves that God exists.[89] This is *not* Anselm's argument, as the briefest reading of the text shows. However, it is not an uncommon form of presentation of the argument.

In his famous 'Anselm book' (first published in 1931), Karl Barth (1886–1968) attempts to subject the text of the *Proslogion* to a rigorous reading that takes seriously the theological and prayerful nature of the entire work as well as what he regards as the problematical chapters (*P*2–4) that constitute the 'main text'.[90] From the outset, Barth's view of the role of philosophy and its relationship to theology influenced his reading of Anselm. Barth always claimed that Anselm

84 Collingwood, *Metaphysics*, p. 190.

85 Ibid., p. 189.

86 Collingwood, *Philosophical Method*, p. 125.

87 Ibid., p. 126.

88 Ibid., pp. 126f.

89 H. Reichenbach, *The Rise of Scientific Philosophy*, Berkeley/Los Angeles 1951, p. 39.

90 K. Barth, *Anselm, Fides Quaerens Intellectum: Anselm's Proof of the Existence of God in the Context of his Theological Scheme*, translated by I.W. Robertson, SCM Press, London 1960 (=*AFQI*), p. 8.

(as he interpreted him) had had a decisive influence on his thought.[91] It seems, however, that Barth's Anselm bears too much the imprint of Barth for us not to see that it is Barth's own thought that decisively influences his reading of Anselm. In the introduction to *AFQI*, Barth reveals precisely how his own theological understanding will influence his exegesis of the *Proslogion*. Tellingly, he omits Anselm's reference to the proof-nature of the argument when he quotes the relevant passage from *P*0.2. Thus, it is not surprising to read:[92] 'What is set out in *Prosl. 2–4* is first described as a 'proof' *(probare, probatio)* by Anselm's opponent Gaunilo' and '[Anselm's] own particular description of what he is doing is not *probare* at all but *intelligere*.' According to Barth, the *argumentum* should not be identified with the proof of *P*2–4. This is correct. But Anselm's *argumentum* is meant to be a proof in a way that cannot be accommodated by Barth's interpretation. The 'proof' of *P*2–4 is not the *argumentum*, but according to Anselm the *argumentum* is a proof.

Barth's account is flawed, because he does not take account of the fact that Anselm is a dialectician who has great confidence in the power of reason.[93] Nonetheless, his stress on the overriding significance of faith has the positive effect of enabling him to see in Anselm someone who has absolute faith in God's revelation in Jesus Christ (as proclaimed by the magisterium of the Church). However, unlike Barth, Anselm is able to hold on to both reason and faith. Once one takes account of the flaw in Barth's account of Anselm, one discovers a serious and detailed engagement with the text. This leads him to stress the distinction between the general (*P*2) and special (*P*3) theories of the being of God, which helps to explain the different moves contained in *P*2 and *P*3. According to Barth, Anselm's main point 'did not come till the narrowed-down Proof of *Prosl. 3* and it was not the general proof of *Prosl. 2*':[94]

> If God were to exist merely generally, in the manner of all other beings, then not only would he not exist as God, but according to Anselm's own account – he did not create himself and therefore does not possess existence as such, as is granted to the creature – he would not exist at all.

God's special existence is associated with the inconceivability of His non-existence. It is not just that this 'God' would not exist, if its existence were not inconceivable, but if someone denies God's existence he must ask himself whether he is really thinking of God as X: 'If he is not thinking of him then obviously he

---

[91] See T. Torrance, *Karl Barth: An Introduction to His Early Theology 1910–1931*, Edinburgh 1962, p. 182. Barth's earlier work, *Die christliche Dogmatik im Entwurf* (1927) already reveals him as engaged in a reading of the *Proslogion*.

[92] *AFQI*, p. 14

[93] Barth sees Anselm in a line of Augustine, Plotinus and Plato, ignoring the important roles played by Aristotle, Boethius and Cicero in the development of Anselm's thought. See *AFQI*, p. 59.

[94] *AFQI*, p. 154.

does not deny his existence. If he is thinking of him then he is thinking of one whose existence cannot be denied.'[95]

In spite of his engagement with the text, what emerges from his account is a Barthian Anselm for whom X is one of the 'various revealed Names of God'.[96] However, Anselm knew this as a human description, which was not unambiguously to be attributed to God. It is not for the revelation of a name, but of the use to which he can put this human description (i.e. the *argumentum*), that Anselm gives thanks to God. He is enabled to understand how X can function successfully as the middle term of a syllogism that establishes the existence of God.

Barth concludes *AFQI* with the following assertion:[97]

> That Anselm's Proof of the Existence of God has repeatedly been called the 'Ontological' Proof of God, that commentators have refused to see that it is in a different book altogether from the well-known teaching of Descartes and Leibniz, that anyone could seriously think that it is even remotely affected by what Kant put forward against these doctrines – all that is so much nonsense on which no more words ought to be wasted.

Although I think one does have to address Descartes, Leibniz, Kant and others, if one is to understand how Anselm's argument has been received, it is still the case that one learns little or nothing from them concerning the argument itself. Barth's *AFQI* represents one of the few serious attempts to understand Anselm's text, a precondition, one would think, for discussing his argument. Barth's reading of the *Proslogion* is impressive, but it stops short of the philosophical debate, not because the debate is over, but because he considers the debate to be theological and therefore not open to philosophers. Knowledge of God is not available to man as a possibility, except as an act of God's grace.[98] Barth's Anselm shares this view, and thus he is not to be placed amongst the proponents of natural theology, such as Aquinas. The reality is, however, that Anselm appears to make greater claims for human reason than Aquinas.

Anselm is swept up by Barth in his task of protecting the Christian gospel from the predations of anti-theists and those within the Church who naively follow them. In his *Church Dogmatics*, Barth cites Feuerbach:[99]

---

95 *AFQI*, p. 145.

96 *AFQI*, p. 75. See *AFQI*, p. 77: 'Thus in no sense is [Anselm] of the opinion that he produced this formula out of his own head but he declares quite explicitly the source from which he considers it to have come to him', i.e. God.

97 *AFQI*, p. 171.

98 H. Meynell, *Grace versus Nature: Studies in Karl Barth's* Church Dogmatics, London 1965, p. 12; see K. Barth, *Church Dogmatics*, I:1, 2nd edn, Edinburgh 1975, pp. 448ff.

99 Barth, *Church Dogmatics*, II:1, Edinburgh 1957, p. 292.

> Theology is anthropology, i.e., in the object of religion which we call in Greek *Theos*, in English God, there expresses itself nothing other than the nature of man; or, the God of mankind is nothing other than the deified nature of man (*Das Wesen der Religion*, 1848, Lecture 3).

Barth defends Anselm against the kind of reading that might follow from this view, which Barth considered many of his predecessors and contemporaries had failed to protect themselves against, 'with their quite open and express projection of human self-consciousness into the transcendent'.[100] Just as the word '*invenire*' can be translated as 'to discover' or 'to invent', Barth seeks to preserve Anselm from a reading of his argument which would see in it '*invenire*' as invention rather than discovery.

The rationale for, and effect of, Barth's theological approach of rejecting a theology of humanity and the world that explains itself in terms of Christian faith is to safeguard Christian faith from the possibility of being turned on its head, so that it can be explained in terms of humanity and the world. Christianity is not reducible to man or the world, and is to be hermetically sealed from explanations that would undermine it. For Anselm, this is not the case. God is knowable, because we are made in God's image. An explanation can be understood by anyone and a proof that establishes a truth of the faith can be grasped by anyone. There is no *rule* that says this is impossible or dangerous. Faith provides us with a knowledge that would render reason superfluous, if we were not required to explain that faith, to expose it to others, to take the risk that they might misunderstand it and misrepresent it, as Anselm believes we are. In *CDH*I:1, Anselm's introduction and his discussion with Boso show how reason has a real (if subordinate) place in the exposition of the faith. The point is not to arrive at the faith through reason, but to delight in understanding and contemplating what we believe and to be able to respond adequately to those who ask us the reason for our belief (cf. *1 Peter* 3:15). Boso responds to this by saying that 'the correct order' is to believe first and discuss rationally afterwards. Nevertheless, Boso says, it would be negligent not to endeavour to understand what we believe. He makes it clear what this means when he goes on to ask Anselm to explain the necessity and reason for the incarnation. In fact, in the preface Anselm had already written that his purpose was to proceed without reference to Christ to prove by necessary reasons that no one could be saved without Him.

The difference and similarity between the positions of Barth and Anselm is highlighted in the following assertion made by Barth:[101] 'Anselm's hypothesis [i.e. X] is certainly an expression, but not as Gaunilo thinks empty words, but the Word of God – … a Word of God within the context of his revelation, to which also belongs the revelation of his existence.' As we have seen, the 'hypothesis' (X) may have been employed by Anselm precisely because it is not the Word of God, but

[100] Ibid., p. 293.

[101] *AFQI*, p. 131.

because it is the word of man (and in fact the word of man who does not know the Christian God). The problem for Barth is that he recognises that Anselm's notion of proof can be interpreted as involving a meeting with unbelievers on common ground. He counters such an interpretation with the assertion that Anselm calls the unbeliever 'on to his own ground'.[102] Anselm could not possibly have meant to enter into a discussion with the unbeliever on equal terms, since if he did he was deceived. Thus, Barth concludes the first part of his book as follows:[103] 'We can only say that if that is how Anselm thought then it was reasonable and so, dismissing the possibility that he was deceived, clearly his attitude to proving is exactly as we have seen.' In much the same vein, near the end of his book, Barth writes:[104]

> From what has been already said and in the whole context, the commonplace explanation of *quia stultus et insipiens* is quite impossible – that the man who says *Deus non est* is a clown who is incapable of following the proof because he cannot think logically. That would be a completely unjustifiable affront to one's fellow mortal.

But the commonplace explanation is clearly the correct one. Anselm added *stultus* to *insipiens* precisely because he wanted to say that anyone who could follow an argument, could follow this and would consequently have to accept God's existence, and if he did not it was because he was *insipiens* and *stultus*.

In response to Karl Barth's interpretation of Anselm, the German Benedictine Anselm Stolz (1900–1942), sought to push Anselm even further away from his roots in the dialectical tradition, stating: 'Nothing is more absurd than to see a philosopher in the author of the *Proslogion*.'[105] He adds: 'There is no trace of a proof of God's existence',[106] and concludes that *P*2–4 constitutes 'a piece of mystical theology'.[107] Stolz argues that there are two styles of writing to be found in Anselm, the doctrinal/dialectical and the prayerful, and concludes that since the former do not contain prayers, then the *Proslogion* must belong to the second group. Consequently it does not involve the dialectic of a philosophical proof of God's existence. Stolz's understanding of the structure and purpose of this work arises out of his belief that it does not contain a philosophical proof. It allows him to overlook the glaringly obvious, that Anselm clearly states he wishes to prove God's existence.

In spite of the influence of Barth's 'theological' reading of Anselm, a growing interest in Anselm's argument was expressed by philosophers in the second half of

102 *AFQI*, p. 67.

103 *AFQI*, p. 72.

104 *AFQI*, p. 159.

105 A. Stolz, 'Anselm's Theology in the Proslogion', in Hick and McGill, *The Many-Faced Argument*, pp. 183–206, p. 188.

106 Ibid., p. 202.

107 Ibid., p. 206.

the twentieth century. This was tied in with a wider interest in ontological arguments, and reinforced a particular reading of Anselm, which attempted to extrapolate one or more ontological arguments from *P*2–3. It is to this contemporary reception of the *Proslogion* that I shall now turn.

Chapter 8
Anselm's Argument Today

The last chapter ended with attempts to understand Anselm's argument from a non-philosophical stance. Nevertheless, arguably the greatest interest in the argument in recent times has been expressed by philosophers, for whom it has raised the possibility that God's existence can be proved in some way or who have felt it possesses sufficient and enduring robustness to be worth responding to and refuting. Although there have been some serious attempts by theologians to get to grips with aspects of the text of the *Proslogion* (for example, de Lubac[1] and von Balthasar[2]), there has been a failure to appreciate the dialectical nature of the argument presented there. Rahner (writing before and during the Second World War) represents a particularly interesting case. He follows Maréchal in rejecting the 'paralogism of the Anselmian proof',[3] whilst producing philosophical and spiritual writings that bear suggestions of an unacknowledged Anselmian influence.[4]

In a contemporary philosophical sub-culture that regards the notion of God as odd, rather than special, we find little awareness of the characteristic feature of Anselm's argument that God as X possesses 'unique logical properties'.[5] Hartshorne, nevertheless, suggests that God is not just another being to be placed in the same logical class with all other beings. He is not just factually, but also conceptually unique.[6] This is not to say that for Anselm there is an exceptional

---

1 De Lubac focuses his attention on *P*14. See H. de Lubac, *Recherches dans la foi: trois études sur Origéne, saint Anselme, et la philosophie chrétienne*, Paris 1979, pp. 81–124; and 'Sur le chapitre XIVe du *Proslogion*' in *Spicilegium Beccense I. Congrés International du IX Centenaire de l'arrivée d'Anselme au Bec*, Paris 1959, 295–312.

2 See H.U. von Balthasar, *The Glory of the Lord: A Theological Aesthetics*, vol. II, Edinburgh 1985, pp. 211–59.

3 K. Rahner, *Spirit in the World*, translated by W. Dych, London 1968, p. 185. See J. Maréchal, *Le point de départ de la métaphysique*, Cahier V, 2nd edn, Paris/Brussels 1949, p. 339. According to Maréchal, the paralogism renders Anselm's proof null and void. However, in a later footnote, Maréchal remarks that such language is intended to refer to the argument propagated by the philosophical tradition as Anselm's, rather than to Anselm's argument itself (p. 473).

4 Philosophical writings: *Geist in Welt* [1939]; *Hörer des Wortes* [1941]. Spiritual writings: *Worte ins Schweigen* [1938].

5 J.N. Findlay, *Language, Mind and Value: Philosophical Essays*, London 1963, p. 9. An exception is Campbell, who is aware that Anselm's formula 'was the only one to which the logic of his Argument could be applied to yield an existential conclusion' (*From belief*, p. 194).

6 C. Hartshorne, 'Is the Denial of Existence Ever Contradictory?', in *The Journal of Philosophy*, 63 (1966) 85–93, 92.

mode of inference to be employed in the case of X, but rather that it is the use of X as the middle term in his argument concerning the existence of God, etc., that renders the argument a special or unique case.

The Logical Form of Anselm's Argument

Graham Oppy treats Anselm's argument as the first of many attempts to formalise ontological arguments for the existence of God. Oppy avoids discussion of whether Anselm's argument is actually an ontological argument, suggesting that this term is like a proper name, which tells us nothing about the nature of arguments to which it refers.[7] Such a view is difficult to defend, since the use of the term 'ontological argument' in Kant's *Critique* appears to play a strategic role in the invalidation of the classical proofs of God of seventeenth and eighteenth century rationalists. It is precisely this 'baggage' that makes the application of the term to Anselm's *Proslogion* argument inappropriate.

As we have already seen, many versions of Anselm's argument have been presented by his interpreters. If it is the case, as Geach and Strawson suggest, that the form of a particular concrete argument is not reducible to a single logical form,[8] then we should not be surprised that numerous, even competing, versions of this argument are constructed. A problem arises, however, when attempts are made to refute the argument on the basis that a particular invalid argument appears to share the form of Anselm's argument, since one would also have to show that his argument did not also share the form of a valid argument, to do which exhaustively is a step no one has yet taken. This is the case even where care is taken to adhere closely to the form of Anselm's argument. Further problems arise when such care is not taken. Thus, Peter van Inwagen assumes that Anselm's argument is sufficiently like that of Descartes that in treating of the latter he is addressing (more or less) the former.[9] However, although Anselm's X and Descartes's 'perfect being' may have similar roles in their respective arguments, it is clear that Anselm's argument does not operate in the same way, if one substitutes 'perfect being' for X.

An example of the failure to appreciate the difference between a revamped 'Anselmian' argument and Anselm's own argument is to be found in Millican,[10] who treats a flaw in his own version of the argument as a flaw in Anselm's argument, although he fails to show that his argument 'is essentially the same as Anselm's'.[11] Millican writes that his exposition is based on a 'theory' that Anselm

---

7 G. Oppy, *Ontological arguments and belief in God*, Cambridge 1995, p. 5.

8 See P. Geach, 'Why logic matters', in H.D. Lewis (ed.), *Contemporary British Philosophy: Personal Statements*, Fourth Series, London 1976, pp. 86–99, p. 95.

9 Peter Van Inwagen, *Metaphysics*, 2nd edn, Boulder, Col. 2002, p. 92.

10 P. Millican, 'The One Fatal Flaw in Anselm's Argument' in *Mind*, 113 (2004) 437–76.

11 Ibid., 458.

would not have endorsed, adding that 'we can ignore this complication here'.[12] But we cannot ignore such complications. If we are to assess Anselm's argument then we should avoid the intrusion of non-Anselmian improvement into the presentation of the argument. For, once we deracinate Anselm's argument from his thought, it is no longer his argument, and we will *inevitably* fail to understand 'the logical progression of his argument'. Millican appears to be in part driven to his interpretation because he refuses to accept the special case nature of X for Anselm. He writes: 'it is simply not in general valid to infer from "I am thinking of an X" to "There is some X of which I am thinking".'[13] Anselm would agree that this is not in general valid, but he is concerned with the unique case of God as X. In this particular case, Anselm argues, this move is valid and is in fact required.

In his treatment of Anselm's argument, David Lewis raises further questions about how one should read and interpret Anselm. When addressing 'Anselm's ontological argument',[14] he is not concerned to show that the argument he presents is in fact Anselm's. This might be because this argument is just 'one of the arguments that can, with some plausibility, be extracted' from *P*2.[15] Lewis does not tell us which arguments he has excluded. But, if his argument is not that of Anselm, it must be the case that, if Lewis identified it, Anselm's argument has been excluded. For what reason could it be excluded? Because this one is more sound?[16] It would have been useful to know what the argument was that Lewis considered to be less sound than the one he presents, which turns out to be not sound at all.

That Lewis's argument is not that of Anselm is easily established. For the purposes of his argument, Lewis construes 'that X' as an 'idiom of universal quantification', rather than as a definite description.[17] But, as Morscher points out, the Latin '*id*' does not possess the characteristic of the universal quantifier.[18] Lewis does not recognise that Anselm distinguishes between 'something X' and 'that X'. The latter bearing the uniqueness assigned by a definite description. An important element of Anselm's argument is that '*aliquid* X' is unique and is therefore '*id* X'.[19] Thus, Lewis is incorrect to limit Anselm's use of 'that X' to that of universal quantification.

---

[12] Ibid., 449.

[13] Ibid., 463.

[14] D. Lewis, 'Anselm and Actuality', in D. Lewis, *Philosophical Papers*, vol. 1, New York/Oxford 1983, pp. 10–25, p. 10. By permission of Oxford University Press.

[15] Ibid., p. 11.

[16] Ibid.

[17] Ibid.

[18] E. Morscher, 'Was sind und was sollen die Gottesbeweise? Bemerkungen zu Anselms Gottesbeweis(en)', in F. Ricken, *Klassische Gottesbeweise in der Sicht der gegenwartigen Logik und Wissenschaftstheorie*, Stuttgart/Berlin/Cologne 1991, pp. 62–86, p. 65.

[19] R. La Croix, *Proslogion II and III: A third interpretation of Anselm's argument*, Leiden 1972, p. 89, translates both '*aliquid*' and '*id*' as 'something', indicating that he too is unaware of the distinction between the definite and indefinite uses of the term.

In his version of Anselm's argument, Lewis presents the following as one of its premises: whatever exists in the understanding can be thought of as existing in reality.[20] In fact, Anselm's view is that such a thing as a mythical beast can be in the understanding, even though it cannot be thought to exist (otherwise it would not be a mythical beast). Lewis then puts forward another premise: whatever exists in the understanding and exists in reality is greater that it would be if it did not exist in reality.[21] Anselm's equivalent premise is that it is greater for X to exist in reality than not to so exist. Lewis glosses this second premise in what appears to be, from an Anselmian perspective, a more acceptable form: 'What excels a hypothetical nonexistent God is not some other being; it is the same being, conceived as existent'.[22] This is then transposed into the language of possible worlds: 'For any understandable being x, and for any worlds w and v, if x exists in w but x does not exist in v, then the greatness of x in w exceeds the greatness of x in v.'[23] But this is not equivalent to what Anselm says of X in *P*2. According to Anselm, the fool 'understands what he hears, and what he understands is in his understanding, even if he should not understand that it exists' (*P*2.5). He is not saying that it is possible to think of X as a hypothetical non-existent God to be compared with a really existent God. If he were saying that, he would have to say that it is possible to think of a non-existent X, whereas the point of his argument is that this is not possible. Anselm is not confused or equivocating here. He is simply acknowledging that understanding something and understanding that something exists are not the same thing (*P*2.6). He is not saying that there are distinct ways of thinking of X – as a really existing X or as a hypothetical existent X. It is an outcome of his argument that there is only one way of thinking of X – as really existing. In this, X is unique.

Richard Campbell identifies a three-fold structure in Anselm's argument: X exists; X cannot be thought not to exist; God is the only such thing.[24] Unfortunately, he does not address the entirety of the text, but focuses on *P*2–3,[25] believing that the identity of God and X is established at this stage. But, as I have already argued, the identity of God (i.e. the God Anselm believes in) and X cannot be established without the later chapters of the *Proslogion*. Campbell attempts to oppose this view by arguing that 'You (i.e. God) are X' acts as a premise in later chapters, including

---

20 Lewis, 'Anselm', p. 11.

21 Ibid.

22 Ibid., p. 12.

23 Ibid.

24 Campbell, *From belief to understanding: a study of Anselm's Proslogion argument on the existence of God*, Canberra 1976, p. 16.

25 His rationale is that these chapters have been the subject of controversy amongst philosophers (Campbell, *From belief*, p. 11). But, given that this controversy has missed the point from Campbell's perspective, that would seem a reason for looking beyond such a limited view of the text. La Croix, *Proslogion II and III*, commits a similar error.

*P*15, and that therefore this identity must already have been established.[26] Anselm has certainly made the claim that God is X, and is in the process of justifying this claim. However, 'You are X' functions as a premise in the way that 'p' functions as a premise in a *modus tollens* argument: 'if p, then q; not q, therefore not p.' Thus, in *P*15, Anselm is making the point that an argument of the form, 'If God is X, then God is greater than can be thought; God is not greater than can be thought, therefore God is not X (i.e. something greater than God can be thought)', leads to a contradiction, since nothing greater than God can be thought. This is further confirmation of the identity of X and God, since if there were known to exist something greater than can be thought, but this was not God, then something greater than God would exist (i.e. X would be greater than God).

Dialectical Effectiveness

Oppy argues that it is not possible for an ontological argument to be dialectically effective, even if it should be sound.[27] What this seems to mean is that: 'There is no *a priori* argument from uncontroversial premises that will persuade any reasonable nontheist that God exists.'[28] However, such a statement is question-begging for Anselm, since for him 'reasonable' and 'nontheist' are not terms that can consistently be applied to the same person, i.e. the fool (who by definition is not reasonable). Furthermore, it would seem that 'reasonable' participants in a debate will judge an argument on its merits, rather than prejudge it. To suggest that it is not the truth of the premises or the validity of an argument but the dialectical tactics of the disputants that determine the *philosophical* success of a proof,[29] would appear to call into question not the proof, but the notion of dialectical effectiveness. However, given his dialectical training Anselm was certainly aware of the tactical possibilities available to any opponent, which may partly explain why he employed a middle term that was not overtly theistic.

It is frequently 'pointed out' that no-one has ever been converted by Anselm's argument. An extreme account of the implications of this position is found in J. Findlay's attempted disproof of God, in which he concludes:[30] 'It was indeed an ill day for Anselm when he hit upon his famous proof. For on that day he not only laid bare something that is of the essence of an adequate religious object, but

---

[26] Campbell, *From belief*, p. 23.

[27] Oppy, p. 119. In *Arguing about Gods*, Oppy has subsequently expressed doubts about his general objection, suggesting that, even though ontological arguments may not always be question-begging or invalid, their conclusions are 'of no religious significance'. (G. Oppy, *Arguing about Gods*, Cambridge 2006, p. 65.)

[28] Oppy, *Ontological Arguments*, p. 282.

[29] For a different version of this kind of objection, see B. Williams, *Descartes: The Project of Pure Enquiry*, 1978, pp. 161f.

[30] J.N. Findlay, 'Can God's Existence Be Disproved?', in *Mind*, 57 (1948) 176–83, 182.

also something that entails its necessary non-existence.' For God's existence must be inescapable, His non-existence inconceivable, in a way that is clearly not the case according to 'modern views'. But, as we have seen, Anselm addressed just this question. How can it be that we do not grasp God? His answer is that if we could, He would not be God. Although, as sinners we see less than we ought, it must be a characteristic of God that He is beyond our understanding because of our limitedness and His greatness. He is inescapable, but not in the way Anselm initially expected and Findlay continued to expect. If we fail to see God clearly and inescapably, this is not because of a limitation in God, but because of one in us. It will always be open to us to misunderstand Him. This is why for Anselm his argument is required, even though God's non-existence is inconceivable.

Argumentum or *Argumenta*

Since the time of Norman Malcolm and Charles Hartshorne it has been commonplace to see more than one argument in the *Proslogion*, to regard *P*2 and *P*3 as almost competing versions of Anselm's argument. Hartshorne considered *P*2 to be 'a blundering preamble' to the real proof in *P*3.[31] But the argument of *P*2 is an essential part of the *unum argumentum*, establishing the premise, 'X exists'. The purpose of *P*3 is to establish that X shares a particular attribute with God, the inconceivability of its non-existence (thus justifying in part the premise, 'God is X'). Thus *P*2 and *P*3 (and the remainder of the *Proslogion*) do not constitute alternative versions of Anselm's argument, but rather the task of finding and justifying the middle term, as the predicate of the minor premise and as the subject of the major premise. Anselm's argument is, as he says, *unum argumentum*, and to misunderstand this point is to misunderstand the *Proslogion*.

Although Malcolm also speaks of different arguments in *P*2 and *P*3, he is aware that there is no evidence that Anselm thought he was offering two different proofs in the *Proslogion*.[32] As we have seen, the evidence is that he sought to provide a single argument. Thus, whatever the merits of Malcolm's argument on its own terms, as an interpretation of Anselm his approach is at least questionable. Anselm could have been mistaken in thinking that he had managed to provide a single argument. But one ought to show that he was wrong. To do that one would need to give an exhaustive account of what Anselm's argument was and how it operated. But Malcolm does not do this.

Desmond Henry too sees more than one proof in the *Proslogion* and others in the *Responsio*, 'provided that one is prepared to concede that the occurrence of "X" within proofs which otherwise differ in form and content does not make those proofs identical'.[33] His view appears to be supported by Holopainen's claim that

[31] Hartshorne, *Anselm's Discovery*, p. 14.

[32] Malcolm, 'Anselm's Ontological Arguments', 45.

[33] D.P. Henry, *The Logic*, p. 148.

X is the *argumentum*. As such it does not mean what contemporary philosophers mean by argument, and so there is no reason to suppose that Anselm would have objected to the likes of Henry and others finding different arguments (in the sense of contemporary philosophers) which make use of his *unum argumentum*. However, I suggested in Chapter 5 that Holopainen's claim does not best fit the evidence, and that Anselm's *argumentum* was the justification of the terms of a syllogism of the form: God is X, X is F, therefore God is F. Anselm would not have agreed that there is more than one argument in this sense in the *Proslogion*.

Brian Leftow speaks of Anselm's *argumentum* as a '*form* of argument',[34] and in doing so comes closer, perhaps, to Anselm's position. However, this description, does not adequately convey the meaning of the term '*argumentum*', since the form of the argument cannot deliver the cogency of the premises and justify the use of the middle term, which for Anselm is a requirement of his *argumentum*. Thus, when he 'unpacks' Anselm's argument, Leftow treats the identification of God and X (or, in Leftow's language, 'that which is in the greatest describable state', 'the greatest of all things') as an assumption. But, if we take seriously what Anselm says in *P*0.2, that he is proving 'whatever else we believe about the divine substance', then his statement in *P*2.3 – 'we believe You to be something than which nothing greater can be thought' – is a statement of something that he intends to prove. To see 'God is X' as an assumption is to misconstrue Anselm's argument.

Parodies

Oppy, like many others, is disappointed with Anselm's response to the lost island objection, since, he states, 'it is not enough for St Anselm simply to assert that Gaunilo's argument does not parallel his own argument for the existence of a being than which no greater can be conceived'.[35] But Anselm does not simply assert this. In fact, he invites his opponent to suggest precisely how he could use an argument concerning X to prove something concerning not-X, particularly when the argument concerning not-X claims to be talking about a kind of X. For an island than which no greater can be thought is not something than which nothing greater can be thought, since I can think of something greater than it, e.g. a world containing the island. Consequently, it is not another member of the class of X, but of the class of not-X.

---

[34] B. Leftow, 'Anselm's perfect-being theology', in B. Davies and B. Leftow (eds), *The Cambridge Companion to Anselm*, Cambridge 2004, pp. 132–56, p. 140. See also B. Davies, 'Anselm and the ontological argument', in Davies and Leftow, *Companion*, pp. 157–78, p. 169; and La Croix, *Proslogion II and III*, p. 124.

[35] Oppy, *Ontological arguments*, p. 17.

The fact that such a serious commentator as R.M. Adams takes the lost island objection seriously requires some explanation. Adams writes:[36]

> The third premise of the lost-island argument appears to have been accepted by Anselm. It expresses a more sweeping claim about the superiority of the real to the unreal.... But Anselm raised not a murmur of protest when Gaunilo in effect attributed to him the still more sweeping assumption that whatever exists in reality is greater than anything that does not.

We have seen that Anselm initially left much of what 'Gaunilo' said unanswered, not because he accepted it, but because rightly or wrongly he did not think it was worth answering. Whilst Anselm might have considered as uncontroversial the statement in *G*1.1, 'whatever exists in reality will be greater', it is not a proposition he requires for his argument to work. Anselm requires that X in the understanding and in reality is greater than X in the understanding alone. The issue of whether the bee buzzing outside my window is greater than Hercules is not relevant to Anselm's argument. There can only be one X, according to Anselm. Everything that can be the subject of comparison in terms of greatness, apart from this one X, is not-X. Thus, there is always something greater than the lost island, even if amongst islands it is unsurpassably great. For it is a property of members of the class of not-X that there is always something greater than them, i.e. member(s) of the class of X. It is a tautology that X is greater than not-X. It is irrelevant which not-X is greater than which not-X. The point at issue is whether an X existing in the understanding alone could be as great as an X existing in understanding and in reality.

Some attempts have been made to invert Anselm's argument and to prove the existence of a devil, understood as an anti-God rather than the devil of Christian belief. But, if God can be shown to exist 'everywhere and always' (*P*13.2, *P*14.2, *P*18.10), then one would expect 'by parity of reasoning' that anti-God can be shown to exist 'nowhere and never'.[37] Anti-God is the opposite of 'whatever it is better to be than not to be' (*P*5.7). If it is better for it to exist in reality than not to do so, then it cannot exist in reality.[38] And, it transpires that it cannot exist in the understanding. The argument runs thus:

---

36 R.M. Adams, 'The logical structure of Anselm's argument', in *The Philosophical Review*, 80 (1971) 28–54, 37. Copyright, 1971, Sage School of Philosophy at Cornell University. All rights reserved. Used by permission of the present publisher, Duke University Press.

37 W. Power, 'Ontological Arguments for Satan and Other Sorts of Evil Beings', in Dialogue, 31 (1992) 667–76, 674.

38 It might be argued that it is less good or less great to exist than not to exist, in which case the existence of anti-God might be proved. But there appears to be no possible justification for this account. It would seem to be employing 'less good' to mean 'better', 'less great' to mean 'greater' and 'anti-God' to mean 'God'.

1. Anti-God is that than which a lesser cannot be thought.

2. Anti-God does not exist in the understanding or it is not anti-God, since it is less great for it not to exist in reality than for it not to exist in the understanding.

3. Therefore Anti-God does not exist in the understanding or in reality, since this is less great than not existing in the understanding alone.[39]

It seems that anti-God is nothing and that this is a 'proof' of the non-existence of anything that is nothing. The properly inverted parody of Anselm's argument does nothing to undermine it.

Shiftiness and Ambiguity

It might be suggested that Anselm commits the quantifier shift fallacy: I think of God, therefore there is a God of whom I think, therefore there is a God. Prior provides an account of the error involved in such a move: the '*main* trouble' with Anselm's argument lies in the premise, 'Some object-in-the-mind has all perfections'.[40] Prior expresses the problem in the form of the following argument:[41]

> *x* thinks that there is a *y* such that *y* is perfect.
> Therefore there is a *y* such that *y* is in *x*'s mind and is perfect.

The weakness for Prior lies in the mistaken belief that 'a relation between *x* and some *y*' is expressed by '*x* thinks that there is a *y* such that *y* is P', as is the case with the proposition, 'It is true of *x* that there is a *y* which he loves' which entails that 'there is a *y* such that it is true of *x* that he loves it'. But how does Prior's account map against what Anselm actually does in his argument? If we adhere to Anselm's expressions, we find an argument which is quite different from that provided by Prior and which cannot be made to fit Prior's account. Anselm's argument is that [i] I think of an X and X is in the understanding, [ii] nothing greater than X can be thought of, [iii] it is greater for X to exist in reality than in the understanding alone, [iv] therefore an X exists in reality and in the understanding, otherwise

---

[39] C. Grant, 'The Ontological Disproof of the Devil', in *Analysis*, 17 (1957) 71–2, 72, points out that if existence is a property of a perfect being, then correspondingly non-existence must also be a property of a being at the other end of the spectrum of perfection. Proponents of the various devil proof parodies, who substitute terms like 'worse' (Haight and Haight) or 'more evil' (Richman), fail to reflect the inverted form of the term 'greater', which is, of course, 'lesser'. See D. Haight and M. Haight, 'An ontological argument for the devil', in *The Monist*, 54 (1970) 218–20; and R. Richman, 'A serious look at the ontological argument', in *Ratio*, 18 (1976) 85–9.

[40] A.N. Prior, 'On Some Proofs of the Existence of God', in A.N. Prior, *Papers in Logic and Ethics*, Gerald Duckworth & Co Ltd., London 1976, pp. 56–63, p. 61.

[41] Ibid., p. 62.

something greater than X can be thought of (which contradicts [ii]). It is not because one thinks of something X that one thinks that there must exist something X that one thinks of, but because it follows from one's possession of X in the understanding and the principle that it is better for X to exist in reality as well as in the understanding than in the understanding alone, that one must conclude that there exists something X in reality. The apparent shiftiness in Anselm's argument arises from the misrepresentation of it by Prior and others.

It is possible to argue that ambiguity exists in the phrase 'something than which a greater cannot be thought exists'. Such a statement can mean either [a] 'if anything is X, then it exists' or [b] 'there is something that exists that is X'. Anselm may appear to be establishing [b] when what he does is to establish [a].[42] However, Anselm's use of the terms, *aliquid* and *id*, shows that he is aware of this distinction. His argument conveys both the universal generalisation expressed by [a] (a statement concerning the members of the class of X), and the existential claim [b] (that this class has at least one, and no more than one, member).

C.J.F. Williams argues that what Anselm proves in *P*3 is ambiguous, since it can be taken as having (in Russell's terms) primary or secondary occurrence.[43] What Anselm wanted to prove (according to Williams) was the primary occurrence, that there is just one thing that is X and whose non-existence is inconceivable. What he actually proves (according to Williams) is the secondary occurrence, that it is not the case that there is just one thing that is X, whose non-existence is conceivable, which of course is not a proof that there is such a thing. To prove the primary occurrence, Anselm would need to prove that there exists just one thing which is X. But that is precisely what he does in *P*2 and the remainder of the *Proslogion*. The argument of *P*3 is not a separate argument containing an unjustified claim about the existence of X.

Unity and Uniqueness

I have suggested that for Anselm X is unique, i.e. it belongs to a class with at least one, and no more than one, member.[44] But Anselm does not appear to establish that

---

[42] See the discussions in J.H. Sobel, *Logic and Theism, Arguments For and Against Beliefs in God*, Cambridge 2004, pp. 35–40 and 60–63 and Van Inwagen, *Metaphysics*, pp. 95–7.

[43] C.J.F Williams, 'Russelm', in *The Philosophical Quarterly*, 43 (1993) 496–9, 499.

[44] It is worth noting that Russell's Paradox does not apply to Anselm's argument, since X is not a class which is a member of itself. It might be argued that the class of not-X contains itself since X is greater than everything else, including the class of not-X. However, the class of not-X is the class of all things that are not God that can be compared to God in terms of greatness. It would make no sense to compare X with the class of not-X rather than its members, since the class of not-X, unlike its members, is not the kind of thing that comparisons of greatness are relevant too. Therefore the class of not-X is not a member

this is the case, although in *R*5.13 he makes it clear that he regarded his argument as having done so: 'Nor is it obvious that, if [something greater than everything] were to exist, something similar to it would not also exist, as is established as certain in the case of what is called "something than which a greater cannot be thought".' In *P*23, Anselm states that (i) one thing is necessary and (ii) this is it. But, by (i) does Anselm mean [a] that there is only one object that is necessary (uniqueness) or [b] that this object is necessarily one (unity)?[45] Anselm's discussion of the Trinity would appear to support the view that he is referring to God's unity rather than His uniqueness, especially as other beings can be said to be necessary. At best, it seems, Anselm has established that there is at least one member of a class of objects of type X, but not that this class of objects has only one member.[46] However, for Anselm, to prove the necessary unity of such an object that possesses the attributes of God is to prove its uniqueness, since if God as X is whatever it is better to be than not to be, it is better to be uniquely X than not uniquely X. Therefore, anything that is not uniquely X is not X, since X is whatever it is better to be than not to be. The justification of the premise 'it is better to be uniquely X than not uniquely X' lies in the tautology that 'an X which is better than any other X is better than an X that is no better than any other X'. X's uniqueness follows as part of the *unum argumentum*.

Anselm's account of the unity of God as X may appear to be problematic. In *P*18.9, he writes, 'Therefore life and wisdom and the rest are not parts of You, but they are all one, and each one of them is all that You are and what all the rest are'. According to Plantinga the implication of such a claim (concerning the identity of God and his attributes) is that God is a property. In other words, He is 'an abstract object', and not a person possessing 'knowledge, awareness, power, love or life'.[47] But it follows from Anselm's argument that God is a unity and that He possesses all these attributes. Of course, others might argue that this simply shows that the notion of God as X is incoherent, and consequently that the class of X admits of having no members. As we saw in Chapter 4, Anselm was aware of the problem posed by the unity of God. He develops a strategy to show that with our limited understanding we cannot experience this unity of God's attributes (*P*18.7). Although this strategy shows how we can understand the difficulty we are faced with, it also shows that it is not something we can resolve, so that we can understand how all God's attributes are one with each other and with Him. If we could understand this, then it would not be God that we understood. We are constrained by our 'narrow understanding'. However, for Anselm, if we possess

---

of itself. This point is missed by C. Viger, 'St. Anselm's ontological argument succumbs to Russell's paradox', in *International Journal for Philosophy of Religion*, 52 (2002) 123–8.

45 In fact, Anselm had attempted to show that God as X must be one in *P*18: 'That there are not parts in God ….'

46 See the comment in Sobel, *Logic*, p. 82, that Anselm presumed that X 'is the *only* one such thing'.

47 A. Plantinga, *Does God have a nature?*, Milwaukee 1980, p. 47.

the concept of X in the understanding, then it cannot be contradictory. The fact that the fool accepts that X exists in the understanding resolves the question of whether X is coherent or contradictory. Thus, Anselm can apparently assume that God as X is coherent, and just needs to provide an explanation of how this is to be understood, given the *prima facie* contradictory nature of His attributes.

X in the Understanding and in Reality

For Anselm, all God's attributes follow from X and can be predicated of X. And, if they can be predicated of X, then they must be compatible as Anselm attempts to show throughout the *Proslogion*, since no object that can be understood and be in the understanding can be the subject of incompatible predicates. In this, X differs from a square circle or the greatest prime number, which are strictly speaking not understood or are only understood in the sense that they are understood to be impossible, and which therefore cannot be said to be in the understanding. But can it really be claimed that Anselm shows that X exists in the understanding? It might be argued that X is unlike the square circle, which exhibits an obvious contradiction. It is not clear that it is unlike the greatest prime number, which appears *prima facie* to have a possible referent. However, there is something distinctive about the concept of X. It concerns the limits of conceivability. We know that there are limits to conceivability; for example, I cannot think simultaneously of everyone I have ever met (although I can think the phrase 'everyone I have ever met'). Thus, a phrase such as X, which expresses the limits of conceivability, does not appear to express contradiction or incoherence in the way that the phrase 'the greatest prime number' does, since the latter implies that there are limits to our capacity to add or multiply, which do not in fact exist. If the concept of X can be shown to be contradictory or incoherent then it is possible to argue that the attributes of God, which follow from an argument employing X as a middle term, are contradictory or incoherent. But, it is not the case that the concept of X has been shown to be contradictory or incoherent by the attributes of God, since there is an account of them, given by Anselm in the *Proslogion*, which indicates how it is possible that they are not contradictory or incoherent. How then could we show that the concept of X is contradictory or incoherent? The answer is, by showing that the concept of the limits of conceivability is contradictory or incoherent. But, as I have argued, this is not the case.

In suggesting a 'set of assumptions about existence and predication', Adams makes the following point: '[I]t is essential to the argument [of *P*2] to assume both that the same thing can exist in the understanding and in reality, and that it must have at least the same *defining* properties in reality as in the understanding.'[48] However, it is not clear that Anselm would accept this supposed assumption of his. According to his treatment of '*mentis locutio*' and '*naturalia verba*' in *M*10, what

[48] Adams, 'Logical structure', p. 34.

is thought is not identical with its object, it is more like an image or reflection of it. It is not the same thing as its object, although it might still be said to share in some sense 'the same *defining* properties'. By X in the understanding, Anselm means that there exists in the understanding something that has the properties of X but in the manner appropriate to the understanding. The concept is not identical with the object, but it is nevertheless the object in the understanding. Thus, the *concept* of fire does not burn my understanding, although it is nevertheless the concept of *fire*. One form of the concept is as image and this helps us to understand the relation between concept and object. The image of the fire reflected in the mirror is cold to the touch, although the fire itself is hot. Nevertheless, the image I see is the image of the fire and is in a sense identical to it (insofar as that can be said of a mirror-image). It is the image of this fire and no other. Similarly, I see the image of a man in a photograph. I am then shown a line-up of half a dozen men I have never previously met. I recognise one of the men in the line-up as the same person as the one in the photo. They are the same man, although one is the image of the other. When Anselm distinguishes between X in the understanding and X in reality, this is what he means.

Defining and Describing God

In the previous section, we noted that Adams spoke of 'defining properties' in relation to X. But, as we have seen, Anselm does not regard God (as X) as definable. This lack of definability is characteristic of that which is supremely real, precisely because it is that which is supremely real. However, Anselm does not come to his conclusion from this direction, but rather draws it out from his *argumentum*: X must be greater than can be thought, otherwise I could think of something greater than it (i.e. something so great that it is greater than can be thought). There is little point in listing the names of those who talk of X as Anselm's definition of God, since this incorrect view is almost universally held amongst recent commentators and interpreters,[49] notable exceptions being Campbell[50] and La Croix.[51]

In 'On Denoting', Bertrand Russell makes a distinction between definite and indefinite occurrences of a 'denoting phrase'.[52] The only thing that distinguishes 'the F' from 'an F' is the former's implication of uniqueness.[53] The suggestion has been made by Barnes that in his argument Anselm shifts between the indefinite and definite descriptions, and as a result is only able to establish the existence of God

---

[49] It is worth noting, nonetheless, that this is one of the main weaknesses of Charlesworth's much-used commentary. See M. Charlesworth, *St. Anselm's Proslogion*, Oxford 1965, esp. pp. 54–72.

[50] *From belief*, pp. 24–8.

[51] *Proslogion II and III*, pp. 14–16.

[52] B. Russell, 'On Denoting', in *Mind*, New Series, 14 (1905) 479–93, 479.

[53] B. Russell, *Introduction to Mathematical Philosophy*, London 1919, p. 176.

because he has assumed that the existence of some God involves the existence of the unique God.[54] Thus, he shifts from talking of '*aliquid* X' (an F) to '*id* X' (the F) in an illegal move.[55] Interestingly, it was Russell himself who points to how such an objection might be rebutted. Having argued that the proof of the existence of a most perfect being fails, because it lacks proof of the premise that 'there is one and only one entity *x* which is most perfect', he comments in a footnote:[56]

> The argument can be made to prove validly that all members of the class of most perfect Beings exist; it can also be proved formally that this class cannot have *more* than one member; but, taking the definition of perfection as possession of all positive predicates, it can be proved almost equally formally that the class does not have even one member.

This describes what Anselm in fact does prove. That there exists a class of objects which are X, that this class has no more than one member and, *pace* Russell, that it has at least one member.[57] Consequently, anything true of a member of this class (*aliquid* X) is also true of the member of this class (*id* X). The objection of Barnes consequently does not succeed, since there is no move of the kind he describes. Anselm does not assume the uniqueness of X. X is 'definitionally' unique, since as Anselm's argument shows, to be 'something X' requires being the unique member of the class of X, in other words, 'that X'.

Anscombe defends Anselm against the charge that X is a definite description, saying that he has left open the question, 'How many things fall under that description?'.[58] But Anselm's reply would surely be that only one thing can fall under that description. If we understand which is meant by X, we understand that it is unique. We cannot possess an understanding of X where this is not the case. If we attempt to think of there being two or more Xs, X′ and X′′, and think of them as possessing exactly the same attributes (since otherwise one would be greater than the other and therefore would be X, whilst the other would be lesser and therefore would not be X), then X′ would have the attribute of being X′′, and vice versa.

---

54 J. Barnes, *The Ontological Argument*, London 1972, p. 80.

55 Ibid., p. 13.

56 Russell, 'On Denoting', p. 491.

57 Anselm's argument attempts to show that these attributes (predicates) can be understood to 'co-exist' in God as X. Only if X is contradictory or incoherent can we argue that possession of these attributes is. See above.

58 G.E.M. Anscombe, 'Russelm or Anselm?', in *The Philosophical Quarterly*, 43 (1993) 500–504, 501. Campbell, *From belief*, also argues that Anselm is not employing X as a definite description (p. 88). Campbell also notes that Anselm differentiates between 'something X' and 'that X', and accordingly suggests that there is 'a logical gap' (p. 127). My view is that for the reasons already stated, there is no gap to be filled.

Existence, Necessary Existence and Predicates

In Chapter 7, I questioned the relevance of Kant's objection that existence is not a predicate. Unfortunately, this objection continues to be seen as central to the interpretation of the *Proslogion* and to the assessment of the validity and soundness of its argument, as if it is 'a magic word' that can 'dissolve Anselm's enchantments'.[59] Of course, Kant did not direct it at Anselm, but others have done so on his behalf, often at the same time identifying Anselm's argument with a Cartesian ontological argument. The origins of this as an objection to Anselm thus lie in a confusion. Nevertheless, it is necessary to look briefly at how contemporary philosophers have handled it and the associated question of whether necessary existence constitutes a predicate.

Davies argues that Anselm does not succumb to Kant's criticism, because his argument does not require that existence be treated as a perfection, or a 'first-level predicate', in Frege's terminology. According to Davies:[60]

> Anselm's argument … asks us to accept (a) that thinking of something than which nothing greater can be thought is not the same as thinking of something than which a greater can be thought, and (b) that something only *in intellectu* cannot be thought of as something than which nothing greater can be thought.

Stating that X is greater than something that only exists *in intellectu* does not require that 'exists' be treated as a predicate in a Kantian sense nor a first-level predicate in a Fregean sense. On this account, Anselm's argument is not addressed by the kind of objections put forward by Kant and Frege.[61] However, it might still seem that existence is a predicate for Anselm, since I spoke in Chapter 7 of 'subtracting' existence from X. The point I was making was that if existence could be subtracted from X, we would be left with something that was not X. Just as adding existence to a concept does not provide us with X, so attempting to subtract existence from a concept cannot provide us with the concept of X minus existence, but only with the concept of something that is not X. Even if it could be shown that it is not a predicate in relation to other things, this would not

---

[59] P. Geach, 'Review of *From Belief to Understanding*', in *Philosophy*, 52 (1977) 234–6, 234.

[60] Davies, 'Anselm and the ontological argument', p. 170.

[61] See G. Frege, 'The Foundations of Arithmetic', in M. Beaney (ed.), *The Frege Reader*, Oxford 1997, pp. 84–129, p. 103. For Frege the 'ontological argument' fails, because existence is a second level predicate (a property of concepts). The argument could only work if existence were a first level predicate (a property of objects). According to Frege, sentences employing singular terms of the form, '*x* exists', are meaningless. (G. Frege, 'On Concept and Object', in Beaney, *Frege Reader*, pp. 181–93, p. 189). However, since we can differentiate between the various senses of 'Julius Caesar exists', 'Tony Blair exists' and 'Mickey Mouse exists', it does not seem that such sentences are senseless.

allow us to draw the conclusion that it is not a predicate in relation to God. Once again, the special case nature of God as X has to be taken into account before we attempt to draw such conclusions. Thus, even if Davies is wrong in suggesting that the question of existence as a property or predicate is not relevant to Anselm's argument, it does not follow that Anselm's argument would be refuted by Kant's objection, which does not concern God as X.

Furthermore, it is possible to argue that 'existence in reality is not expressed by the "existential" quantifier, if it is assumed that the universe of discourse is not restricted to things that exist in reality'.[62] Thus, if 'exists' can apply to something that exists in the understanding alone (as Anselm holds in the case, for example, of a chimera), then 'exists' does not illegitimately and covertly force existence in reality on anything of which it is predicated.

Norman Malcolm writes: 'Anselm's ontological proof of *Proslogion* 2 is fallacious because it rests on the false doctrine that existence is a perfection (and therefore that "existence" is a "real predicate").'[63] As we have seen, Malcolm and others, such as Charlesworth,[64] believe that there is a quite different argument in *P*3, concerning the necessary existence of God (even though Anselm's argument does not employ this language of God). According to Malcolm: 'Although it is an error to regard existence as a property of things that have contingent existence, it does not follow that it is an error to regard necessary existence as a property of God.'[65] Malcolm states that Anselm maintains 'not that existence is a perfection, but that the logical impossibility of nonexistence is a perfection. In other words, necessary existence is a perfection'.[66] This cannot claim to be a literal account of Anselm's argument, since Anselm eschews the language of necessity and perfection concerning X. In fact, Malcolm provides some interesting exegesis concerning what Anselm is trying to do in his argument, for example: 'In *Responsio* I Anselm adds the following acute point: if you can conceive of a certain thing and this thing does not exist then if it *were* to exist its nonexistence would be *possible*.'[67] As Malcolm asks in conclusion: 'Can anything be clearer than that the conjunction "God necessarily exists but it is possible that He does not exist" is self-contradictory?'[68] Thus, it is not the case that 'God necessarily exists' is equivalent to 'If God exists then He necessarily exists'.[69] There is no element of contingency in God: 'What Anselm has proved is that the notion of contingent existence or of contingent nonexistence cannot have any application to God.'[70] Language about not-X cannot

62 Adams, 'Logical Structure', 34.

63 Malcolm, 'Anselm's Ontological Arguments', 44.

64 Charlesworth, *St Anselm's Proslogion*, pp. 73f.

65 Malcolm, 'Anselm's Ontological Arguments', 52.

66 Ibid., 46.

67 Ibid., 48.

68 Ibid., 58.

69 Ibid., 57.

70 Ibid., 49.

be applied to X. As a consequence, the class of contingent objects, which is a subclass of the class of not-X, cannot be said to contain X as a member. Of course, the class of not-X may also include necessary objects. The important distinction is then between X and not-X rather than between necessary and contingent objects. It might be true that, as Malcolm argues, 'Anselm is right to deduce God's necessary existence from his characterisation of Him as a being a greater than which cannot be conceived'.[71] However, this would not be central to Anselm's argument unless one could show that necessary existence were a unique characteristic of God as X. The concept of X appears to be more basic than that of a 'necessary being'. Whilst X may be said to refer to a necessary being, it does not follow that the term 'necessary being' refers to X. (There may be non-divine necessary beings, for example, in Boethian cosmology.[72])

God and Possible Worlds

One interesting question arising from the special case nature of God is whether He is susceptible to arguments in modal logic concerning possible worlds. If one takes seriously the point that Hartshorne makes above concerning God's conceptual uniqueness, then it certainly seems strange to talk of God as if he is one object in a possible world. Plantinga writes that a 'possible world is a possible state of affairs'.[73] To talk of God in terms of possible worlds is to talk of possible states of affairs in which God exists or does not exist. But that is question-begging. If God exists, He cannot not exist – in which case, to talk of possible worlds in relation to God (i.e. his possible existence/non-existence) is to assume that He does not exist (*modus tollens*). In fact, Plantinga's version of Anselm's argument is a proof that if God is possible, He exists in all possible worlds, i.e. He necessarily exists. In *The Nature of Necessity*, Plantinga presents a simplified version of his modal ontological argument, in which he equates *unsurpassable greatness* with *maximal greatness in every possible world*:[74]

(1) There is a possible world in which unsurpassable greatness is exemplified.
(2) The proposition *a thing has unsurpassable greatness if and only if it has maximal excellence in every possible world* is necessarily true.
(3) The proposition *whatever has maximal excellence is omnipotent, omniscient, and morally perfect* is necessarily true.
(4) *Possess unsurpassable greatness* is instantiated in every world.

---

71 Ibid.

72 See D.P. Henry, 'Proslogion Chapter III', in F.S. Schmitt et al. (eds), *AA*, 1, pp. 101–5, p. 103.

73 A. Plantinga, *The Nature of Necessity*, Oxford 1974 p. 96. By permission of Oxford University Press.

74 Ibid., p. 216.

(4) follows from (1) and (2). It follows then that 'possess unsurpassable greatness' is instantiated in this world. Therefore, there exists in this world an omnipotent, etc., being who exists and has these properties in every world. This is not Anselm's argument, but it shows that for modal arguers to prove God exists, it is necessary to prove that He exists in all possible worlds. God's non-existence cannot be entertained, since to think of Him as not existing in any possible world is to think of Him as existing in no possible world. In this sense, such arguments share an important insight with that of Anselm.

The 'Anselmian Sin'

According to Findlay, 'The proofs based on the necessities of thought are universally regarded as fallacious: it is not thought possible to build bridges between mere abstractions and concrete existence'.[75] Leaving aside the question of the unwarranted nature of this universal assertion, it is the case, as Plantinga points out, that it cannot suffice as a refutation of Anselm's argument, since Anselm 'claims to have an *argument* for the necessity of at least one existential proposition'.[76] Nevertheless, F. Zabeeh has asserted that we should not 'commit the Anselmian sin', which is to move from 'conceptual inquiry' to 'ontological commitment'.[77] This 'sin' arises from a refusal to accept the empiricist assumption that all knowledge is limited to as well as by sense experience. Thus, Hume's claim – 'Whatever *is* may *not be*. No negation of a fact can involve a contradiction. The nonexistence of any being, without exception, is as clear and distinct an idea as its existence'[78] – has serious implications for Anselm if it can be justified. It would indicate that we require evidence apart from the idea of something before we can know that it exists, whereas Anselm's *reductio* proof for the existence of X is intended to support the claim that God's existence cannot be denied and to do this apart from supporting evidence. The question is whether the empiricist assumption can be justified. Note that this assumption as expressed above by Hume involves a claim about 'any being'. What one wonders could come under the category of any being? Does God fall under this category? For the assumption to work against Anselm He will need to. But surely this is to assume that God is a being in the sense that other things are beings. Anselm's point is that He is not, that He is uniquely distinct. However, if God does not fall under this category of beings, then the assumption and all that follows from it is irrelevant to the case of God. For the assumption to have any force it must entail a claim that God is not a special case, that X falls under the same category as not-X. It is necessary to show that a rule

[75] Findlay, 'Can God's Existence Be Disproved?', 176.

[76] Plantinga, *The Nature of Necessity*, p. 197.

[77] F. Zabeeh, 'Category-Mistake', in *Philosophy and Phenomenological Research*, 23 (1962), 277–8, 278.

[78] D. Hume, *Enquiries concerning Human Understanding*, London 1777, sect. 12 part 3.

such as Hume's can justifiably be applied 'without exception' to both not-X and X. Simple assertion of the rule does not constitute such a justification.

Conceivability, Possibility and Magicians

The need to adhere to the terms of Anselm's argument is brought out by the discussions of Sobel and Rowe concerning the question of the possibility of X. According to Sobel, 'Ontological proofs would show by doing that God's existence is demonstrable'.[79] This description is particularly appropriate in the case of Anselm's argument, given its special case nature. For Anselm does not and cannot justify the form of his argument except by showing that it works in the case of X and that attempts to undermine it by reference to cases of not-X cannot work. Since the form of his argument is not applicable to not-X and all other arguments sharing this form would need to concern not-X (if they are not to be mere repetitions of his argument), it should be clear that one can only provide an assessment of Anselm's argument by adhering to his argument, the form he gives it and its middle term.

Sobel argues that the burden of proof is on what he calls Anselm's 'preliminary argument': that there exists in the mind at least one thing that is X.[80] However, he considers Anselm's argument to be question-begging, because it does not show that X is in the mind '*in the sense needed by the argument*'.[81] In other words, Anselm has not proved the possibility of X, since '[u]nderstandability and conceptual coherence do not entail logical possibility'.[82] According to Sobel, Anselm's argument concerning '*existence in the mind*' is essentially the same as that concerning '*logical possibility*'.[83] But, since Anselm does not equate conceivability and logical possibility, this is to introduce into Anselm's argument the weakness Sobel intends to find there.

That Anselm's view of the relation between conceivability and logical possibility is not as Sobel describes it, can be seen in the analysis of the term '*aliquid*' in the so-called *Philosophical Fragments* contained in Ms Lambeth 59.[84] Anselm includes amongst things that can be understood, things that do not exist, citing the example of the chimera.[85] A chimera is a mythical animal and is by definition non-existent. Thus, it cannot be said to be logically possible in Sobel's

79 Sobel, *Logic*, p. 30.

80 Ibid., p. 64.

81 Ibid., p. 65.

82 Ibid., p. 66.

83 Ibid., p. 66.

84 See F.S. Schmitt, *Ein neues unvollendetes Werk des hl. Anselm von Canterbury* (*Beiträge zur Geschichte der Theologie und Philosophie des Mittelalters*, 33/3), Münster 1936.

85 Ibid., pp. 42f.

sense – i.e. as having the possibility of actually existing – otherwise it would not be a chimera. For Anselm, it is generally the case that understanding something does not entail the logical possibility of something. His argument is that in the specific case of X, understanding X entails understanding that X exists.

To support the view that the weakness in Anselm's argument relates to the possibility of X and the error in identifying this with conceivability, Sobel makes use of an analogy developed by Rowe concerning magicians, magicans(=existing magicians) and magicos(=non-existing magicians).[86] The real life Houdini was a magician and a magican, whilst the mythical Merlin was a magician and a magico. A non-existing thing cannot be a *magican*, and an existing thing cannot be a *magico*.[87] Incorporating 'existence' in its definition does not mean that a magican exists – just that no non-existing thing is a magican. The existence of magicans is dependent on the existence of magicians. If no magicians ever existed, then there would not be any existing thing that would exemplify the concept, 'magican'.[88]

Sobel puts in more general terms the point made by Rowe's magician analogy. He writes that 'corresponding to *every* kind K that can be thought or conceived without contradiction to be instantiated, there are kinds, for example, *actually or truly existing K's*, which can also be thought or conceived without contradiction to be instantiated, *which* kinds are instantiated only if the corresponding kinds K are instantiated'.[89] But, all this shows is that for not-X (magicians, lost islands, etc.) *a posteriori* work is required. In the case of X there is no kind X′ that can be distinguished from kind X′′. There is no 'being that is *in every* ***non-existential*** *respect* exactly like a being than which (according to Anselm's lights) nothing greater can be thought'.[90] Sobel assumes on Anselm's behalf what Anselm argues cannot be the case, and then detects a fault in Anselm's argument based on this assumption. He tries to employ the distinction between X′ and X′′ to produce a parallel argument to that of Rowe,[91] which leads to the conclusion: 'so it can be known *a priori* that it is possible that there is an Anselmian god, only if it can be known *a priori* that there is an absolutely magnificent being'.[92]

Rowe's critique of Anselm also concludes that his argument is question-begging, since in assuming the possibility of God it introduces a premise that is

---

86 W. Rowe, 'The Ontological Argument', in J. Feinberg and R. Shafer-Landau (eds), *Reason and Responsibility: Readings in Some Basic Problems of Philosophy*, 12th edition, pp. 11–21.

87 Ibid., p. 18.

88 Ibid., p. 19.

89 J.H. Sobel, 'Born Again! Anselm and Gaunilo in the Persons of Charles Hartshorne and William Rowe' [forthcoming in *Oxford Readings in the Philosophy of Religion*], 25th April 2008 (http://www.scar.utoronto.ca/~sobel/OnL_T/AnselmBornAgain.pdf), p. 25.

90 Ibid., pp. 25f.

91 Ibid., p. 27.

92 Ibid., p. 28.

almost equivalent to the conclusion that he is setting out to prove.[93] But it is Rowe who has introduced the notion of possibility into Anselm's formula. He states that our understanding of Anselm will be helped by replacing 'can be thought' by 'is possible' in the formula, X.[94] The idea that Rowe's alteration will assist our understanding of Anselm is simply incorrect. It introduces the idea that for Anselm the conceivable is the possible and therefore that he has assumed what is to be proved. Thus, Rowe writes without qualification (apparently having forgotten that this is *his* version of X) that Anselm thinks of God as that than which nothing greater is possible.[95]

The Conceivability and Inconceivability of God

Kenny asks whether it is 'self-refuting' to speak of an inconceivable God,[96] and how it is possible to know what a word means if one cannot think of what it means.[97] But as Anselm points out in the example Kenny cites from *R*9, we can know what ineffable means even though we cannot 'by definition' understand something that is ineffable. Both in the *Proslogion* and *Responsio*, Anselm makes it clear that we can think and speak of God 'to some extent'. As we saw in *P*1.33, Anselm seeks to understand to some extent, and he believes God can make this possible (*P*2.2). In *P*14.5, in the chapter where Anselm addresses the question that Kenny raises, he writes: 'Or is it that it has seen both the truth and the light, but at the same time has not yet seen You, since it has seen You to some extent, but has not seen You as You are?' In the *Responsio*, he seeks to get his Catholic opponent(s) to admit that if X cannot be thought of in some way, then neither can God (*R*1). Here he uses the example of the sun and daylight. One sees daylight (it is what allows us to see), but cannot look directly at the light of the sun, although they are the same light. Again, as noted in Chapter 4 (§14.8), according to Anselm when we speak of or see the ineffable God, we can only do so through another, '*per aliquam similitudinem aut imaginem*' (*M*65). This similitude or image is the rational mind, where God is seen, if only indirectly (*M*67). In *R*7, Anselm explains that it might be possible to say we cannot talk of God, because we may not understand what the word 'God' means. But, this is not true of X, since we can have some idea of

---

93 Rowe, 'The Ontological Argument', p. 20. See also Sobel, *Logic*, p. 94.

94 Rowe, 'The Ontological Argument', p. 13.

95 Ibid., p. 18. Others too make this identification of 'conceivable' and 'logically possible'. See, for instance, Adams, 'Logical Structure', 29: 'I interpret "can be thought" as meaning "is logically possible".' Plantinga says much the same, but qualifies it with 'or so, at any rate, I shall take him' (*The Nature of Necessity*, p. 199). He is not really interested in Anselm's 'actual intentions' (ibid., p. 199 n. 1).

96 A. Kenny, *The Unknown God: Agnostic Essays*, London 2004, p. 29. See also Leftow, 'Anselm's perfect-being theology', p. 141: *P*15 'casts a pall over Anselm's whole method'.

97 Kenny, *The Unknown God*, p. 33.

what X means. The point is not that we understand fully all the implications of being X, but that we can understand a phrase such as 'nothing greater than this can be thought'. That is all that is required for Anselm's argument. And as Anselm shows in *P*15, it follows from the fact that God is X that He is greater than can be thought. This does not mean that He is outside the limits of our thought, but that He extends beyond those limits. We can think of Him (for He is within the limits of thought) and not think of Him (since he is also beyond those limits). Just as when water is poured continuously into a small jug, there is still water in the jug when it overflows.

Kenny writes:[98] 'The distinction between understanding words and understanding the thing which they describe can only be effective if the things in question are to some *extent* describable.' These are words with which the author of the *Proslogion* could have agreed. Even in its limited way, X constitutes an understandable description. It transpires from Anselm's argument that what we to some extent understand by X is 'greater than can be thought'. As the analogy of the water jug suggests, this does not remove our limited understanding of X, but reveals just how limited that understanding must be. Kenny sees the issue as one of metaphor and the irreducibility of theological metaphor to 'literal language'.[99] For Anselm it is a question of what one might call theological anthropology. God created man in His image – i.e. as rational and free. It is in this image that God is to be found by rational investigation. For Anselm this is not a metaphor. The *imago dei* is a scriptural truth, which expresses a real similarity (a point of contact) between God and man. But, if Anselm's argument is not intended to employ metaphor, how is it supposed to be operating? This question is bound up with that of the nature of Anselm's argument. I have discussed the dialectical form of Anselm's argument. But the form is not the argument itself, as Anselm would hold (*DG*4). I will now turn to the nature of Anselm's argument and attempt to show how it constitutes the central expression of Anselm's theological anthropology.

---

98 Ibid.

99 Ibid., p. 40.

Conclusion
The Significance of Anselm's Argument

Anselm's Argument and the *Imago Dei*

The outcome of Anselm's argument in the *Proslogion* is not simply that the God of Catholic belief exists, but that this God cannot be eradicated by or from human reason. Anselm had already given an account in the *Monologion* how and why this should be the case, in his description of human *ratio* as *imago dei*. Whilst there Anselm develops a thoroughly Augustinian understanding of the trinitarian image of God in man, he also shows himself to be sympathetic to the approach to dialectic being championed by thinkers such as Berengar, in which dialectic is acknowledged as the expression of reason, and for which rejection of dialectic, and hence reason, constitutes a rejection of the *imago dei*: 'to have recourse to dialectic is to have recourse to reason; and he who refuses this recourse, since it is in reason that he is made in the image of God (*cum secundum rationem sit factus ad imaginem dei*), abandons his glory….'[1] It is this trinitarian image of God in man that allows Anselm to achieve his objective in the *Monologion* of establishing 'by reason alone' (*M*1) the necessity of the Catholic doctrine of God as Trinity. Thus, even prior to the *Proslogion*, Anselm is involved in a 'turn to the subject', to the understanding itself as the basis on which God is to be understood. In *M*66, Anselm writes that it is only through the rational mind itself that the rational mind 'is most able to progress in the discovery' of the supreme essence. The more studiously it endeavours to learn about itself, the more able it is to ascend to knowledge of the supreme essence.[2] This chapter, entitled 'That through the rational mind one approaches most nearly to knowing the supreme essence', follows on directly from the discussion of how anything can be rationally postulated concerning the ineffable in *M*65. At one point the language is very close to that of the *Proslogion*: 'we say and do not say, see and do not see' the same thing. This is because, 'we speak and see through another' (*M*65). Just as when we look at a face in a mirror, we see not the face itself but its image or likeness, so when we speak of the ineffable God, we do so (are only able to do so) through another, '*per aliquam similitudinem aut imaginem*' (*M*65). The mind is the mirror and image of God, in which it sees Him, whom it cannot see directly (*M*67). If the human mind can remember and understand itself and God, then *a fortiori* God remembers Himself

---

1 See Berengar, *Rescriptum contra Lanfrannum*, quoted in T. Holopainen, *Dialectic and Theology in the Eleventh Century*, Leiden 1996, p. 116. Reprinted with permission of Koninklijke Brill N.V.

2 See also *M*68.

and understands Himself, and does so eternally.[3] Although the *imago dei* is an hypothesis that permits Anselm to reach his conclusion, he does not establish its truth in the *Monologion*. Yet his ability to establish the trinitarian doctrine by reason alone depends on its truth. Whether Anselm was explicitly aware of what he needed to do in order to provide a justification for the *Monologion* (i.e. to establish that the human reason is made in God's image) is unclear. He certainly says nothing to suggest that he thought there was a weakness in the role he gave to the *imago*. Nevertheless, his desire to find a self-sufficient argument to supplement, rather than replace, that of the *Monologion*, indicates that he was aware of a lacuna in his argument there.

In the *Proslogion* Anselm indicates that he expected to achieve more by his argument than he did. He needs to explain why it is that, in spite of the fact that he has found God, he does not experience Him. This can be understood in the terms of the *Monologion* argument as a questioning of the reality of the *imago dei*, of how, if we are made in God's image and remember, understand and love Him, we do not recognise Him. This, of course, leads to the central question of the *Proslogion* itself, how the fool can say that there is no God. For the fool too is made in God's image.

'X' as the Proper Word for God

I have argued that X operates as the middle term of Anselm's argument and that this term was not arbitrarily arrived at, but was the result of Anselm's endeavour to discover the *unum argumentum*. To understand the significance of this term for Anselm, it is necessary to look at his understanding of words and concepts in the *Monologion*. In *M*10, Anselm develops the notion of '*naturalia verba*'. The 'natural word' is the 'proper and principal word' for a thing. It is the means by which reason identifies, for example, man's 'universal essence' as 'rational, mortal animal'. These words are basic, underpinning the words of particular languages, and are what allow us to think and speak of the objects we think and speak of. Nothing can better represent what we think of than the natural word. Although Anselm does not say one cannot substitute another term for the natural word of an object, he makes it clear that to do so is to move away from its real meaning. Thus, defining man as 'a mammalian bi-ped' whilst not inaccurate cannot deliver to rational thought what the definition, 'rational, mortal animal' does. It is not the 'proper and principal word' for man.

In the absence of a definition of God that can capture His essence, it transpires that there is nevertheless a word which functions as a natural or proper word for God. This word is 'X'. The importance of this point must not be overlooked, since it means that no other word will do for Anselm. As we have seen, attempts to replace X by other terms lead to or arise out of misunderstandings of Anselm's argument.

---

[3] See *M*32.

This irreplaceable word contains a reference to the act of thinking. Thought about God cannot be separated from thought about the thinking subject. This assertion is both deducible from the fact that X is the natural word for God in the *Proslogion*, and from the methodological role of the *imago dei* in the *Monologion*. The reference to the thinking subject does not happen by chance to be included in this natural word, but is rather an important indicator as to this word's origin in the rational mind as the *imago dei*. Anselm was aware that the discovery of his *argumentum* would (or, at least, could) be achieved through a reflection on the implications of the fact that man is made in God's image, and has an immediate relationship with God which underlies his rational activity. It transpires that the natural word of God is a human word about that which is totally Other, a word that seeks to unite the human subject and the Other. This human word for God (Anselm's natural word) reflects this relation of man and God, in which God is both at man's centre (in the image) and totally Other (beyond comprehension). This natural word does not arise simply out of the act of thinking about God, but, in a sense, is a word about human thinking. It is also a transcendental word, for it refers to that which man experiences at his core as the cause and enabling condition of all that he is.

The Retrieval

Although it is impossible to completely recapture the process by which Anselm, the author of the *Monologion*, came upon the argument of the *Proslogion*, the extent to which we can understand the explanatory power of his argument would seem to be dependent upon such a retrieval, which it is therefore necessary at least to attempt.

Our starting-point is the task Anselm set himself – to find a self-sufficient proof of God. It is not difficult to discover the reason for his confidence that such a proof was possible, since 'not to be able to be thought not to be' is a unique characteristic of God, distinguishing Him from all other (even necessary) beings in Boethian cosmology.[4] And, for Anselm, if God is 'that which is not able to be thought not to be', then it must be possible to show that He cannot be thought not to be. There is a real need to prove what *prima facie* should not need proving, since the fool says in his heart, 'There is no God'. Atheism should not be possible for man, yet the fact that he attempts to deny God (as scripture itself recognises) requires explanation. The proof of God is the proof of what cannot be thought not to be. Given his knowledge of Augustine and in particular of the *De Trinitate*, it would have been clear to Anselm where this undeniability of God in man is situated – in the fact that man is the *imago dei*, in the mind, not the body.[5] God's undeniability is inextricably connected with the rational mind's remembrance and understanding of Him as the

---

[4] Cf. Henry, *The Logic*, pp. 146f. and *Medieval Logic and Metaphysics*, London 1972, p. 109.

[5] Augustine, *In Ioannis Evangelium*, XXIII, 10.

enabling condition of rationality as expressed in *M*32: 'For if the human mind could have no memory or understanding of itself or the supreme wisdom, it would not distinguish itself from irrational creatures and the supreme wisdom from all creatures.' Anselm identifies this rationality with the power to distinguish 'the just from the not just, the true from the not true, the good from the not good, the greater good from the lesser good' (*M*68). Thus, it is in investigating what it is that allows such distinguishing to take place that Anselm's enquiry proceeds.

We can hypothesise that Anselm's process of reflection went something like this:

- Man is the *imago dei*.
- Therefore, man remembers God.
- This remembrance of God is not a purely theoretical premise, but is attested to by Christian experience.
- It is because of this experience that man knows that he is God's image.
- The remembrance of God is a precondition of rational activity, which is characterised by the power of distinguishing true from untrue, greater from lesser, etc.
- If through reasoning, we wish to find God, since He is not directly accessible to our intellectual 'vision', we should look at His image in man.
- We must look at rational man if we wish to find God.
- In particular, we shall find God in the thinking subject's rational distinguishing between what is God and what is not God, between what is greater and what is lesser.
- That which is experienced as a condition of rational activity must be articulated in terms appropriate to this method of reflection.
- A middle term must be found which expresses properly the meaning of what it is that is thought of when we think the word 'God'.
- This middle term must be characterised by a rational distinguishing between what is greater and what is lesser.
- It will also be the case that this middle term will function as natural words function in relation to non-divine things, as 'the proper and principal word for a thing' (*M*10).
- Although this 'word' cannot be a definition, it nevertheless will play a similar function in our talk of God.
- Furthermore, no other word or term will do (as Anselm points out in his *Responsio*).

It is the discovery of the middle term 'X', 'the proper and principal word' for God, that permits Anselm to carry out his programme of establishing that God exists and cannot be thought not to exist, and vindicates the argument of the *Monologion* with its anthropological assumption of the *imago dei*.

The Ineradicability of the Concept of God

Although Anselm does not explicitly identify God's undeniability with our remembrance of Him, the proof of this undeniability is the proof of the *imago dei* in man, that God is remembered and understood in man's rationality. If man were not made in the image of God, he would not be able to remember and understand Him. He would not be able to provide the proof that Anselm provides. But since Anselm does provide this proof, then man can be known to be made in God's image and the underlying assumption of the argument of the *Monologion* is vindicated. In language borrowed from transcendental philosophy, we might say that the *Proslogion* represents the reduction – going from the particular experience (the possession of the concept of X in the understanding) to the condition of its possibility (the affirmation that X exists in reality), whilst the *Monologion* represents the deduction – the explanation of how it is that such a condition is the condition of possibility of not just this act of thought about God, but of all thought (i.e. from my remembrance of God to the acknowledgement that this remembrance is required for all thought or better all acts of judgement).[6]

It is the success of the argument of the *Proslogion* that justifies the method of the *Monologion* and indeed vindicates Anselm's (and Augustine's) understanding of man as made in God's image. In the *Monologion* Anselm explains *how* this is the case, he deduces knowledge of God from the trinitarian image of God. But without establishing the reality of this image, Anselm's *sola ratione* argument can be no more than suggestive. It is the proof of the *Proslogion*, the demonstration *that* God exists and cannot be thought not to exist, that uncovers the ineradicable connection with God in man's rational activity. Anselm did not develop, and perhaps could not have developed, this relation of the *Monologion* and *Proslogion*, although he must have been aware that his briefest of treatments of the Trinity in *P*23 could not replace that of the *Monologion*. It was sufficient for him to show in the *Proslogion* the strategy to be employed in proving the God of Catholic belief. But, in doing so he also vindicates the theological anthropological role of the *imago dei*.

In today's world, the word 'God' appears as just one word among many. Yet, for Anselm, the word 'God' is the undeniable word for that which man encounters within as the ground of his being. When this fact is grasped, man knows that even if he desires to deny it, still he cannot do so, except in a lie, in an act of self-denial: 'even if I should not want to believe it, I would *not* be able *not* to understand that You exist' (*P*4.6). The real meaning of Anselm's argument is that God cannot be denied by anybody, except in a wilful refusal with no basis in reason. Accepting God is part of accepting oneself and one's own experience. Thus, faith is not rendered superfluous by Anselm's 'transcendental' understanding of the knowledge of God, rather it is seen as a 'categorical' necessity if man is to

---

6 See Kant, *CPR*, A85; B117: 'The explanation of the manner in which concepts can thus relate *a priori* to objects I entitle their transcendental deduction.'

be what he should. Acceptance of God requires a will that acts with rectitude, a choice not to be '*stultus et insipiens*'.

In his 'Meditation on the word "God" ', Karl Rahner stated that 'man exists only when he says "God"'.[7] By this word he does not mean the phonetic sound or the word found in a dictionary, but the 'real' or 'true' word, which reveals the unfathomable mystery at the heart of language and thought.[8] For Anselm, too, the word 'God' is constitutive of being human. Although it is not possible to develop a whole theory of man out of Anselm's writings, we find nevertheless in Anselm a drawing together of philosophical reflection and human experience, in which philosophical argument arises out of, and is determined by, that experience. The *unum argumentum* involves the solution to a problem encountered explicitly in Christian experience: how do we know God and not know Him, experience God and not experience Him, at the same time? Anselm's answer is: X is necessarily affirmed; God is X; God dwells in inaccessible light, yet, as the light that enables us to see, is the precondition of our 'seeing' (and it might be said of our knowledge that we do not 'see' Him); we find this light, not externally, but by studying the image of God, the rational mind; thus, although we can and do (in fact, as image of God, must) have a direct relationship with God, we can only conceptualise this indirectly. The experience of God, which all men have, is not accessible to them directly. It is mediated to them in other experiences. Thus, the fool remembers God, and can only think rationally (if he thinks rationally) because of this remembrance, yet he still believes he can say meaningfully, 'There is no God'. The lesson perhaps is that the fool cannot eradicate God by attempting to deny Him, and that the ineradicable nature of Anselm's argument is the result of the ineradicable nature of the God it purports to demonstrate.

---

7 K. Rahner, *Grace in Freedom*, London/New York 1969, pp. 183–90, p. 188.

8 Ibid., p. 190.

Bibliography

Manuscripts

Avranches, Bibliothèque d'Avranches:	Ms 159
London, Lambeth Palace:	Ms 59
Oxford, Balliol College:	Ms 62
Oxford, Bodleian Library:	Ms Bodley 271
	Ms Bodley 830
	Ms Laud misc. 363

Printed Primary Sources

Anselm

Charlesworth, M.J., *St. Anselm's Proslogion*, Oxford 1965.

Corbin, M. (ed.), *L'oeuvre de S. Anselme de Cantorbéry*, vols 1–[5], Les éditions du Cerf, Paris 1986–[1990].

Henry, D.P., *The Logic of Saint Anselm*, Clarendon Press, Oxford 1967.

Schmitt, F.S., *Ein neues unvollendetes Werk des hl. Anselm von Canterbury (Beiträge zur Geschichte der Theologie und Philosophie des Mittelalters*, 33/3), Münster 1936.

Schmitt, F.S. (ed.), *Sancti Anselmi cantuariensis archiepiscopi Opera Omnia,* vols I–VI, T. Nelson and Sons, Edinburgh 1946–1961.

Southern, R.W., and F.S. Schmitt (eds), *Memorials of St Anselm*, British Academy, London 1969.

Others

Albert the Great, *Summa Theologiae, sive De Mirabili Scientia Dei*, edited by D. Siedler et al., Monasterii Westfalorum, Aschendorff 1978.

Alexander Nequam – R.M. Thomson (ed.), *Alexander Nequam: Speculum Speculationum*, British Academy/Oxford University Press, Oxford 1988.

Alexander of Hales, *Glossa in Quatuor Libros Sententiarum Petri Lombardi*, vols 1–4, Collegium S. Bonaventurae, Quaracchi 1951–57.

——, *Summa Theologica*, vols 1–4, Collegium S. Bonaventurae, Quaracchi 1924–48.

Aristotle – J. Barnes (ed.), *The Complete Works of Aristotle*, vols 1–2, Princeton University Press, Princeton NJ 1984.

Augustine, *Confessiones* – Augustine, *Confessions*, translated by R.S. Pine-Coffin, Penguin, London 1961.
——, *De Dialectica* – J. Pinborg (ed.), *De Dialectica*, Reidel, Dordrecht 1975.
——, *De Ordine* – Augustine, *Contra academicos; De beata vita; De ordine; De magistro; De libero arbitrio*, Brepols, Turnhout 1970.
——, *De Doctrina Christiana – On Christian Teaching*, translated with an Introduction and Notes by R.P.H. Green, Oxford 1997.
——, *De Trinitate* – J. Rotelle (ed.), *The Trinity*, New York City Press, Brooklyn NY 1991.
Aulus Gellius, *The Attic Nights of Aulus Gellius*, vol. 2, translated by J.C. Rolfe, Harvard University Press, Cambridge Mass. 1952.
Boethius, *The Theological Tractates & The Consolation of Philosophy*, translated by H.F. Stewart and E.K. Rand, revised by S.J. Tester, Harvard University Press, Cambridge Mass. 1973.
——, *Commentaria in Porphyrium a se Translatum*, PL64 cols 71–158D.
——, *De Consolatione Philosophiae*, *PL*63 cols 579–862C.
——, *De Differentiis Topicis Libri Quatuor*, *PL*64 cols 1173–1216D.
——, E. Stump, *Boethius's De topicis differentiis*, Cornell University Press, Ithaca/London 1978.
——, *De Divisione* – J. Magee (ed.), *Anicii Manlii Severini Boethii De divisione liber*, critical edition, translation, prolegomena and commentary by John Magee, Brill, Leiden 1998.
——, *Liber De Persona Et Duabus Naturis Contra Eutychen Et Nestorium*, *PL*64 cols 1337–1354D.
——, *In Categorias Aristotelis Libri Quator*, *PL*64 cols 159–294C.
——, *In Librum Aristotelis De Interpretatione Libri Duo*, *PL*64 cols 293–392D.
——, *In Librum Aristotelis De Interpretatione Libri Sex, Editio Secunda, seu Maiora Commentaria*, *PL*64 cols 393–640A.
——, *In Topica Ciceronis Commentariorum Libri Sex*, cols 1039–1174A.
——, E. Stump, *Boethius's In Ciceronis Topica*, Cornell University Press, Ithaca/London 1988.
Bonaventure, *Commentaria in IV libros Sententiarum Magistri Petri Lombardi, Opera Theologica Selecta*, vols 1–4, Collegium S. Bonaventurae, Quaracchi 1934–1949.
——, *Itinerarium Mentis in Deum – The soul's journey into God, etc.*, translated by E. Cousins, SPCK, London 1978.
——, *Quaestiones Disputatae de Mysterio Trinitatis – Disputed Questions on the Mystery of the Trinity*, translated by Z. Hayes, Saint Bonaventure University, St Bonaventure NY 2000.
Cajetan, Thomas de Vio, *Sancti Thomae Aquinatis Opera Omnia, vol. 4: Pars Prima Summa Theologiae (ad q. 49) cum commentariis Thomae de Vio Caietani*, Rome 1888.

Daniels, A., *Quellenbeiträge und Untersuchungen zur Geschichte der Gottesbeweise im Dreizehnten Jahrundert, mit besonderer Beruchsichtigung des Arguments im Proslogion des Hl. Anselm*, Münster 1909.

Descartes, R. – C. Adam and P. Tannery, *Oeuvres de Descartes*, vol. III, Paris 1899.

——, J. Cottingham, R. Stoothoff and D. Murdoch (eds), *The Philosophical Writings of Descartes*, vols I–III, Cambridge University Press, Cambridge 1984–1991.

Duns Scotus, *Opera Omnia*, vols 1– , Typis Polyglottis Vaticanis, Vatican City 1950–.

——, *De Primo Principio* – A. Wolter, *John Duns Scotus: A Treatise on God as First Principle*, Forum Books, Chicago 1966.

Feuerbach, L., *Sämmtliche Werke*, edited by W. Bolin and F. Jodl, vols 1–10, Stuttgart 1903–1910.

Gabriel Biel, *Collectorium circa quattor libros Sententiarum: Prologus et Liber primus*, vols 1– , edited by W. Werbeck and U. Hofman, Mohr, Tübingen 1973–.

Gilbert Crispin, *De Angelo Perdito*, in A. Sapir Abulafia and G.R. Evans (eds), *The Works of Gilbert Crispin Abbot of Westminster*, British Academy/Oxford University Press, London 1986.

Hegel, G.W.F., *Werke*, vols 1–20, 3rd edn, Suhrkamp, Frankfurt 1993–96.

Henry of Ghent – J. Decorte and R.J. Teske, *Henry of Ghent's* Summa: *The Questions on God's Existence and Essence (Articles 21–24)*, Peeters, Louvain 2005.

John of Salisbury, *Metalogicon*, *PL*199 cols 823–946C.

John Scotus Eriugena, *Homilia in Prologum S. Evangelii secundum Ioannem*, *PL*122 cols 283–296D.

John Wyclif – M. Dziewicki (ed.), *Johannis Wyclif De ente liborum duorum excerpta: Libri I, Tractatus tertius et quartus: Liber II, Tractatus primus et tertius, et fragmentum De annihilatione*, Wyclif Society/C.K. Paul, London 1909.

Kant, I. – *Immanuel Kant's Critique of Pure Reason*, translated by N. Kemp Smith, 2nd impression with corrections, Macmillan, London 1933.

——, *Kant's Gesammelte Schriften*, hrsg. von der Königlich Preussischen Akademie der Wissenschaften, vols 1– , G. Reimer, Berlin 1900– .

Lanfranc, *Epistola B. Pauli Apostoli ad Colossenses*, *PL*319–332A.

Leibniz, G.W., *New Essays on Human Understanding*, translated and edited by P. Remnant and J. Bennett, abridged edition, Cambridge 1982.

Luther, Martin – *D. Martin Luthers Werke: Kritische Gesamtausgabe*, vol. 9, H. Böhlau, Weimar 1893.

Migne, J.-P., *Patrologiae cursus completus. Series Latina*, vols 1–221, Paris 1844–1865.

Nicholas of Amiens – M. Dreyer, *Nikolaus von Amiens: Ars Fidei Catholicae – Ein Beispielwerk axiomatischer Methode*, Aschendorff, Münster 1993.

Nicholas of Cusa, *Opera Omnia*, vol. 12: *De Venatione Sapientiae/De Apice Theoriae*, Felix Meiner, Hamburg 1982.
Paul of Venice – F. Ruello (ed.), *Paul Venetus: Super primum Sententiarum Johannis de Ripa lecturae abbreviatio. Prologus*, L.S. Olschki, Florence 1980.
Peter Damian, *De Divina Omnipotentia*, *PL*145 cols 595–622D.
——, *De Sancta Simplicitate*, *PL*145 cols 695–704B.
Peter Lombard, *Sententiae in IV libris distinctae*, vols 1–2, Editiones Collegii S. Bonaventurae, Grottaferrata 1971–1981.
Peter of Tarentaise, *In IV libros Sententiarum commentaria* [facsimile reprint of Toulouse edition 1649–52], Gregg Press, Ridgewood NJ 1964.
Peter Olivi, *Quaestiones in secundum librum Sententiarum quas primum ad fidem codd. mss.*, vols I–III, edited by B. Jansen, Collegium S. Bonaventurae, Quaracchi 1922–1926.
Richard of Middleton, *Super Quattor Libros Sententiarum*, Brixiae 1591.
Richard of Saint Victor, *De Trinitate Libri Sex*, *PL*196 cols 887–992B.
Robert Grosseteste, *De Decem Mandatis*, edited by R. Dales and E. King, British Academy/Oxford University Press, Oxford 1987.
Robert Holcot, *Quaestiones super quatuor libros sententiarum*, Lyons 1497.
Schelling, F.W.J. von, *On the History of Modern Philosophy*, translated by A. Bowie, Cambridge University Press, Cambridge 1994.
Schopenhauer, A., *On The Fourfold Root of the Principle of Sufficient Reason and On the Will in Nature*, translated by Mme. K. Hillebrand, Revised edition, George Bell, London 1907.
——, *The World as Will and Idea*, vol. II, translated by R. Haldane and J. Kemp, 3rd edn, Boston 1887.
Spinoza, B. de, *Opera*, vol. II, edited by C. Gebhardt, C. Winter, Heidelberg 1925.
Suarez, F., *The metaphysical demonstration of the existence of God: metaphysical disputations 28–29*, translated and edited by J. Doyle, St. Augustine's Press, South Bend Ind. 2004.
Thomas Aquinas, *Sancti Thomae Aquinatis doctoris angelici (de Aquino) opera omnia iussu Leonis XIII edita*, vols 1– , Rome 1882– .
Thomas of Buckingham, *Questiones in quattuor libros Sententiarum*, Paris 1507.
Walter of Saint Victor, *Excerpta ex Contra Quatuor Labyrinthos Franciae*, *PL*1129–1172A.
William of Auxerre – J. Ribaillier (ed.), *Magistri Guillelmi Altissiodorensis Summa Aurea [: Liber Primus]*, CNRS, Paris 1980.
William of Conches – G. Maurach (ed.), *Philosophia Mundi: Ausgabe des 1. Buchs von Wilhelm von Conches' 'Philosophia'*, University of South Africa, Pretoria 1974.
William of Ockham, *Opera Theologica*, vol. 9, edited by J. Wey, Editiones Instituti Franciscani Universitatis S. Bonaventure, Bonaventure NY 1980.
Wolff, C., *Philosophia prima sive ontologia methodo scientifica pertractata qua omnes cognitionis humanae principia continentur*, Frankfurt 1730.

——, *Theologia Naturalis – Pars II*, Editio Novissima Emendiator, Verona 1779.

Printed Secondary Sources

Anselm

Spicilegium Beccense I. Congrés International du IX Centenaire de l'arrivée d'Anselme au Bec, Paris 1959.
Adams, R.M., 'The logical structure of Anselm's argument', in *The Philosophical Review*, 80 (1971) 28–54.
Anscombe, G.E.M., 'Russelm or Anselm?', in *The Philosophical Quarterly*, 43 (1993) 500–504.
Balthasar, H.U. von, *The Glory of the Lord: A Theological Aesthetics*, vol. II, T. and T. Clark, Edinburgh 1985, pp. 211–59.
Barnes, J., *The Ontological Argument*, Macmillan, London 1972.
Barth, K., *Anselm, Fides Quaerens Intellectum: Anselm's Proof of the Existence of God in the Context of his Theological Scheme*, translated by I.W. Robertson, SCM Press, London 1960.
——, *Church Dogmatics*, I:1, 2nd edn, T. and T. Clark, Edinburgh 1975.
——, *Church Dogmatics*, II:1, T. and T. Clark, Edinburgh 1957.
——, *Die christliche Dogmatik im Entwurf*, Chr. Kaiser, Munich 1927.
Becker, G., *Catalogi bibliotecharum antiqui*, Bonn 1885.
Boschung, P., *From a Topical Point of View: Dialectic in Anselm of Canterbury's* De Grammatico, Brill, Leiden 2006.
Brecher, R., *Anselm's Argument: the Logic of Divine Existence*, Ashgate, Aldershot 1985.
Campbell, R., *From belief to understanding: a study of Anselm's Proslogion argument on the existence of God*, Australian National University, Canberra 1976.
Davies, B., 'Anselm and the ontological argument', in Davies and Leftow, *Companion*, pp. 157–78.
Davies, B., and B. Leftow (eds), *The Cambridge Companion to Anselm*, Cambridge University Press, Cambridge 2004.
Eadmer, *The Life of Saint Anselm, Archbishop of Canterbury*, edited with introduction, notes and translation by R.W. Southern, Clarendon Press, Oxford 1972.
Evans, G.R., *Anselm and a New Generation*, Clarendon Press, Oxford 1980.
Flint, R., *Theism: The Baird Lecture for 1876*, 9th edition, W. Blackwood, Edinburgh 1895.
Gasper, G., *Anselm of Canterbury and his Theological Inheritance*, Ashgate, Aldershot 2004.
Gasper, G., and H. Kohlenberger (eds), *Anselm and Abelard: Investigations and Juxtapositions*, Toronto 2006.

Hartshorne, C., *Anselm's Discovery: A Re-examination of the Ontological Proof for God's Existence*, Open Court, LaSalle Ill. 1965.
Henry, D.P., 'Proslogion Chapter III', in *AA*, I, pp. 101–5.
Holopainen, T., *Dialectic and Theology in the Eleventh Century*, Brill, Leiden 1996.
——, 'Anselm's *Argumentum* and the Early Medieval Theory of Argument', in *Vivarium*, 45 (2007) 1–29, 24.
——, 'Logic and Theology in the Eleventh Century: Anselm and Lanfranc's Heritage', in Gasper and Kohlenberger, *Anselm and Abelard*, pp. 1–16.
Hume, D., *Dialogues concerning Natural Religion*, 2nd edn, London 1779.
——, *Enquiries concerning Human Understanding*, London 1777.
Kienzler, K., *International Bibliography – Anselm of Canterbury*, Edwin Mellen Press, Lewiston/Queenston/Lampeter 1999.
La Croix, R., *Proslogion II and III: A third interpretation of Anselm's argument*, Brill, Leiden 1972.
Leftow, B., 'Anselm's perfect-being theology', in Davies and Leftow, *Companion*, pp. 132–56.
Lewis, D., 'Anselm and Actuality', in D. Lewis, *Philosophical Papers*, vol. 1, Oxford University Press, Oxford 1983, pp. 10–25.
Logan, I., 'Ms Bodley 271: Establishing the Anselmian Canon?', in *The Saint Anselm Journal*, 2 (2004) 67–80.
——, '"Whoever understands this…": On translating the Proslogion', in *New Blackfriars*, 89 (2008) 560–74.
Lubac, H. de, *Recherches dans la foi: trois études sur Origéne, saint Anselme, et la philosophie chrétienne*, Beauchesne, Paris 1979.
——, 'Sur le chapitre XIVe du Proslogion', in *Spicilegium Beccense I*, 295–312.
Malcolm, N., 'Anselm's ontological arguments', in *Philosophical Review*, 69 (1960) 41–62.
Millican, P., 'The One Fatal Flaw in Anselm's Argument', in *Mind*, 113 (2004) 437–76.
Morscher, E., 'Was sind und was sollen die Gottesbeweise? Bemerkungen zu Anselms Gottesbeweis(en)', in F. Ricken, *Klassische Gottesbeweise in der Sicht der gegenwartigen Logik und Wissenschaftstheorie*, Kohlhammer, Stuttgart/Berlin/Cologne 1991, pp. 62–86.
Omont, H., *Catalogue général des mss des bibilothèques publiques de France, départements*, vol. II, Paris 1888.
Perkams, M., '*Rationes necessariae – rationes verisimiles et honestissimae*: Methoden philosophischer Theologie bei Anselm und Abaelard', in Gasper and Kohlenberger, *Anselm and Abelard*, pp. 143–54.
Schmitt, F.S., et al. (eds), *Analecta Anselmiana*, vols I–V, Minerva Verlag, Frankfurt 1969–1978 = *AA*.
Southern, R.W., *Saint Anselm: A Portrait in a Landscape*, Cambridge University Press, Cambridge 1990.

——, *Saint Anselm and his Biographer*, Cambridge University Press, Cambridge 1966.

——, 'St. Anselm and his English pupils', in *Medieval and Renaissance Studies*, I (1941–43) 3–34.

Steiger, L., 'Contexe Syllogismos: Über die Kunst und Bedeutung der Topik bei Anselm', in *AA*, I, pp. 107–43.

Stolz, A., 'Anselm's Theology in the *Proslogion*', in J. Hick and A.C. McGill (eds), *The many-faced argument: recent studies on the ontological argument for the existence of God*, pp. 183–206, Macmillan, London 1968.

——, '"Vere esse" im *Proslogion* des hl. Anselm' in *Scholastik*, 9 (1934) 400–409.

Viger, C., 'St. Anselm's ontological argument succumbs to Russell's paradox', in *International Journal for Philosophy of Religion*, 52 (2002) 123–8.

Williams, C.F.J., 'Russelm', in *The Philosophical Quarterly*, 43 (1993) 496–9.

Others

Adams, M.M., *William Ockham*, vols 1–2, University of Notre Dame Press, 1987.

Beyssade, J.-M., 'The idea of God and the proofs of his existence', in J. Cottingham (ed.), *The Cambridge Companion to Descartes*, Cambridge University Press, Cambridge 1992, pp. 174–99.

Biard, J., 'The Middle Ages in Hegel's History of Philosophy', in *The Philosophical Forum*, 31 (2000) 248–60.

Bonansea, B., 'Duns Scotus and St. Anselm's ontological argument', in *Studies in Philosophy and the History of Philosophy*, 4 (1967) 128–41.

——, 'The ontological argument: proponents and opponents', in *Studies in Philosophy and the History of Philosophy*, 6 (1973) 135–92.

Chadwick, H., *Boethius: The Consolations of Music, Logic, Theology, and Philosophy*, Clarendon Press, Oxford 1998.

Chatillon, J., 'De Guillaume d'Auxerre à saint Thomas d'Aquin: l'argument de Saint Anselme chez les premiers Scolastiques du XIIIe siècle', in *Spicilegium Beccense I*, pp. 209–31.

Colish, M., *The Stoic Tradition from Antiquity to the Early Middle Ages*, vol. 1, Brill, Leiden 1990.

Collingwood, R.G., *An Essay on Metaphysics*, Clarendon Press, Oxford 1940.

——, *An Essay on Philosophical Method*, Clarendon Press, Oxford 1933.

Coreth, E., 'Dialectic of performance and concept', in F.E. Crowe, *Spirit as Inquiry: Studies in Honor of Bernard Lonergan*, Continuum, Minnesota 1964, pp. 147–54.

Davies, B., *The Thought of Thomas Aquinas*, Clarendon Press, Oxford 1992.

Ebbesen, S., 'Ancient Scholastic Logic as the source of medieval scholastic logic', in Kretzmann, N., et al. (eds), *The Cambridge History of Later Medieval Philosophy*, Cambridge University Press, Cambridge 1982, pp. 101–27.

Emery, G., 'Brief Catalogue of the Works of Saint Thomas Aquinas', in J.-P. Torrell, *Saint Thomas Aquinas*, vol. 1: *The Person and His Work*, Revised edition, Catholic University of America Press, Washington DC 2005.

Findlay, J.N., 'Can God's Existence Be Disproved?', in *Mind*, 57 (1948) 176–83.

——, *Language, Mind and Value: Philosophical Essays*, Allen and Unwin, London 1963.

Frege, G., 'The Foundations of Arithmetic', in M. Beaney (ed.), *The Frege Reader*, Blackwell, Oxford 1997, pp. 84–129.

——, 'On Concept and Object', in Beaney, *Frege Reader*, pp. 181–93.

Gál, G., 'Viae ad exsistentiam Dei probandum in doctrina Richardi Rufi OFM', in *Franziskanische Studien*, 38 (1956) 177–202.

Geach, P., 'Review of *From Belief to Understanding*', in *Philosophy*, 52 (1977) 234–6.

——, 'Why logic matters', in H.D. Lewis (ed.), *Contemporary British Philosophy: Personal Statements*, Fourth Series, pp. 86–99, Allen and Unwin, London 1976.

Ghellinck, J. de, *Le Mouvement Théologique du XIIe siècle*, 2nd edn, Éditions 'De Tempel', Bruges/Brussels/Paris 1948.

Gibson, M., *Lanfranc of Bec*, Clarendon Press, Oxford 1978.

——, 'The *Opuscula Sacra* in the Middle Ages', in M. Gibson (ed.), *Boethius: His Life, Thought and Influence*, pp. 214–34, p. 214, Basil Blackwell, Oxford 1981.

——, 'The Study of the "Timaeus" in the eleventh and twelfth centuries', in *Pensamiento*, 25 (1969) 183–94.

Gilson, E., *The Philosophy of Thomas Aquinas*, 2nd edn, W. Heffer and Sons, Cambridge 1929.

Grabmann, M., *Die Geschichte der scholastischen Methode*, vol. 1, Wissenschaftliche Buchgesellschaft, Darmstadt 1969.

Grant, C., 'The Ontological Disproof of the Devil', in *Analysis*, 17 (1957) 71–2.

Haight, D., and M. Haight, 'An ontological argument for the devil', in *The Monist*, 54 (1970) 218–20.

Hartshorne, C., 'Is the Denial of Existence Ever Contradictory?', in *The Journal of Philosophy*, 63 (1966) 85–93.

Henry, D.P., *Medieval Logic and Metaphysics*, Hutchinson, London 1972.

Hessbrüggen-Walter, S., 'Augustine's Critique of Dialectic: Between Ambrose and the Arians', in K. Pollmann and M. Vessey (eds), *Augustine and the Disciplines: From Cassiacum to* Confessions, pp. 184–205, Oxford University Press, Oxford 2005.

Hine, H., 'Natural Questions', in L. Reynolds (ed.), *Texts and Transmission: A Survey of the Latin Classics*, Clarendon Press, Oxford 1983, pp. 376–8.

Hopkins, J., 'Nicholas of Cusa's intellectual relationship to Anselm of Canterbury', in P. Casarella (ed.), *Cusanus: The Legacy of Learned Ignorance*, Catholic University of America Press, Washington DC 2006, pp. 54–73.

Hunt, R., 'Studies on Priscian in the eleventh and twelfth centuries', in *Mediaeval and Renaissance Studies*, I (1943) 194–231.

Inwagen, Peter van, *Metaphysics*, 2nd edn, Westview, Boulder Col. 2002.

Kenny, A., *The Unknown God: Agnostic Essays*, Continuum, London 2004.

Kneale, W., and M. Kneale, *The Development of Logic*, Clarendon Press, Oxford 1962.

Knox, R., *The Trials of a Translator*, Sheed and Ward, New York 1949.

Kretzmann, N., 'Faith Seeks, Understanding Finds: Augustine's Charter for Christian Philosophy', in T. Flint (ed.), *Christian Philosophy*, pp. 1–36, University of Notre Dame Press, Notre Dame Ind., 1990.

Lapidge, M., 'The Stoic Inheritance', in P. Dronke (ed.), *A History of Twelfth-Century Western Philosophy*, Cambridge University Press, Cambridge 1988, pp. 81–112.

Lauer, Q., *Hegel's Concept of God*, State University of New York Press, Albany 1982.

Logan, I., 'Whatever happened to Kant's ontological argument?', in *Philosophy and Phenomenological Research*, 74 (2007) 346–63.

Long, R., and M. O'Carroll, *The Life and Works of Richard Fischacre OP: Prolegomena to the Edition of his Commentary on the Sentences*, Verlag der Bayerischen Akademie der Wissenschaften, Munich 1999.

MacKinney, L., *Bishop Fulbert and Education at the School of Chartres*, University of Notre Dame Press, Notre Dame Ind. 1957.

McEvoy, J., *Robert Grosseteste*, Oxford University Press, Oxford 2000.

——, 'Robert Grosseteste's use of the argument of Saint Anselm', in J. McEvoy (ed.), *Robert Grosseteste: new perspectives on his thought and scholarship* (*Instrumenta Patristica*, vol. XXVII), Brepols, Turnhout 1995, pp. 257–75.

Maréchal, J., *Le point de départ de la métaphysique*, Cahier V, 2nd edn, Desclée de Brouwer, Paris 1949.

Marenbon, J., *Boethius*, Oxford University Press, Oxford 2003.

Maritain, J., *The Dream of Descartes*, London 1946.

Matthews, S., *Reason, Community and Religious Tradition: Anselm's Argument and the Friars*, Ashgate, Aldershot 2001.

Meynell, H., *Grace versus Nature: Studies in Karl Barth's* Church Dogmatics, Sheed and Ward, London 1965.

Minio-Paluello, L., 'The Text of the Categoriae: The Latin Tradition', in L. Minio-Paluello, *Opuscula: The Latin Aristotle*, Adolf M. Hakkert, Amsterdam, 1972, pp. 28–39.

Nelis, S., 'What Lanfranc Taught, What Anselm Learned', in *The Haskins Society Journal*, 2 (1990) 75–82.

Nothdurft, K., *Studien zum Einfluss Senecas auf die Philosophie und Theologie des zwölften Jahrhunderts*, Brill, Leiden 1963.

Oppy, G., *Arguing about Gods*, Cambridge University Press, Cambridge 2006.

——, *Ontological arguments and belief in God*, Cambridge University Press, Cambridge 1995.

Pegis, A., 'Four medieval ways to God', in *The Monist*, 54 (1970) 317–58.

Plantinga, A., *Does God have a nature?*, Marquette University Press, Milwaukee 1980.

——, *The Nature of Necessity*, Clarendon Press, Oxford 1974.

Power, W., 'Ontological Arguments for Satan and Other Sorts of Evil Beings', in *Dialogue*, 31 (1992) 667–76.

Prior, A.N., 'On Some Proofs of the Existence of God', in A.N. Prior, *Papers in Logic and Ethics*, Gerald Duckworth & Co. Ltd., London 1976, pp. 56–63.

Raedts, R., *Richard Rufus of Cornwall and the Tradition of Oxford Theology*, Clarendon Press, Oxford 1987.

Rahner, K., *Grace in Freedom*, Burns and Oates, London 1969.

——, *Spirit in the World*, translated by W. Dych, Sheed and Ward, London 1968.

Reichenbach, H., *The Rise of Scientific Philosophy*, University of California Press, Berkeley/Los Angeles 1951.

Richman, R., 'A serious look at the ontological argument', in *Ratio*, 18 (1976) 85–9.

Rohls, J., *Theologie und Metaphysik: der ontologische Gottesbeweis und seine Kritiker*, Mohn, Gütersloh 1987.

Rorty, R., 'The historiography of philosophy: four genres', in R. Rorty et al. (eds), *Philosophy in History: Essays on the historiography of philosophy*, Cambridge University Press, Cambridge 1984, pp. 49–75.

Ross, G., 'Seneca's Philosophical Influence', in C. Costa (ed.), *Seneca*, Routledge and Kegan Paul, London 1974, pp. 116–65.

Rowe, W., 'The Ontological Argument', in J. Feinberg and R. Shafer-Landau (eds), *Reason and Responsibility: Readings in Some Basic Problems of Philosophy*, 12th edn, Thomson Learning, London 2005, pp. 11–21.

Russell, B., *Introduction to Mathematical Philosophy*, Allen and Unwin, London 1919.

——, 'On Denoting', in *Mind*, New Series, 14 (1905) 479–93, 479.

Sobel, J.H., 'Born Again! Anselm and Gaunilo in the Persons of Charles Hartshorne and William Rowe' [forthcoming in *Oxford Readings in the Philosophy of Religion*], 25th April 2008 (http://www.scar.utoronto.ca/~sobel/OnL_T/AnselmBornAgain.pdf).

——, *Logic and Theism, Arguments For and Against Beliefs in God*, Cambridge University Press, Cambridge 2004.

Steiner, G., *After Babel: Aspects of Language and Translation*, 3rd edn, Oxford University Press, Oxford 1998.

Stump, E., *Dialectic and its Place in the Development of Medieval Logic*, Cornell University Press, Ithaca/London 1989.

Tennemann, W.G., *Geschichte der Philosophie*, vols 1–11, Leipzig 1798–1819.

Torrance, T., *Karl Barth: An Introduction to His Early Theology 1910–1931*, T. and T. Clark, Edinburgh 1962.

Vignaux, P., 'La preuve ontologique chez Jean de Ripa', in *AA*, IV/1, pp. 173–94.

Weisheipl, J., *Friar Thomas D'Aquino: His Life, Thought, and Works*, Basil Blackwell, Oxford 1975.

Wenzel, S., 'Robert Grosseteste's Treatise on Confession, "Deus est"', in *Franciscan Studies*, 30 (1970) 218–93.

Williams, B., *Descartes: The Project of Pure Enquiry*, Penguin, Harmondsworth 1978.

Wittgenstein, L., *Zettel*, 2nd edn, Blackwell, Oxford 1981.

Wood, A.W., *Kant's Rational Theology*, Cornell University Press, Ithaca/London 1978.

Zabeeh, F., 'Category-Mistake', in *Philosophy and Phenomenological Research*, 23 (1962), 277–8.

Index